KENTUCKY BOURBON & TENNESSEE WHISKEY

STEPHANIE STEWART-HOWARD

Globe
Pequot

Guilford, Connecticut

All the information in this guidebook is subject to change. We recommend that you call ahead to obtain current information.

Globe Pequot

An imprint of Rowman & Littlefield

Distributed by NATIONAL BOOK NETWORK

Copyright © 2016 by Rowman & Littlefield
All photography by the author, unless otherwise noted

British Library Cataloguing in Publication Information Available

Library of Congress Cataloging-in-Publication Data Available

ISBN 978-1-4930-0864-3 (paperback)
ISBN 978-1-4930-1834-5 (e-book)

♾™ The paper used in this publication meets the minimum requirements of American National Standard for Information Sciences—Permanence of Paper for Printed Library Materials, ANSI/ NISO Z39.48-1992.

*This book is dedicated to my husband,
Seth Howard, who followed me to
so many distilleries I can't count,
and to Paul and Anne Koonz, who
introduced me to so many bourbons.*

CONTENTS

~ ABOUT THE AUTHOR ~

Stephanie Stewart-Howard is a journalist and author whose resume also includes work as an artist, actor, costume designer, and researcher. After spending several years as managing editor and primary writer at *Nashville Lifestyles* magazine, she decided to leap into the book and freelance world. She is the author of *Nashville Chef's Table* and regularly contributes to *Nashville Arts*, Gannett's 12th and Broad, *Renaissance* magazine, and a host of other national and regional publications.

ACKNOWLEDGMENTS

This book would not have been possible without a lot of help. Every single distiller I talked to made a huge impact, and I owe them a huge debt, but I have to say special thanks to Darek Bell at Corsair, Billy Kaufman at Short Mountain, James Hensley at Nelson's Greenbrier, and Jeff and Jenny Pennington at Speakeasy Spirits, without whom this never could have happened. Long before I learned anything real about whiskey, you guys were already teaching me. Thanks also to Marc Coffman, Jim Rutledge, and Jimmy Russell for being extra helpful.

Thanks to Mike Veach at the Filson County Historical Society, for putting up with my questions and being a terribly fun interview.

Thank yous also need to go, in no particular order, to my dad, Joe Stewart, who came with me on crazy rides for this book, and my mom, Yvonne Stewart; also Ben Palos, Amy Preske, Cary Ann Fuller, Eric Byford, Karen Lassiter, Paul Newton, Jennifer Matthews, Micaela Burnham, Shawn Reed, Kathleen Cotter, and Laura Kimball at TruBee Honey. Finally, to all my whiskey drinking girls in Lexington—Missy, Abby, Stephanie, Dena, and Theresa (ok, you live in Ohio), thanks so much!

~ INTRODUCTION ~

There's no denying that brown spirits are undergoing an amazing renaissance. Depending upon whom you speak with, that may have begun as recently as five or six years ago, or it may have been percolating since the late 1980s; but it's very true that right now, whiskey, bourbon, and scotch are all hot. From a plethora of interest in scotch and the broad expansion of its popularity worldwide, to the growth of American whiskeys and bourbons not only in the United States but also in unexpected, emerging spirits markets in Australia, China, Korea, Japan, Russia, India, and Eastern Europe, something big happened and it is changing the way we view brown spirits across the board.

While Scots and Irish products are a big part of this market, this book chooses to focus on the American cousins, very specifically those made in Kentucky and Tennessee, the traditional homes of American bourbon and whiskey. We're seeing a rise in craft distilling across the nation. You'll now find whiskey being made in small-batch distilleries in the Midwest, the Northeast, and on the Pacific coast. Kentucky bourbon and Tennessee whiskey are the spirits that have come to define us nationally as much as anything else we produce. If you ask a Kentuckian or Tennessean, they might say that if you drink whiskey made anywhere else in

Photo courtesy of Nelson's Greenbrier Distillery

the United States, you might just be kidding yourselves. We are the real deal.

From the 1950s through the 1980s, bourbon and whiskey brands came to be associated with celebrities, sometimes those with rebellious or devil-may-care attitudes—from writing powerhouses like William Faulkner and Tennessee Williams to Frank Sinatra, the Rolling Stones, Guns 'N Roses, and outlaw country icon Willie Nelson singing "Whiskey River (Take My Mind)." More recent artists across genres—take Frankie Ballard for example, or Rihanna, or Sundy Best—have kept up the tradition.

In 1964 President Johnson—a whiskey drinker himself—along with Congress, officially declared bourbon to be a native spirit, a "distinctive product of the United States." Bourbon was the first product of any kind to get this special designation. I suspect LBJ never anticipated what Kentucky bourbon and Tennessee whiskey would become a few decades later. Back then, bourbon was generally regarded as the drink of the Southern gentleman, the kind of thing you consumed while playing cards, and perhaps smoking a cigar—LBJ would have been very familiar with that world.

Today bourbon and whiskey woo customers from a wide-ranging collection of men and women across all walks of life. They are the focus of a thriving revival of artisan cocktail culture, in which drinks familiar to the Johnson White House, like mint juleps and Old-Fashioneds, are just the introduction. They are still made here with loving care by distillers with a lifelong commitment. Some, like Jimmy Russell, the eighty-year-old master distiller at Wild Turkey, have been at it for sixty years and are passing the role along to sons, grandsons, and nephews. Others, including the Nelson brothers at Nelson's Greenbrier or John Pogue at Old Pogue, have only just begun, even though their family traditions date back to the nineteenth century.

All of them make up part of this ongoing, developing heritage. I am proud to introduce you to these distillers and their art and give you a bit more background on them, in hopes that you decide to do more than just buy a bottle.

The Changing Face of Bourbon

The goal of this volume is not to give you the concise history and science behind these spirits. There are other good books that do that out there, including Michael R. Veach's excellent *Kentucky Bourbon Whiskey: An American Heritage*. I also highly recommend Eric Byford's documentary film *Straight Up: Tennessee Whiskey* and his forthcoming follow-up on Kentucky bourbon. You'll also want to follow a good blog or two—I recommend Chuck Cowdery's (chuckcowdery.blogspot.com).

The goal here is to introduce you to many of the distilleries in these states, the personalities of their distillers and owners, and the character of the whiskey and bourbon they make. The hope is to interest you enough to get you out traveling across the two states, discovering not only fantastic spirits but also a culture with roots dating back two hundred years, and developing an understanding and appreciation of a spirit that is quintessentially our own.

Whiskey and bourbon have a very long history in this part of the country, inexorably tied to key moments in history, from the Whiskey Rebellion and the Louisiana Purchase to Prohibition. Since World War II there have been moments in which the industry struggled to survive in a Southern culture where the notion of Prohibition continues to cling. Indeed, a surprising number of counties in Tennessee and Kentucky remain dry. Famously, Moore County, home of Lynchburg, Tennessee, and the iconic Jack Daniel's distillery, remains dry as of this writing, even though it produces

Photo courtesy of Jack Daniel's Distillery

one of the best-known and best-loved whiskeys in the world. (Though as filmmaker Eric Byford says, the new understanding of revenue potential from distilleries is making some of these counties damper.)

Prior to Prohibition, each of these states had hundreds of distilleries in operation. Robertson County in Tennessee alone is reputed to have had as many as seventy-two distilleries in operation. Some of them served a national and international market; others served the local grocery store or the distiller's farmer friends on a Saturday evening. Almost every distiller had his (or her) own techniques for making whiskey and bourbon, though the basic rules—like 51 percent corn or better in the mash—were established early on.

Bourbon and whiskey taxes funded almost every American war until Prohibition; the country was carried on the back of that revenue. It was because of Prohibition that a national income tax became necessary: So much revenue was lost in making alcohol illegal. Despite its repeal on December 5, 1933, many of the country's longtime distilleries never came back.

The two states handled their distilling communities in very different ways in Prohibition's aftermath. Kentucky embraced its distilleries and the families that controlled them, and worked tirelessly to grow its bourbon tourism to the point that today it brings in hundreds of thousands of visitors each year to the state. The Kentucky Bourbon Trail program, in which ten of the state's distilleries participate together, has claimed more than 1.4 million visitors over the past five years, with more than 400,000 guests from all over the world visiting at least one of those distilleries in 2012. Clearly, those tourists have significant impact in the state, resulting in not only tours and purchases of the state's products (and the associated state taxes that come from alcohol) but also in filled restaurants, hotels, and other tourist attractions.

With this rebirth of the industry's popularity, Kentucky has also seen a distinct rise in its craft distillery population, so much so that there is now a Kentucky Bourbon Trail Craft Tour that runs from Bardstown down to Bowling Green, across to Louisville and Lexington, and includes eight smaller distillers, many of whom are producing excellent small-batch products. Some of them are brand-new iterations, like Town Branch, Corsair, and Barrel House, while others, Old Pogue and Willett for example, are reinventions of older brands whose distilleries closed up shop some time ago, often by members of the original family.

Tennessee, by contrast, has been much slower to the mark. Tennessee whiskey, led by Jack Daniel's and George Dickel, has long had a good reputation, but until the 1990s, when Phil Prichard came on board with his craft distillery, that was the only real legal spirit making of note in the state, and more was not anticipated. When Prichard decided to set himself up in the 1990s, he took advantage of locating in one of the three counties (Moore, Lincoln, and Coffee) in Tennessee that at the time allowed for distilling when he opted to open in Kelso in an old school building in Lincoln County. It would take almost another decade before the efforts of lobbyist Mike Williams of Franklin (founder of Collier and McKeel) and craft distillers like Darek Bell and Andrew Weber of Corsair, who at the time were operating entirely out of their Bowling Green facility, would manage to influence a change in Tennessee's laws in late 2009 under Governor Phil Bredesen.

How that change will affect tourism is still an open question. I like to think that the arrival of new craft distillers and the potential for a third large-scale distillery in Nashville coming from Speakeasy/Pennington's, will begin to draw even more travelers than those who make the annual pilgrimage to Lynchburg for Jack Daniel's or to nearby George Dickel. And surely those crowds get bigger every year. With the promise of some more-diverse openings in places like Memphis, how big the Tennessee Trail might eventually become is also an open question, but whether you follow Interstate 65 from the Kentucky border through Nashville to Alabama or get off on Interstate 24 and head to Chattanooga, there are now a growing number of spirit-related stops that didn't exist before.

As this book went to press, Chattanooga Whiskey just got their new facility under way, and H Clark Distillery in Thompson's Station cut the ribbon on its new building. (Find them via hclarkdistillery.com.)

Where the Bourbon Industry Is Headed

In 2013 current Tennessee governor Bill Haslam signed into law the long-term traditional requirements that any product labeling itself "Tennessee

Whiskey" or "Tennessee Sour Mash Whiskey" must be required to meet the federal required standards for bourbon production, plus follow what's known as the "Lincoln County Process," which is the step that separates Tennessee whiskey from Kentucky bourbon.

The federal requirements for a spirit to be called "bourbon" declare that the spirit must be produced in the United States (to be Kentucky bourbon, it must be produced in Kentucky). It must contain a grain mixture that is at least 51 percent corn (most bourbons and Tennessee whiskeys are additionally made with rye and malted barley, but there are variations as to how much—Kentucky bourbon tends to have a higher rye content than traditional Tennessee whiskey made by Jack and George). The spirit must be aged in new, charred oak barrels, distilled to no greater than 160 proof, cut as it goes into the barrel to not more than 125 proof, and bottled at 80 proof or higher. (If you're a true novice, the proof is twice the percentage of alcohol by volume, so 80 proof is 40 percent alcohol.)

Those rules are very specific, and part of the bourbon and whiskey resurgence has been a close testing of them. Of course, the added step in Tennessee whiskey, the Lincoln County Process, demands that the distillate be mellowed by running it through a layer of sugar maple charcoal before it is put in the barrels to age. That process makes Jack Daniel's and George Dickel mellower and sweeter than many of their Kentucky bourbon counterparts.

The burgeoning world market, and the reality that many of the large distillers are now owned at least in part by multinationals with their own business concerns, means that corporate culture has begun to challenge the stringent requirements long set down in tradition, especially in Tennessee. The question of whether or not whiskey must be aged in new barrels has recently been a source of much discussion across the Tennessee whiskey world, and while that seems to be a settled issue now, it will most likely continue to rear its head over time.

Simply put, the reuse of barrels might be economical for some companies, but the vast majority of the state's distillers, craft and otherwise, believe it would produce a lesser-quality product. Nearly universally, distillers told me over and over that the importance of fresh charred oak barrels in giving whiskey its flavor and character as it sits for years cannot be over-emphasized, and to change the process would be to produce something that is not Tennessee whiskey.

The other big question that surrounds the industry, which anyone who follows the news of the whiskey world must be aware of, is the issue of "rectifying" versus producing. That's not one you'll see go away anytime soon. The pages of the *Daily Beast*, the *Wall Street Journal*, the *New York Times*, the *Washington Post*, and the airwaves of NPR covered it in depth in 2014–15. The Tennessee legislature discussed the issue of what constitutes the nomenclature "Tennessee whiskey" twice during the writing of this book alone. By the time you read this, they will have taken it up again, one suspects. While it may seem like a simple issue, it's not at all. The situation is not unique to Tennessee and Kentucky—it has affected a huge number of distillers. Many so-called craft distillers have labeled their products as local, but in reality have been sourcing them from mass producers—and with luck, aging them locally, though not producing them.

The most obvious example has been the recent controversies—everywhere from Iowa to Kentucky—over rye whiskey, which in fact is produced and distilled by companies like Midwest Grain Products (often abbreviated MGP) in Lawrenceburg, Indiana, a company that sources whiskey—often very good whiskey, most frequently rye whiskey—of various kinds for a huge number of producers. Bulleit Rye, Templeton Rye, and George

Dickel Rye all start their existence with MGP. MGP also produces neutral grain spirits used in the production of gin and vodka for various companies. At issue, however, is the right to label something as a product of the state even if it is not.

Some of those producers include craft distillers and large distillers here in Tennessee. It seems like it's an easy question, but the reality is full of complexities. Most agree it's wrong to mislabel a so-called "rectified" product—bought from another company elsewhere who made it, tweaked to meet your needs, and then bottled and labeled as your own as if made in your state. However, the larger truth is that, first, rectifying has been going on for centuries and in some cases is part of the tradition, and second, the more obvious reality is that young distilleries have to age their products, and meanwhile, they need to make a profit to keep running while their whiskey ages. That takes years and makes things more complex.

Starting a distillery is no small financial endeavor. Ingredients and the necessary equipment don't come cheaply. Those young distilleries have a couple of options—they can produce other spirits, from unaged whiskeys (sometimes mistakenly called "moonshine") to products like rum or vodka that don't require the time commitment and can quickly make it to market without years of aging.

Even so, there are *very* strong feelings on the subject at every distillery you go to, some pro and some con. Expect this issue to be ongoing, something that will involve both large court cases and small local conundrums for quite some time. In Tennessee and Kentucky the labeling laws are such that if the product isn't genuinely made in the state, it can't be labeled as Kentucky bourbon or Tennessee whiskey. Where it is labeled as such, it's understood that the product matches the legal requirement and definition.

You'll see the same thing happening with unaged products as well, including products labeled "moonshine" or "white dog," which are, in fact, grain alcohol from large producers that has been flavored and altered to meet the palates of consumers. That doesn't mean these products are necessarily bad; more often than not they are flavored to appeal to buyers and answer their needs. It does mean the national discussion about what some spirits are and are not is a long-term prospect we'll be dealing with for some time. The debate should be interesting, because producers making true white whiskey and true moonshine have an investment in consumers understanding what those words mean, and to likewise have expectations based on those meanings.

What comes to mind most is the number of distillers who take pride in the fact that their product is made in this region, with a slow-aging process, and that it's natural—a combination of good grain, yeast, and limestone-filtered water. Most of the new distilleries that source whiskey are now honestly laying down their own whiskey. Their biggest challenge will be to create something the market likes as much or more than the rectified product. Many craft and small-batch distillers have made that transition admirably over the past few years. Look at Brown-Forman's Woodford Reserve, for a great example, originally sourced via the company's Old Forester label. Others will succeed too, and bear in mind, many of those rectified products are in fact actually good drinking. The public is glad to buy them.

Meanwhile, from those newer distilleries that have launched other products to keep themselves financially sound while the aging process takes place, there has arisen a collection of really interesting artisan non-brown spirits in the area. Barrel House distilling company in Lexington, Kentucky, is making some pretty fine barrel-aged rum right now; Corsair Artisan offers up an assortment of products—their gin is outstanding if you like juniper and citrus on the front, and I'm excited about the apple brandy they're starting to produce; and Tenn South in Lynnville, Tennessee, has an artisan take on gin with a distinctly Southern palate that really will impress you with the potential of the New American gin category. As this book went to press, Speakeasy Spirits brought their splendid Picker's Vodka to market as well.

In those cases the entrepreneurial spirit drove the invention of some outstanding products. Pay attention. Plenty of the small distilleries in this book don't have much in the way of marketing budget, but they're worth looking for in your liquor store, and many of their products are available online. If you have the urge to try something, please do.

There are also a few distilleries that have taken on the challenge of unaged whiskeys and done exceptionally well with them, and a few who are committed to real, old-school moonshine whiskey made like the boot-leggers and wildcatters did back in the day. Short Mountain in Woodbury, Tennessee, stands out in that category. Also included is a distillery in Ashe-ville, North Carolina, right over the border, Troy and Sons, because they have deep ties to Tennessee. Their view on unaged whiskey is worthy of your consideration.

In the end, this book is being written at a wild time in the industry. Business is booming as artisan cocktails and craft distilleries intrigue popular culture and classic American brown spirits have attained a new and profound respect in the worldwide market. Whether you're a longtime fan of Jim Beam or Maker's Mark, Woodford Reserve or Jack Daniel's, if you're a fan of true Kentucky bourbon or Tennessee whiskey, this is your time. If you are excited by new iterations on the theme—by Corsair's outstanding experimental small-batch whiskeys or the brand-new bourbon from Barrel House or the wickedly good moonshine at Short Mountain—this is your time too.

If you're brand new to drinking bourbon and whiskey, the answer to the best way to drink it is the way you like it best. As Jimmy Russell, Bill Samuels, or Fred Noe III will tell you, "Drink it neat, drink it on the rocks, drink it in a cocktail—the way you like it is the right way." Most of the distilleries generously provided their own recipes for you to try, if cocktails are your thing. Also included is a short chapter with traditional and basic cocktail recipes that you can try on your own. Most are incredibly easy to make.

With that in mind, welcome to this odyssey across the bourbon and whiskey world. Each chapter is different and distinct—some more personal adventure, some more serious conversations with distillers—but all are guides to the spirits and the places where they're made. Each chapter tells you something different about the history, the technology, and the experience of bourbon and whiskey in this part of the world. Still, don't take it on word alone. Come down and visit.

Kentucky and Tennessee have everything you need to make whiskey. The
two states, with their eastern mountains, rivers for transport, rolling hills,
ideal agricultural climates with four distinct seasons, and abundant natural
limestone for filtering iron and other minerals out of water, provide anything you could want for the production of good brown spirits. Whiskey
production followed the settlement of the area. It didn't so much come
with them as develop as a resource after they arrived, not just for the enjoyment of drinking but as a tool for barter and exchange as well. During the
colonial era, neither had yet achieved statehood on their own: Kentucky
was a westward extension of Virginia, and Tennessee of North Carolina.
From the 1770s to 1790s, an influx of population, including colonial offi-
cers given land grants for their service during the Revolution, encouraged
the development of good-sized towns and eventual recognition by the
fledgling nation. Kentucky became a state in its own right in 1792, Tennessee in 1796.

When you talk about colonial America, of course, the most popular
spirit isn't whiskey—rum and gin easily surpass it in terms of regular production and use. Rum, the still-popular Caribbean spirit whose history we
know today mostly by references in movies about seventeenth- and early
eighteenth-century pirates, was made from molasses, produced from sugarcane. Demand for it helped build up the massive sugar plantations in
the Caribbean, supplying not only the American colonies but Europe as
well. The first rum distilleries in the United States were built as early as the
1660s in New York and New England, and they quickly became successful. The drink's popularity was not limited to the north. Virginia and the
Carolinas developed a taste for it as well. If you're a fan of the STARZ
series *Black Sails*, which follows eighteenth-century pirates, you might have
a sense of what rum meant to the colonial Americas.

Other spirits, including gin—a spirit that dates back medicinally at
least to the Middle Ages, made by adding botanicals, especially juniper,

to fermented grain mash—developed a popularity with colonial Americans as well. Beer, of course, had come to the colonies with the settlers at Jamestown and Plymouth, and remained a mainstay in the colonial diet. Most beers were made in the home, just like bread and other staples, while distilled spirits were more likely to be purchased. In some cases, beer was regarded as a safer alternative to local water for drinking, a not unreasonable choice in the colonial era when sanitation was not at modern levels of refinement.

Whiskey, or whisky, as the Irish and Scots spelled it, was nothing new to the colonists. Distilled spirits made from grain mash had been produced for centuries in various forms. Immigrants from both areas settled in Virginia and the Carolinas, and many moved westward during the colonial era. The Scots-Irish, particularly, made it into the area early on and are credited with bringing the tradition of mashed-grain distilled spirits with them.

(By way of clarification, "Scots-Irish" is an American term that largely refers to people of Scots and English descent whose families moved to Ireland during the early seventeenth-century settlement of the Irish "plantations"—they remained Protestant [often of dissenting sects, Calvinist rather than high church Anglican] in the Catholic majority country, mostly settling in Ulster in Northern Ireland. In the seventeenth and eighteenth centuries, they migrated, along with other Irish and British citizens, to the colonies in significant numbers.)

Historian Mike Veach counters the notion that whiskey was strictly a product of immigrants from the British Isles by pointing out that the names of the big early distillers, many still around today, are fairly diverse—Williams, Pepper, Craig, Beam (the German Boehm), Weller, Spears, Davis, and Myers.

For those coming from the British Isles, the making of whiskey was not unfamiliar, but what they made for the most part in colonial America was unaged—what today we'd call white whiskey or white dog. According to Mike Veach, author of *Kentucky Bourbon Whiskey*, who graciously allowed me to interview him for this book, people started distilling their own whiskey in Kentucky, Tennessee, and western Virginia because the price for importing rum and other spirits proved prohibitive. Whiskey, he says, could be made from what settlers had at hand, and what they had a lot of was grain. It became so commonplace that coppersmiths in the western parts of the colonies began building pot stills themselves, so more expensive ones didn't have to be imported from Europe.

Dub Cornett, Nashville music producer, dynamic marketing voice for Troy and Sons, and a native of the western mountains of Virginia, waxes poetic on the circuit riders who traveled the western territories of the Appalachians, carrying jugs of unaged whiskey with them to help open up new audiences to their preaching. There's perhaps some irony these days in the notion of whiskey being used to spread the gospels through those hollows and mountains, but evidence suggests he's got the right idea. Of course, even today, those areas, including my mother's native Virginia Blue Ridge Mountains, have a reputation for producing moonshine of their own. It is and always has been a part of the landscape there. My mom went to school with the children of bootleggers.

By the time of the American Revolution itself, residents of the western territories had themselves a useful cash crop in whiskey—as Mike Veach tells me, they regarded it the same way they might other commodities they could produce and use for sale or barter, with farmers making small quantities from grain they raised, such as corn and rye, but also wheat. One of the earliest versions, the "Pennington method" (circa 1800), cited to me by both Veach and Jeff Pennington at Speakeasy Spirits, was made primarily of corn, mixed with malted barley and rye. The Pennington method is a "sweet" mash, according to Veach, starting from scratch, cooking grain, and adding yeast; a "sour" mash also adds some of the liquid materials from the previous batch back into the new mash. Sour mash is by far the most common method used today in bourbon and whiskey production here.

Early on, filtering a distillate through charcoal wasn't that unusual, though Tennessee's Lincoln County Process, which filters that distillate through sugar maple charcoal specifically, had not yet made itself commonplace, though Jack Daniel seems to have learned it from the distiller who taught him at least as early as the 1850s.

As Eric Byford of Beardforce Films, maker of *Straight Up, Tennessee Whiskey*, will tell you in no uncertain terms, from this era onward whiskey became the primary funding source for our young country's wars. Many of our founders were distillers themselves. For example, George Washington had his own distillery at Mount Vernon. They understood the value of liquor in the new country's culture. After the Revolution, when money was needed to pay off the debts incurred during the war, the young government established taxes and tariffs by which to do so. Among those was an excise tax on distilled spirits, which went into effect in 1791.

Photo courtesy of Jack Daniel's Distillery

The problem came when the tax imposed proved much tougher on the western territories and states than it did back East. In the West, as Mike Veach says, we had a largely barter-based economy, and whiskey itself was essentially a currency used by many small distillers. Back East, the large distilling companies making rum and gin had real currency—the return on their product. That made it much easier for them to pay the tax than for western distillers to do so. Veach points out that in the East it was easy to gauge how much whiskey each distillery made and tax it accordingly. In the West, with small, haphazard production, federal regulators were making educated guesses and ultimately taxing the farmer-producers for things they hadn't produced. This is an oversimplified picture, and the federal regulators, according to Veach, did indeed try to show some sympathy to the Kentucky producers, but it underlines the elements that led to the Whiskey Rebellion.

The worst of the Whiskey Rebellion centered on western Pennsylvania, where troops were ultimately called up to quell the threats of violence coming from the small distillers and farmers producing in that region. In 1794, when a US marshal showed up to issue writs to those who hadn't paid their taxes, a threatening group of some five hundred insurrectionists arrived at the home of General John Neville, the official tax inspector. President George Washington sent men to negotiate with the angry distillers and farmers, but he also stood his ground. He asked the governor of Pennsylvania, and those of Virginia, New Jersey, and Maryland, to send a militia to enforce the tax. Washington himself rode to Pennsylvania with some 13,000 or so militia men, showing he wasn't willing to be cowed by the situation. In the end the protesting producers packed up and went home without any physical violence on either side. A few suffered arrest, no one was killed, and ultimately everyone was pardoned or let off.

While this particular tax was repealed under Thomas Jefferson in 1801, taxes on whiskey and distilled spirits continued to fund the government throughout the nineteenth century, including paying for the Civil War and nearly every other armed conflict we entered into. It was only with the coming of national Prohibition, with the passage of the 18th Amendment in 1919, that it became necessary to pass a national income tax to make up for the revenue that was lost.

Distilling, however, continued apace, including in the new states of Tennessee and Kentucky. At some point over the stretch of the next twenty-five years, the production of what we call "bourbon" whiskey began. There are a number of popular theories as to how that happened. What we know for sure is that in Kentucky at the time, the Ohio River had become a driving force of commerce, with flatboats carrying goods from the areas around Louisville and Owensboro down the river to where it met with the Mississippi, and from there all the way south into New Orleans.

In 1803 Jefferson's Louisiana Purchase made the markets there even more readily available for merchants in Kentucky. At some point merchants started putting their unaged whiskey in barrels and sending it down the river to those markets too.

What makes Kentucky bourbon and Tennessee whiskey what they are, in no uncertain terms, is the aging process that takes place when the distillate is put into charred oak barrels and set for years to age. Contemporary distillers use words like "magic" and "alchemy" when they talk to me (read the interviews that follow) about it. The distillate goes in as something smooth, but as it sits in those barrels, the changing seasons encourage it to ooze into the charred wood in the summer heat, absorbing oakiness and tannins and deep brown color, then come flowing right back out when the weather is cool. The fact that Tennessee and Kentucky have not only the raw materials to make the distillate perfect but also the ideal climate for aging these products, is what makes them special. With modern climate control, it's indeed possible to make whiskey in Florida, Maine, or Montana, but for going on two centuries, the perfect process has been a natural occurrence here.

Barrel aging is nothing new—the Romans used charred oak barrels, and the medieval fortified wine makers and producers of fine brandies did so too. The question is, when did Kentucky and Tennessee distillers and merchants decide it was a good idea to put their white dog whiskey

Photo courtesy of Dan Cohen, Jim Beam

into them to age? If you surf through any of the bourbon websites online, chances are good you will see credit going to one Rev. Elijah Craig.

Craig, a preacher of the kind I mentioned earlier, was a Virginian who migrated into the Kentucky territories in the 1780s. He served as pastor of a church in Fayette County, started a school in 1787 to provide classical education, and made a good deal of money as a businessman, building mills and factories focused on everything from fulling cloth and making paper to a lumber mill. Craig's distillery was built, like his other businesses, in what was then called Fayette County, which would eventually become Woodford County and finally Scott County. That's relevant because the origin of the name "bourbon" is often credited to Bourbon County, named in honor of the French royal family prior to the French Revolution, for their aid in the American Revolution. Records show he started the distillery in 1789, but there is no concrete evidence that he was the first to create Kentucky bourbon whiskey.

"I think it's the favorite propaganda to credit Elijah Craig as the first bourbon maker," says Mike Veach with confidence. "Everyone does it, but the story was used to fight the growing Temperance Movement in the late 1870s." Presumably because there's no question Craig was a man of the cloth. In his excellent book, Veach further points out that in 1827, a eulogy offered in Craig's memory lists his many, many firsts, but doesn't make mention of bourbon, and that tribute, offered by a fellow distiller, Lewis Sanders, is fairly damning to the argument for Craig as the founder of the tradition.

"Craig was certainly a distiller making the same kinds of spirits as his contemporaries at that time," says Mike Veach. "But he wasn't the inventor of bourbon. The fact is no one can be precisely identified. I would love someone to claim the invention of bourbon in writing . . . " Veach believes very strongly that the origins of bourbon have little to do with Bourbon County, and everything to do with the growing trade in the very early nineteenth century between Kentucky and New Orleans.

"They were drinking brandy there, and they had some type of distillation going on in New Orleans," he says, referencing the continuation of French tastes in New Orleans, and the difference between them and the raw whiskeys being produced in Kentucky and the region.

"In Kentucky, we were making this because corn is what we grew," says Veach. "Whiskey preserves corn, and makes it even more marketable. It's an added value product. At that time, most of it was sold or transported in jugs and crocks, not in barrels, and most distillers had small stills. Working all day, they'd fill maybe five to ten gallons; it would take them a good seven to ten days to fill a barrel. In the meantime, they end up losing about three gallons that will be absorbed by the wood. Jugs and crocks are a better economic choice—you don't lose anything, and it's much easier for you to sell by the gallon or by the quart as a small producer. Remember, this still isn't much of a cash economy, especially early on; they're bartering goods, and that makes the smaller amounts preferable too. You need nails for your barn from the blacksmith? Ok, that's two gallons of whiskey."

The way Veach tells it, there wasn't much of a market for Kentucky whiskey in New Orleans, where the taste ran to aged French brandies brought on trade ships directly from France. The goal for the savvy merchant who wanted to sell that whiskey in New Orleans was to make it taste a lot more like French brandy. "And to do that, you age it in barrels," he asserts. "Cognac has been aged in barrels since the fifteenth century; they knew, like the Romans knew, that the barrels keep the alcohol from going bad for a much longer period. That's my argument here, that the point was to make our product much more like French brandy."

In the 1820s, the point where Craig and company were supposedly making bourbon in and around Bourbon County, references to "bourbon whiskey" are notably lacking. Veach, looking at the records for production and taxation of whiskey in the early nineteenth century, and noting the potential loss from tax on an aged product, since part of the whiskey is absorbed into the barrel wood, concluded that a merchant or grocer was a far more likely inventor than distiller. This puts him, Veach admits, at odds with the status quo, but after speaking with him at length, I think his argument makes tremendous sense.

According to Veach, the earliest reference to charring barrels comes from a Lexington grocer in 1826, writing to a liquor producer and commenting that if the barrels are charred one-sixteenth of an inch on the inside, the whiskey would be improved. The implication, of course, is that the notion of charring the barrels is a fairly new thing in the 1820s, and Craig died in about 1808.

"I think the natural candidates for the actual creators of bourbon are the Tarascon brothers, Louis and John," says Veach. They fled France in the aftermath of the 1789 Revolution and started a shipyard in Pittsburgh first, then, according to Veach, after losing a vessel at the Falls of the Ohio, decided to move their business farther to the southwest to trade with New Orleans. They didn't build another shipyard, instead constructing a mill and shipping warehouse below the falls at Shippingport, Kentucky, by 1807.

"They were probably purchasing the whiskey cheaply, aging it themselves, and shipping the product to New Orleans. I'd suggest it's more likely that 'bourbon' was named for Bourbon Street in New Orleans, where it was being sold. They would transfer the whiskey they bought in jugs to the charred oak barrels, because it was cheaper to buy the jugs already made, and the process was less labor intensive. Before long they could send it down the Ohio on steamships—the first steamboat was traveling the river in 1817 or earlier, and by the 1820s, they were becoming common."

Tennessee, meanwhile, Veach says, had a very similar history to Kentucky's, adopting many of the same techniques around the same time, but Tennessee was at a disadvantage in that it lacked the Ohio River as a departure point. Memphis, which provides Tennessee's major point of departure for New Orleans, doesn't seem to have developed the kind of whiskey production the mid-part of the state did as the nineteenth century progressed.

"In Kentucky there are different cultures—the merchant river towns and then the rest of the state," says Veach. Indeed, the blend of cultures in both states, which resulted in so much in-state conflict during the Civil War, comes down to the fact that there tended to be two types of aristocracy, according to Veach—a merchant class, especially around the river towns, and a "landed gentry" across the other regions, known for things like horse breeding but with larger, slave-holding estates of cotton and other crops farther south in Mississippi and Louisiana.

Indeed, Tennessee's greatest success as a trader in whiskey seems to have taken off with the coming of the railroads, and the true rise of big name distillers like Jack Daniel, George Dickel's Cascade Springs, and Charles Nelson's Greenbrier took place in the last quarter of the nineteenth century, while many Kentucky names were well established before the Civil War. Veach tells me Tennessee was also much slower to adopt aging in barrels over jugs and crocks; Jack Daniel himself seems to have learned the barreling practice by about 1860, suggesting it was at least used in Tennessee by that time. Daniel seems to have been adamant about charcoal mellowing, something that Veach says was also typical in Kentucky early on but was never a requirement there.

The recipe was also refined and decided during the early and mid-decades of the nineteenth century. Veach tells me there are at least a dozen recipes dating from the early nineteenth century in Kentucky that are very similar, suggesting the process defined itself fairly quickly, and again, barrel aging became crucial to the value of the product. Barrels became such the norm that the best whiskey was always aged in barrels.

The recipe, blending corn, rye, and barley, seems to have evolved early on, with the use of wheat (still typical in some distilleries, Buffalo Trace's highly in demand Pappy Van Winkle brand being an obvious example) and other grains less common. Rye tends to grow best in cooler climates than Tennessee and Kentucky, but Veach says the colonial residents did raise it, especially those of German background, some of whom were among the migrants who came from western Pennsylvania. Rye was often added for flavor, perhaps to counter the sweetness of the corn. Today most distilleries source corn locally and regionally but get rye from northern states, and in some cases from northern Europe. Corn and barley are both crops that grow in this region with ease.

Joking a bit, Veach says his farmer grandfather raised barley one year on a farm in Indiana. "Wild onions grew up in the field, and they got harvested along with the barley—they're the same size as barley grains. That's also true for rye and wheat, and wild onions are fairly common here. I suspect that was a problem in Tennessee and Kentucky as well," he says. The comment underlines the potential problem nineteenth-century distillers had in maintaining flavor profiles—something that would change for the better after Prohibition and World War II with technological advances.

The nineteenth century also saw a wide selection of rectified spirits appear, in an era before there were food and drug regulation laws. Rectifiers generally made cheap distillate with a high alcohol content and, rather than aging it, added flavorings and color to create cheap, easily sellable spirits. Veach notes in *Kentucky Bourbon Whiskey* that the added extras included "burnt sugar" (possibly just brown sugar), fruit juice, creosote, conchineal (a red-purple dye made from insects), starch, acetic ether, oil of wintergreen, and a host of even less palatable options. He cites an 1860 text that advises using the same neutral grain spirit to make multiple varieties of whiskey (including Irish and scotch), with various additives to give it artificial color and flavor, not to mention a very desirable sweetness.

The ultimate showdown between Kentucky's distillers and rectifiers would be one of the leading reasons for the 1906 Pure Food and Drugs Act, which forbade interstate commerce in adulterated and misbranded food and drugs. While whiskey was only one of the many food and beverage products involved, the issue of producing versus rectifying spirits remains one of contention even today.

The difference today comes from the fact that it's easily possible to purchase ready-made whiskey, aged or unaged, from producers like MGP in Indiana, and there's been a recent controversy about craft distillers especially, all over the country, doing so and not acknowledging their sources on the label. Some of these products are excellent, make no mistake, and some big name distillers are doing the same thing, most notably with rye products. At issue is the labeling of a product as being made somewhere and bottled somewhere else.

The other contemporary rectifying issue involves purchasing neutral grain spirits and adding flavor to them to produce products that are then referred to as "moonshine" and the like. There are voices on both sides of this debate, but ultimately it comes down to two things: the necessity of honesty in labeling laws, including the need to define more clearly and legally just what "moonshine" really is, and the reality that young distilleries, while aging a whiskey product, also need to be producing something they can make a profit from, to keep their businesses afloat.

Starting a distillery today is a huge expense. Sometimes, that means buying whiskey from producers like MGP, and sometimes that means a rectified white whiskey or other product. Some young distilleries opt instead to produce unaged products to get a foothold in the business. It varies from distiller to distiller, but in the long run the majority end up releasing products that they've made themselves.

Expect this issue to be prominent in the news for the next several years, and don't expect there to be easy answers. There are strong feelings on every side of the issue.

Prohibition clamped down on the distilling industry across the United States. In Tennessee it began long before the 18th Amendment, passing in 1909, going into effect in 1910, and not ending until 1937, leaving a nearly twenty-year gap that resulted in every distillery in the state except Jack Daniel's and George Dickel vanishing—and even Dickel survived only by moving to Kentucky and remaining there for decades after Prohibition ended, coming back after the company was sold to a larger spirits brand. Even now we are just regaining our reputation as a true distilling state, in spite of Dickel and Daniel's having powerful and long-established names in the industry. Everyone in the world knows Jack Daniel's.

Kentucky revived its industry and committed to it in the years after Prohibition. A few distillers remained open, producing medicinal spirits. They were further interrupted by World War II, which kept distillers busy making products for the war effort rather than spirits for personal use. After the war, most well-known distilleries focused on making a product that was sweeter and lighter, designed to truly please the palate. Maker's Mark provides a great example of a distillery that was very up front about its efforts to make a truly drinkable, milder bourbon. Its success is unquestionable.

Mike Veach's account to me underlines the changes that took place through those years and why Americans post-Prohibition wanted a lighter product.

"There are a lot of different factors that impact how the flavors changed. The biggest here was that during Prohibition and right after, there was still aged whiskey, but there was very little of it. Much of the whiskey made was used as medicine during Prohibition, you know. At the time, whiskey wasn't designed to be that old, either, the bonding period was eight years, and really old whiskey was very heavy and likewise not that desirable. During Prohibition, people used to smuggle much lighter Canadian and Scottish whiskeys in, or they'd dilute what they had with neutral grain spirits (essentially vodka) and rebottle and sell it.

"After Prohibition was repealed, the distilleries in many cases decided to lighten the flavor; they didn't have anything old, the new was much lighter, and that defined the public taste. It was likely true of beer too, by the 1960s all those American pilsner-style beers tasted alike. I think I'd rather drink water than American light beer today. It's kind of that Monty Python joke about making love in a canoe—it's too close to water," he laughs. Bourbon and whiskey didn't become watery, obviously, but they did aim for a taste that matched the new palate. Some of the old qualities like sourness or bitterness began to disappear, and the results were very much appreciated by the audience.

The rise of the craft brewing craze in the 1980s had a profound impact on the larger industry in the United States—suddenly the larger companies were looking at the interesting and flavorful beers being made and their popularity, and striving to buy those small companies or emulate them. The advantage was, they could get a product out quickly, but craft products had to be unique to have an impact, Veach says. By the 1990s, when the resurgence in the popularity of cocktail culture and brown spirits started, the big distillers were already making very good products that got even more attention. Craft distilling requires four to eight years of aging, so there developed the aforementioned problem of what to do in the short-term while the new whiskey ages.

"It's a problem even the big guys have. Woodford Reserve was first sourced from another Brown-Forman product, Old Forester. Fortunately, people were pleasantly surprised at just how good Woodford was when they started to release their own product," he says.

Taste issues for customers began to shift at the same time as those of packaging, and packaging was a primary concern, given the need for cost-effective means of passing on your product to the consumer. In the 1850s merchants and grocers had barrels and customers would bring their own jugs in to fill. Bottles were expensive, and it didn't make business sense to use them. Companies like Nelson's Greenbrier in Tennessee were among the first to mold bottles in standard sizes, and the brown glass machine-blown bottles didn't come along until the very early twentieth century.

At the time, when bourbon and whiskey came right from the barrel, it was typically bottled, according to Veach, at 90 to 105 proof, and drinkable right from the barrel. In the 1850s there were no multistory warehouses, so the product stayed around the same proof. Blending your whiskey to cut it came in via Hiram Walker's Canadian Club about this time. Even by the beginnings of Prohibition, the standard was still about 100 proof, though some companies like George T. Stagg were building multistory warehouses, where the variations in heat and cooling meant barrels of the same distillate matured quite differently.

Since the end of Prohibition, consumers and their demands have changed, and the industry has risen to meet that, big and small. While the 1960s to the 1980s saw a continuation of the spirits' popularity among its traditional audience, the rise of cocktail culture worldwide suddenly brought brown spirits back to the public eye in new ways in the 1990s, and started an unprecedented market for them not only in the region, but across the country and around the world. Today's biggest markets include Eastern Europe, Japan, China, and India. No more is the ideal whiskey and bourbon drinker an older Southern gentleman, sipping as he plays cards. The market has evolved to include young and old, urban and rural, international, and anyone educated about good spirits.

"Consumers have grown more knowledgeable about the product and know more about what they want in recent years," says Larry Kass at Heaven Hill Distilleries, which makes many of the well-known bourbon brands, including Elijah Craig and Evan Williams. "They have more tools at their disposal. This is a very unique time in bourbon history, and it's keeping makers on our toes.

"What's a good bourbon today? There's greater variety than there ever has been; the category has changed. There's been premiumization. In the 1960s there were no super premium brands. Single barrel has become a big thing—the goal is making one perfect bourbon, with nuance, at an epicurean level. For me that's something like Evan Williams Black Label. Small batch and single barrel are becoming like single malt scotch, ideally pure expressions of the whiskeys. They're priced that way too.

"We had to have demand to start making those things, and ironically, our first single barrels were made for Japan, but the trend made its way back here quickly. Today things like age and proof are more important distinctions than ever before. Consumers are helping us carve out new categories, and there's a new currency and connoisseurship that only dates back twenty years when you look at it. Now, if you go into a good bar, a good liquor store, there's more variety, the staff has more education—these are all the manifestations of a continuously maturing category."

I've heard similar words from every distiller, marketing person, and bartender I spoke with. The category is changing, maturing differently. The goal, though, is still the same, and the tight rules and regulations that define Kentucky bourbon and Tennessee whiskey for what they are remain in place, and that's a good thing. "There's a contrast between the old image and the new quality," Larry Kass says.

The torch is being passed still, from parents to children in long family lines of distillers. New distillers are taking it into their heads to make whiskey, and they're learning in an incredibly open industry from the Jimmy

Russells, the Bill Samuels, the Fred Noes. With the overwhelming growth of the industry over the past twenty years, you can only imagine what it will become in another twenty—but I expect it will still be true to its origins as well.

KENTUCKY

Kentucky's history as a distilling state is an unbroken line back to the colonial era. From the very first settlers, all the way through to today, lineages can be traced that are still deep in the branches of the bourbon family tree. It is a history unlike any other, rich with characters and full of adventure. Even Prohibition didn't stop them—six distilleries kept operating, producing alcohol for medical purposes and other uses. After Prohibition, when things could have gone badly, the families with bourbon history—and a few newcomers—set out to save the industry, and within a few years it was flourishing again. Kentucky has a tradition unlike any other state when it comes to the production of spirits, and that tradition has in turn created a rich, deep, thriving culture for the state that many don't even recognize. Anyone who thinks that Kentucky is all about coal and horses has missed its most powerfully impactful contribution to American culture today.

Kentucky has always loved its own product too, shamelessly purchasing and drinking it, and celebrating the culture it has created. The result of that love has been the creation of the epic Kentucky Bourbon Trail, which encourages tourists to make their way from distillery to distillery, learning how the state's signature product is made and coming to understand the incredible handcrafted nature of it all.

The Kentucky Distillers' Association actually conceived and created the Kentucky Bourbon Trail tour back in 1999, with the aim of sharing with visitors the art and science of crafting bourbon, and educating them about its traditions. The Bourbon Trail to date has been wonderfully successful, bringing hundreds of thousands of tourists to the state as they peruse the goings on at some of the biggest distilleries in the country. The

DISTILLERIES

There are many distilleries, large and small, in Kentucky. If you have the time, visit as many as possible, because the styles of bourbon and whiskey actually do differ from place to place. Many of the newer distilleries also offer alternative spirits—places like Barrel House and Corsair Artisan that made their names and got their businesses up and running while they aged their bourbon.

Many of these are covered in the book, but some of them you can explore on your own. As noted in the chapters, many of the big distilleries make multiple products. In addition, there are also a plethora of barreling and packaging houses that are putting out products as well. Some of those may have original distilled products in coming years.

Barrel House—Lexington
Barton's 1792—Bardstown
Brown-Forman (Old Forester)—Shively
Buffalo Trace—Frankfort

program allows you to get a "passport" with which you're encouraged to experience each individual distillery.

Among those included are Four Roses, Heaven Hill and the Bourbon Heritage Center (the company's two locations), Jim Beam, Maker's Mark, Town Branch, Wild Turkey, and Woodford Reserve. Between them, those distillers make a huge percentage of Kentucky's bourbons (note in each chapter where I've included lists of all the products made by those who make more than one). Heaven Hill, for example, is the source of a prodigious amount of bourbon under a variety of names—the most recognized being favorites Elijah Craig and Evan Williams, while the iconic Jim Beam also produces several other major favorites, including Knob Creek.

Most of Kentucky's large distilleries have long histories. Indeed, the Beam family has been distilling in Kentucky since before the American Revolution, and members of that family now have their hands in the

Bulleit—Louisville
Corsair Artisan—Bowling Green
Four Roses—Lawrenceburg
Buchanan Macley—Paris
Heaven Hill—Louisville
Jim Beam—Clermont and Boston
Limestone Branch—Lebanon
Maker's Mark—Loretto
MB Roland—Pembroke
New Riff Distilling—Newport
Old Pogue—Maysville
Paducah Distilled Spirits—Paducah
Wadelyn Ranch Distilling—Waynesburg (awaiting whiskey release)
Whiskey Thief Distilling Co.—Frankfort
Wild Turkey—Lawrenceburg
Wilderness Trail—Danville
Willett—Bardstown
Woodford Reserve—Versailles

distilling of more than just the Jim Beam brand. They have unquestion-ably built a powerhouse legacy for this art—the sort you perhaps expect in the European dynastic wine families but are pleasantly surprised to find duplicated in the United States.

As I spoke with so many of these distillers and the representatives for their companies, what struck me most was the passion they retain for the art and craft of spirit making, and the openness with which so very many of them share their knowledge and understanding across the discipline—and indeed, across the state lines into Tennessee. Almost universally, distill-ers at the new craft distilleries that have risen up in recent years sang the praises of Jimmy Russell, Fred Noe, Bill Samuels, Jim Rutledge, and all the rest for their tireless support and aid. Many of them also praised the help that came from Dr. Pearse Lyons and his crew at AllTech, for their help with yeast.

While exact details of proprietary mash bills may be secret, the atmosphere is incredibly open and welcoming. It's clear that Kentucky has a very vested interest in the industry continuing to thrive and grow. In doing so, it's created a solid economic opportunity for the state and an industry that continues to provide jobs and revenue, even through difficult situations like the economic downturn of 2008.

The success of the Kentucky Bourbon Trail has been echoed in its younger brother, the Kentucky Bourbon Trail Craft Tour, which opens up a longer path up Interstate 635 starting in Bowling Green and up along the Bluegrass Parkway. The Craft Tour highlights the new distilleries that have cropped up in recent years, in some cases distillers so new that as of this writing they were just getting their bourbon out.

Those distilleries include Barrel House Distilling Company, Corsair Artisan Distillery, Limestone Branch Distillery, MB Roland Distillery, New Riff Distillery, Old Pogue Distillery, Wilderness Trace Distillery, and Willett Distillery. Some of these are independent, some are owned by larger companies but operate independently, and some are old family distillers that have revived the family practice. Indeed, the revival of bourbon as a spirit nationally and internationally seems to have excited the heirs of bourbon distillers several times removed to reignite the family passion and take risks they never would have expected.

(Until recently the craft trail included the Silver Trail Distillery, but in April 2015 an explosion and fire destroyed the distillery, gravely injuring two employees, who suffered burns from the hot liquid and vapor and were literally blown out of the distillery's doors. The admirable way in which the distilling community has rallied around those injured and the distillery's ownership underlines the close-knit nature of this industry.)

As you tour the region, you'll notice that the drive from place to place is stunningly beautiful. Distilleries old and new seem to have made an effort to turn their manufacturing centers into places you want to go visit—whether you enjoy your bourbon or are a complete teetotaler. Many of the larger distilleries—and a few of the craft—are now National Historic Landmarks. You'll find buildings dating back two hundred years in some cases and be able to trace the changes that have occurred in the industry since Prohibition.

THE DISTILLERY CAT

I had never thought about the necessity of a distillery cat before visiting Woodford Reserve, but it turns out they're not all that uncommon. These days, while they may hunt mice in the warehouse, distillery cats are perhaps more mascots than anything else, but when most of the old distilleries got started, cats were vital to the industry.

Bourbon, you see, depends on grain, and grain draws rodents. No one wants mice and rats living in a grain storage bin, so enter the distillery cat. At Woodford Reserve I had the good fortune to make the acquaintance of Elijah, the nineteen-year-old resident cat who fulfilled the role there. By the time I met him, the old orange tabby Tom was pretty much devoted to lounging in patches of sunlight, oblivious of the tour, but he added a warmth to it all.

Sadly, Elijah went on to the great barrelhouse in the sky in October 2014, but since then I've met a number of other cats who keep the mice away at a variety of distilleries. I've even met one distillery dog, Shafer at Speakeasy Spirits in Nashville.

So don't be surprised, when you make your visits, to see a cat carefully minding the barrel storage. He's hard at work. (Or she, in the case of Pizza, Corsair's cat shown here.)

Photo courtesy of Darek Bell, Corsair Distillery

Even traveling in Lexington and Louisville, the evidence of the power bourbon has had in the state over the past few centuries is in evidence. Whiskey Row, as it is known, in downtown Louisville has brought the bourbon experience back into an urban area once renowned for its connections to the industry. Formerly a stretch of Main Street with ties to at least fifty distillers, it now offers a plethora of restaurants and bars celebrating the city's cocktail and culinary culture. My own favorite is easily Proof on Main, but there are so many good options, you need to take time to try them yourself. (Find the details for all the restaurants at www.bourbon country.com/things-to-do/urban-bourbon-trail.) Meanwhile, with the addition of urban distilleries like Town Branch and Barrel House, Lexington is bringing distilling itself back into the heart of the city.

Between the two cities, where a host of the distillers lie, you'll find rolling hills, wonderful small towns, and gorgeous scenery. It's some of Kentucky's heritage bluegrass country, and horse farms dot the rich, verdant landscape. When you come as a tourist, be prepared for a sophistication and culture some people foolishly don't associate with Kentucky. The proximity of distilleries on the Kentucky Bourbon Trail means you can plan a weekend around your trip, staying in Louisville or Lexington and visiting the big and the small places nearby with just a little driving.

In the chapters that follow, you'll sample a little bit of my own odyssey and get a sense of what some of the tours were like for me. I hope those chapters in particular get you excited about travel here—it's well worth it. Kentucky's bourbon history is unique—in the true sense of the word. You won't find anything else remotely like it, anywhere in the United States.

BARTON 1792

501 Cathedral Manor, Bardstown, KY 40004;
(502) 331-5879; 1792bourbon.com

Set in a revitalized nineteenth-century distillery, Barton makes a truly good-quality product, and some of its brands, especially the Very Old Barton, are overlooked gems—and very hard to find outside of Kentucky. The brand is owned by the Sazerac Company, which also owns the better-known Buffalo Trace. Barton is a small distillery, but the tour gives you a good look at the business side of the industry, with the added advantage of a brand-new visitor center, and master distiller Ken Pierce clearly knows what he's about. Outside the Bluegrass State, it's easiest to find Barton 1792 Ridgemont Reserve, and you won't find much more on the website. Even so, don't discount this tour and the chance to purchase the Very Old Barton if you have the opportunity.

Products: Ridgemont Reserve 1792 Small Batch Bourbon Whiskey, Very Old Barton Bourbon Whiskey, Ten High, Kentucky Gentleman, Kentucky Tavern and Tom Moore Bourbon Whiskey (most of these are hard to find commercially outside Kentucky)

Barton is something of a dark horse for a company making such a well-received product. Its distillery once upon a time was the old Tom Moore Distillery, founded by its namesake in 1879. The Barton company purchased it in 1944. Master distiller Ken Pierce says the historical record is fairly weak, and only the most basic details are known with any certainty.

We know with reasonable certainty that Tom Moore, a distiller, married a member of the Willett family in the 1870s and worked with his brother-in-law Benjamin Mattingly (also married to a Willett daughter) at the Mattingly & Moore Distillery (previously it had belonged to their father-in-law, John Willett). Mattingly appears to have sold his percentage

Photo courtesy of Amy Preske, Barton 1792

early on in the 1880s to other investors, but Moore maintained his until the end of the century. Upon selling his share, he bought land nearby and built a new distillery, eventually also purchasing the land on which the Mattingly & Moore site was built during World War I and combining the two properties.

Tom Moore kept the distillery going until Prohibition, and his son reopened it afterwards. The family sold the property in 1944 to a Chicago distiller named Oscar Getz, who renamed it Barton Distillery. Over the years, it became Barton Brands, Ltd., acquiring the production of a variety of products, including Kentucky Tavern from Glenmore in Owensboro, and purchasing several former Hiram Walker brands, including Ten High, as well as producing an assortment of other straight and blended whiskeys.

In 1993 the company sold to the Canandaigua wine company, which eventually became Constellation Brands. In 2009 the company sold Barton Brands, this time to the Sazerac Company of New Orleans. The distillery, which now is referred to as the Barton 1792 Distillery, is not part of the promoted Kentucky Bourbon Trail, but it truly is a good choice for a visit, and it's quite close to a number of other sites, including Heaven Hill and Beam.

Photo courtesy of Amy Preske, Barton 1792

Right now the company's flagship product is absolutely the 1792 Ridgemont Reserve, with its high rye mash bill. "It's a very bold, spicy bourbon," says Ken Pierce. "It's what we like; we enjoy the robust character." The name 1792 was given to commemorate Kentucky's attaining statehood and independent status from the Commonwealth of Virginia, of which it had formerly been a part.

The bourbon is complex and full-bodied, and lacks the overt sweetness you find in lower rye content bourbons. The spice notes are terribly and wonderfully present on the front, with middle notes of apple, cream, and vanilla, and you get the oak on the finish, with a hint of coffee and more pepper spice.

Pierce, the master distiller at Barton, took a bit of time out of his day to talk with me. Pierce is soft-spoken and outgoing compared to the likes of a Mark Coffman or Fred Noe, but he is clearly focused on his role and making sure the product continues to be outstanding.

"I'm a chemist by training," he says. "I made dairy and juice drinks before I came to Barton's. There are certain commonalities to observe there, but this of course, this is the king of the hill as far as beverages go." He's been in the bourbon making industry for twenty-six years and says that once people get into the business, they tend to stay around. A Georgia native, he started out at the Barton Brands' Atlanta facility, then came to Bardstown. Of Barton, Pierce says, "We're the quiet guys. We let the quality of our product do the talking. We make every effort to source as close as possible to the distillery; we love locally grown grains."

When I ask him about the little known Very Old Barton, he makes it clear he loves it. "It's a beautiful bourbon," he says. "We've had a loyal following for it for years, but only in Kentucky, and some in Tennessee and Indiana. Like the 1792, it tends to be rye heavy. It's got a nice bold, robust flavor, and it's aged eight years." He's been involved in its creation for quite some time.

With regard to the 1792, he says, "I've been involved with it since its inception. We started talking about it in 1994, and put the first of the whiskey away in 1995. It hit the market, oh, in 2003, I believe. I've been here for production since then. For me it's a labor of love; it's the nectar of the gods."

Pierce keeps a very close watch on his bourbon from grain to bottle. When we talk about flavor and how he achieves it, he says simply that "when I start evaluating, I'm looking for four components—wood, fruit, vanilla, and caramel. The wood, the oakiness, comes from the barrel, obviously. The fruit esters come from the maturation process; with this, they're like a Granny Smith apple. Then you look for vanilla, which is floral, and a caramel note, a brown sugar. Each bottle will have those things; they're a benchmark I look for in an aged product." The goal is a good-quality bourbon meant to be sipped and savored, he tells me.

I ask him to take me through a day in his life as master distiller at Barton. "A day in my life? I'm just always looking for consistency and continuity, making sure, for example, that I have quality grains. I monitor the fermentation process, so nothing goes 'sideways' at any point. I evaluate the distillate—I think it's what most master distillers spend their day doing. And then further down the road, I need to evaluate the aged product, as it gets dumped from the barrels, filtered, and bottled.

"When you have good-quality distillate, you can generally just leave it alone completely until it comes of age, then you get to decide which groups of barrels need to be dumped—after eight years for the 1792. You just let time and the magical charred wood do its work. There's incredible transformation from liquid in to liquid out, in the color, smell, and taste."

Unlike the Very Old Barton, the 1792 is available in all fifty states and has some international distribution. When you taste this bourbon—or any good bourbon—Pierce suggests pouring yourself a very small amount in your glass. Swirl the whiskey, smell it, take a small taste, and let it move around your mouth. Make note, he says, of

Photo courtesy of Amy Preske, Barton 1792

what flavors you get—everyone has a different palate and their own first take on flavor. "Our products are skewed toward very bold, spicy characteristics from the additional rye," he says.

He gently reminds me that they produce other products, noting the Kentucky Gentleman, Ten High, and Kentucky Tavern brands, all of which have a great following in the region. "They're all my children in a sense," he says. "I love them all, even though they're all very different. Each one of our products has a benchmark flavor profile. I make sure that each time we have a consistent product."

Pierce adds that every time he does a tasting it hits him again that "Wow, this is good stuff!" All his bourbons, he says, have a different mash bill, though they all maintain a higher rye content. "Mild" doesn't fit in with what they aim to do at 1792. That works just fine, because they're doing excellent high rye variations.

"How do you drink your bourbon?" I ask.

"Personally, for me? I like 1792 at room temperature, neat. It's 93.7 proof, and that's my 'fault.' I wanted to concentrate the flavor without too much alcohol sting; it's just below the break point—that's why we have a slightly odd proof."

I ask him what visitors to 1792 should expect. "I don't think there's necessarily an expectation . . ." he says meditatively. "Just come by and see exactly how we make our bourbon. You'll have a better appreciation for the amount of craft that goes into the product when you're through. When I talk about 'craft,' so much of this business is hands on, even to the point where we're rolling barrels into place, watching them age, then getting them back on a truck from the rackhouse to dump—it's all hands on, as we evaluate the aging product. And we do it all here on one site—distilling, aging, bottling."

Pierce says that he continues to learn things about the process of creating bourbon every single day, even after twenty-six years in the business. "It's a work in progress, and the day you stop learning, you've got a problem. The thing I think is my first charge here is consistency and continuity. The base of it, for me, is that I want you to be able to pick up a bottle of 1792, and if you've had it once, there's no surprise, you know exactly what you've got."

BARTON 1792 DISTILLERY COCKTAILS

The Barton Brooklyn

2 ounces 1792 rye
1 ounce dry vermouth
¼ ounce Luxardo Maraschino
  liqueur
2 dashes Angostura Bitters

Combine in a mixing glass, add ice, and stir till chilled. Pour into a fresh-chilled glass.

Rosemary's Ride

1 cube bourbon-smoked sugar*
Sprig rosemary
1 ounce fresh lemon juice
1 ounce White Dog infusion**
2 ounces 1792 Kentucky Straight
  Bourbon Whiskey
Can ginger ale

Muddle 1 cube bourbon-smoked sugar and rosemary leaves with lemon juice. Add ice, White Dog Infusion, and 1792. Shake until chilled. Double strain cocktail into a chilled martini glass. Add a splash of ginger ale. Garnish with lemon rind on a rosemary skewer.

*To make bourbon-smoked sugar: Mix four parts sugar with one part 1792 bourbon. Smoke over bourbon barrel bungs and char to dry. Cut dried sugar into chunks or cubes.

**To make White Dog infusion: Mix 2 cups sugar, 1 cup spring water, peel of one orange, and one sprig rosemary and simmer until sugar is completely dissolved. Turn off heat and allow mixture to cool, then stir in 375 ml White Dog. Pour White Dog mixture into infusion jar with peeled orange slices and allow infusion to sit for at least forty-eight hours.

BARREL HOUSE

1200 Manchester Street, Building #9, Lexington, KY
40504; (859) 259-0159; barrelhousedistillery.com

Barrel House is a charming, tiny spot that probably doesn't yet have enough room for you to bring in a whole busload of tourists, but the distillery and its owners have a great perspective on making bourbon—and some darned good alternative spirits that got the place up and running as well.

The Products: Pure Blue Vodka, Devil John Moonshine, Oak Rum, RockCastle Bourbon

The tiny Barrel House distillery is set in the old James Pepper Distillery bottling house in Lexington, and that's important to remember, because their locale is devoid of grassy hills and vistas most of us expect with our bourbon distilleries—it's set in a reclaimed industrial location destined to become part of the city's distillery district. It's also on the National Register of Historic Places, something that seems almost a point of pride for Kentucky's distillers. The original distillery operated from the 1870s to 1958 (right through Prohibition, producing "medicinal" spirits).

Barrel House proves a revelation, a marvelous reminder that upstart new distilleries thrive and grow in this region, more every day. Surrounded by what look like warehouses, only a small sign confirms that you haven't made an error; there's definitely a distillery here. Ok, that sounds good. You enter into a room that seems terribly small by comparison to the larger distilleries, where the decor looks more Old West than Old Kentucky. Shelves and plank-and-barrel tables hold books and local products—and plenty of bottles. To the left is a makeshift bar with a mirror behind it that might be a prop from *Deadwood* if you don't look too closely.

At the time of my visit, Barrel House had not yet bottled its first bourbon, though bourbon should be flowing by the time you read this page. Owners Pete Wright and Jeff Wiseman have, however, done all the right things to get their distillery started, beginning with products requiring short, if any, aging while they get the bourbon aged and right. This is one distillery I haven't made an advance appointment for, so I wander up to Robert Downing, the only part of the team present at the moment and explain what I'm there for—the hospitality is immediate, and I'm whisked into the story of the distillery.

Robert proves a study in enthusiasm. He's game for a short interview before the founders, Pete Wright and Jeff Wiseman, get back from making a run for grain. As we talk, however, other customers—clearly tourists—make their way in, and it's showtime. Robert leads us expertly through a tasting of the current products, and before long, Wright and Wiseman make their appearance and sit down for a chat that's pretty focused on product at first.

"Our tasting room is a pretty significant thing for us," says Pete Wright. "We value the tourists, and I think we have a pretty down-home, hands-on approach here. It makes distilling seem accessible. And really, we have it all in one room." He indicates the side door leading to the adjacent distilling and storage area, because they really do have everything in one place. Nothing is mechanized, which makes it a very, very different animal than what you experience down the road at the larger distilleries.

As mentioned, the bourbon is coming, but they needed something while it matured. That line stretched first to a very solid "moonshine" whiskey. On tasting, it's got a bit of bite, like white lightning ought to have, and then some sweetness on the finish. "It's an unaged product, so we could get it out quickly," Wright says.

They call it "Devil John," and it's made from a family recipe and named for a relation of owner Pete Wright. "That's really my heritage," he says. "Eastern Kentucky. Devil John served in the Civil War, was a local lawman, and on the side made moonshine. He happens to be a very colorful great-great-uncle of mine. It's a good name fit." The shine comes from a mix of cane sugar with milled corn, so you get both sweetness and character. One suspects this might have been the nature of Wright's relation as well. Regardless, it proved a good choice, hitting as it did a few years ago, at the point when the "moonshine" trend really took off across the country with a plethora of new distillers. Barrel House caught the zeitgeist and didn't look back.

From there we move on to corn-based Pure Blue Vodka. My whole crew recognizes this as something we can get behind. Pure Blue, it turns out, was the first spirit Barrel House produced. It's quick to make, for one thing.

"There's a real market for Kentucky vodkas," Wright tells me later. "We started making it as a wise economic choice; the goal was bourbon, but that takes time to produce, and we didn't have unlimited resources, so we needed to get a product on the market fairly quickly. It was a no-brainer. We started with the tag line 'Vodka in bourbon country? The answer has never been so clear.'" The vodka is made with 100 percent corn—none of that potato stuff—and I've got to admit it makes for a really sippable drink at 80 proof. "Like bourbon, you actually want to sip this vodka on the rocks," says Wright.

Well, yeah, but I also see cocktail potential crying out from it, without question. Even for a simple vodka-soda with a twist of lime, this is pretty terrific. Maybe toss in a dash of a favorite citrus bitters. Ah. The potential of good vodka.

They're using limestone-filtered spring water, just as with the bourbon, and that makes for smooth vodka. They source it at nearby Climax, Kentucky, and bring it to the distillery with a water tank. For that matter, one of the truly impressive qualities at Barrel House is their general commitment to source locally where they can for grains and sugarcane, something that's easier for small-scale distilleries, but which also makes for a pretty distinctive taste.

Last but not least, we try a bit of the OAK Rum. It goes down smooth, with an unexpected vanilla-butterscotch note that comes from aging in reused charred oak whiskey barrels, which they source largely from Buffalo Trace these days.

"In the early days, we sourced a lot from Four Roses, but we really only needed five to ten per order, so Buffalo Trace became easier. The goal is eventually to age the rum in our own bourbon

barrels," says Wright. He waxes on the subject of the close relations that exist between Kentucky distilleries. You hear that a lot up here, and it's very reassuring (you hear it in Tennessee too). The thing is, what's driving this industry's resurgence is in part due to the fact that distillers make an effort to help one another and build good relationships.

"The rum is a newer product because it requires aging, and we've only had it on the market for about two years, likewise. But rum is a classic American drink; they were making it all over back in the colonial era," says Wright. "The aging in bourbon barrels just seems to be right; it gives it a Kentucky touch."

Of course, we're inching closer to the bourbon release date. "We're optimistic," Wright says. "We'd like to have it out by September or October [2014], but I don't want us to release it, then be at a point where we can't release more to meet demand for several months, so we're saying definitely by spring of 2015. We're just so close—part of us just wants to get it out, but we've waited so long, so what's another six months?"

If the current products are any indication, there's good reason to be bullish on the bourbon and want to get a bottle to taste as soon as it becomes available. More is still to come, and Wright and co-owner Jeff Wiseman point out they're still learning the ropes of it all. Part of the intrigue here is just how good they got so quickly for a pair of mostly self-taught guys who started in other careers. "We read books, we went to the American Distilling Institute conferences and sat in on sessions, and then we had a lot of trial by experience. We have good advisors, Mr. Russell [the master distiller] comes by from Wild Turkey—the big distilleries have been very friendly."

Over in the corner through this conversation (held at a bourbon barrel table) is a ten-gallon still, the first one they used, Wiseman and Wright inform me, laughing about trying things over a turkey fryer burner. "We never intended that to be production," says Wiseman, "but to learn to produce good product from the process, so that was a great still for us."

Wiseman and Wright's story is not that unusual these days. They'd been friends since childhood and made their way in other industries. For Wiseman, that was air freight, for Wright, medicine. One night the pair of them started discussing the concept of a distillery over a poker game with a few other friends, and an idea was born. By the time it came to fruition—because they were serious—they were the only ones left. "We knew Lexington had a long history of distilling through the 1700s and 1800s. That ended with Prohibition in 1919. We thought, hey, it might be neat to have one again, so why not us?" says Wright. "The craft distilling movement hadn't really taken off yet—this was in about 2006—and we kept throwing it around. It started with six of us, and a year later it had whittled down to Jeff and me. It really took us a year to research and get all our licenses together. By the time we did all that, it was spring 2008. In June we initially leased this building. Now we own it. It was the bottling house for the Pepper Distillery."

He says they originally sought out barns and land out of town, but ultimately this space seemed a natural fit for them. Barrel House became the first craft distiller member of the Kentucky Distilling Association and one of the founding members of the Kentucky Bourbon Trail Craft Tour.

Currently Barrel House has statewide distribution in eight states, with more coming.

BARREL HOUSE DISTILLERY OAK RUM RECIPES

Old-Fashioned

1 teaspoon sugar
1 splash water
2 dashes bitters
1 maraschino cherry
1 orange wedge
2 ounces OAK Rum

Mix sugar, water, and bitters in an Old-Fashioned glass. Drop in a cherry and an orange wedge. Muddle. Pour in OAK Rum, fill with ice cubes, and stir.

OAK Rum Manhattan

1 ounce OAK Rum
½ ounce sweet vermouth
1 maraschino cherry

Add OAK Rum and sweet vermouth. Mix and serve in a martini glass. Garnish with a cherry, if desired.

Buffalo Trace

113 Great Buffalo Trace, Frankfort, KY 40601;
(502) 696-5926; buffalotracedistillery.com

Buffalo Trace is a great stop along the Kentucky Bourbon Trail, perhaps the oldest operating distillery in Kentucky. The National Historic Landmark is absolutely worth the stop. As far as the products go, Buffalo Trace itself is popular for good reason—it's exceptionally drinkable, and several of the company's other premium brands, including Blanton's, hold their own with distinctive character and flavor.

Products: Buffalo Trace, Ancient Age, Blanton's, Col. E. H. Taylor, Eagle Rare, Elmer T. Lee, George T. Stagg, Hancock's President's Reserve, Old Charter, Old Taylor, McAfee's Benchmark, Rock Hill Farms, Van Winkle, R. L.Weller, Rain Organic Vodka, Sazerac, Thomas H. Handy

Buffalo Trace, now owned by parent company Sazerac of New Orleans, may not be the oldest brand of bourbon by name made in the state, but it's surely made at one of the oldest distilleries in Kentucky, competing only, perhaps, with Burk's Distillery, now better known as the Maker's Mark distillery, for length of operations. The site is designated a National Historic Landmark for good reason, and several of the original buildings still survive, including warehouses dating back to the nineteenth century that are still in use today.

The history of the distillery dates at least to 1792, when the single-story stone house that still stands on the property, the "Old Taylor House," was constructed by one Commodore Richard Taylor. The narrative suggests that distilling on the site may go back as far as the 1770s, but there is no remaining physical evidence of that. The earliest established proof of its role in the fledgling bourbon industry comes from the building of a sizable warehouse for goods destined to be shipped down the Kentucky River

around 1811. Shortly thereafter, a gentleman named Benjamin Blanton is said to have begun his distilling there.

If those names sound familiar, it's because they lend their monikers—commemorating the distillery's illustrious history—to some of Buffalo Trace's bourbon products today, such as Old Taylor and Blanton's. (That's typical of the company, so keep paying attention to the names associated with the site—chances are good you'll see them repeated in product names, whether large or small batch.) In 1858 the first contemporary distillery was constructed on the site by Daniel Swigert.

After the Civil War, in 1870 the distillery changed hands, bought by Col. E. H. Taylor (another fine present-day brand), who the company says renamed the place "Old Fire Copper," a reference to the favored wood-fueled copper stills used in production during the era. Taylor spent a prodigious amount of money rebuilding the distillery, which he then sold a few years later to one George Stagg, along with other nearby property, though Taylor continued to operate the business himself. During this time, warehouses A and B were constructed, and they can still be seen today on the property, though Taylor's pricey distillery burned to the ground, reputedly after being struck by lightning in a storm, in 1882.

Photo courtesy of Amy Preske, Buffalo Trace

True to form, Stagg and Taylor rebuilt the distillery almost instantly, spending not only his insurance settlement, but more than $40,000 beyond it, adding a vast mashing and fermenting wing. Taylor apparently envisioned a distillery that would set the standard of the day, and he seems to have gotten it right. In 1886 they introduced a steam heating system for the warehouses, marking the first time the industry made use of climate control, and the same method—steam heat—that's used in the current industry. The distillery finally took on the name of its owner and became the George T. Stagg Distillery in 1904, more than thirty years after the purchase.

In 1897 one Albert Blanton, a sixteen-year-old at the time, went to work for the company; three years later, still a teenager, Blanton became

22 KENTUCKY BOURBON & TENNESSEE WHISKEY

Still House, Warehouse, and Bottling Superintendent. The company continued on very well until the passage of the Volstead Act in 1919. But when Prohibition hit the industry, the distillery was allowed to remain open, producing primarily medicinal product. In 1921, while Prohibition was still in full force during the Hoover administration, Albert Blanton became president of the distillery. He was just forty years old.

In 1929 the company was sold again, this time to Schenley, though it remained recognized as the George Stagg Distillery and would until the 1990s, when it became Buffalo Trace. By the time Prohibition ended in 1933, the Kentucky distilling industry was a mess. Schenley had the forethought to start a huge renovation at the Stagg Distillery, and between 1935 and 1937 he completely overhauled the place while others were struggling to survive. A huge percentage of the state's distilleries closed their doors for good as a result of Prohibition or in a failed attempt to overcome its effects afterwards. Other old established distilleries, like Burk's, ended up sold off cheaply (that sale worked very well for the Samuels' clan and the development of Maker's Mark).

By 1937 Schenley had turned the Stagg Distillery into a state-of-the-art facility, ready to go again. By 1942 the distillery had filled over a million barrels since the end of Prohibition, by 1953 that total hit two million.

From the 1950s to the 1980s, the distillery thrived. In 1984 came the introduction of Blanton's, one of the industry's very first single-barrel bourbons, which continues to have an impressive following today. Less than a decade later, in 1992, the family-owned Sazerac company purchased the distillery and began renovations.

Those renovations were completed in 1999, at which point the distillery's name was changed to Buffalo Trace as it launched the newest product: Buffalo Trace bourbon. In 2005 Harlen Wheatley, who had been with the company for ten years, became the master distiller, a position he holds today.

Wheatley, like many of the master distillers in Kentucky, comes from a family history of bourbon-makers. When I ask if he has a family history that ties him to the company or to Kentucky's distillery culture, he responds, "Not to [Buffalo Trace]; however, all good Kentuckians have a

OLD RIP VAN WINKLE

The Old Rip Van Winkle distillery, which produces the product, is a recent addition to Buffalo Trace and Sazerac. Its founder, Julian P. "Pappy" Van Winkle, worked for the W. L. Weller & Sons wholesale house in Louisville in the late nineteenth century, and eventually he and Alex Farnsley, a good friend, went in together and purchased the place themselves, along with the A. Ph. Stitzel Distillery, which made the warehouse's bourbon. The Stitzel-Weller Distillery, as it became known, produced several brands, including Old Fitzgerald, and was one of the few distilleries licensed to make medicinal bourbon during Prohibition.

From 1935 until his death at the ripe age of ninety-one, "Pappy" had a huge hand in the running of the distillery. After he passed away, Julian Jr., his son, took over, and maintained the distillery until he sold it in 1972, along with the rights to most of the brands, under pressure from stockholders. The only one he retained was Old Rip Van Winkle (one they hadn't done much with since before Prohibition).

After the sale Julian decided to bring that label back from the dead, using stock from the old distillery. Julian III took over the company in 1981, upon his father's passing, and continued the tradition (his own son, Preston, joined the company in 2001, making a fourth generation).

Today's version is a high-quality wheated bourbon using "Pappy's" original recipe—made with corn, wheat, and barley instead of using rye, which allows for a smooth finish and benefits from the long

history in the business. My grandfather distilled and barreled whiskey, and we have relatives that owned and operated the Jett Brother's Distillery, that went out during Prohibition."

I ask him about tasting Buffalo Trace, and he modestly refers me to the company's website, where you can find good details of the products aging—and all current production happens at Buffalo Trace, though the family maintains the same bar-setting standards they always have.

The product is outstanding, and the current fuss is worth it. With a myriad number of major awards, the Van Winkle brand is likely to continue as a rare favorite. If you have the opportunity and budget to pick up a bottle, and you truly like a smooth aged bourbon, make time for Van Winkle.

To gauge the popularity of Pappy and its legend, as well as Kentucky bourbon as a whole, consider this cautionary tale—it's the bourbon crime of the decade. In 2013 some 222 bottles of Pappy Van Winkle—barrel aged since the mid-1990s and worth a pretty penny (perhaps as much as $1,000 per bottle on the black market)—vanished from the distillery without a trace, leaving a mystery for more than a year. In April 2015 Frankfort County prosecutors indicted nine people allegedly responsible for thefts of bourbon worth up to $100,000, including the missing Pappy Van Winkle, as well as a number of barrels worth from $3,000 to $6,000 each from Buffalo Trace and Wild Turkey. The thieves' ring included two employees of Buffalo Trace, one of whom had multiple barrels stored at his home, and one from Wild Turkey. This discovery, according to police statements, may be only the tip of the iceberg.

they have available. But Buffalo Trace, speaking from my own tastings, is a pleasant but not overwhelmingly sweet bourbon, with lots of vanilla and brown sugar to start, spice on the back, then a finish of oak and toffee or brown sugar that lingers. There's a lot of complexity to it, and that makes it a favorite among serious drinkers.

I'll mention Blanton's because it really does have a huge following, and it's a very nice single-barrel product. Blanton's is nutmeg-y on the front, followed by a mix of vanilla, caramel, honey, and a little graininess, with a finish more modest than you'd expect. It's a very nice sipping bourbon.

Both Buffalo Trace and Blanton's have won a fair share of accolades and medals, as have many of the distillery's products. Of course, the biggest deal right now is probably Pappy Van Winkle, a truly aged bourbon that seems to be the big sensation in the bourbon world.

The young Van Winkle products are the ten- and twelve-year versions; the oldest come in at twenty and twenty-three years, respectively. It's a sipping bourbon, something to be consumed neat or not at all. My friend Robert Hicks (see the chapter on Speakeasy Spirits in Tennessee) is a huge lover of Pappy, and he likes the younger versions, as he's not a big fan of the woodsiness of the older variations, but each and every option Pappy Van Winkle offers is a good example of how well-aged bourbon ought to be.

These are absolutely limited-edition products that require true experience and understanding of the nature of bourbon itself on the part of its distillers to produce. The methods are expensive, and the aging increases the expense. When you make product and can't use it for at least a decade, let alone two, you have to offset that expense, and the allotment method by which it's distributed means it's very hard to come by—it's not just a matter of getting a bottle when you want it. Allotment means the number of bottles distributed in most areas is limited, so once it's sold out at the local liquor emporiums in Nashville or Lexington or Louisville, it's gone unless you can source it elsewhere (people have been known to fly off to another city to obtain more Pappy). At this writing, it's the hottest trend in the bourbon world.

How do you blend your barrels for the perfect flavor, I ask Wheatley. "The process is a bit proprietary," he says. "However, the key is matching the standard that has been agreed upon. So for Buffalo Trace, for example, we continue to compare each batch to the original batch that was produced in 1999. We vary the aging of each product, of course, from three to twenty-three years. Buffalo Trace is a premium small-batch bourbon that truly goes above and beyond to deliver authentic, independent, high-quality whiskey and value to each customer."

Photo courtesy of Amy Preske, Buffalo Trace

The life of a master distiller is never easy, obviously, and Wheatley acknowledges that. "Every day is different, but the idea is to preserve the legacy of our brands and consistently deliver the highest-quality bourbons and whiskeys for all our brands—and all that entails. From raw ingredients to maturing the bourbons, it's all important."

The Buffalo Trace production season focuses on spring and fall production, but Wheatley says they do run year-round. The company, says Wheatley, is notably protective of their mash bills, but he'll admit that they "use a combination of corn, rye, wheat, and barley, all at different ratios. We have six large recipes, with multiple experimental recipes. We source materials from area farmers and use a variety of water sources."

He continues, "We have a saying we use here, 'Honor Tradition, Embrace Change,' which pretty much embodies what we do. In many respects we're still doing things the way they have been done (as far as the bourbon-making process) for hundreds of years. We pride ourselves on our consistency in our taste profiles for our bourbons, but we've always got an eye on the future and love to experiment and find new bourbons to create while staying within the confines of bourbon. We believe the perfect bourbon hasn't been created yet, and we're doing our best to create it. I think customers can feel confident that they are getting an authentic, high-quality bourbon backed by 240 years of tradition."

What does he drink? "Typically a Buffalo Trace Manhattan, but it does depend on the occasion . . . "

Buffalo Trace is one of those distilleries I encourage visiting. Its proximity to both Louisville and Lexington makes it easy to be part of a planned trip. Like many of the historic distilleries in the area, it's lush, green, and welcoming. The National Historic Landmark status and the fact that they stake a reasonable claim to be the very oldest continuously operating distillery in the United States definitely add to the interest here. Like Woodford Reserve, there are several different touring options depending on what aspect of the distillery most interests you, including a seasonal ghost tour, so check the website for the most current options before you come.

BUFFALO TRACE COCKTAILS
(courtesy of Buffalo Trace Saloon)

Buffalo Beatdown

¼ ounce Buffalo Trace Bourbon
1 part orange juice
1 part pineapple juice

Add ingredients to shot glass, in order—Buffalo Trace, orange juice, pineapple juice—sip or shoot, and enjoy!

Buffalo Blood
(created by David Valiente)

1 ½ ounces Buffalo Trace Bourbon
½ ounce blood orange bitters
3 dashes Peychaud's Bitters
1 ounce fresh honey tangerine
 juice
Ginger ale

In a mixing pint combine Buffalo Trace, both bitters, and tangerine juice; stir well. Strain into bucket glass over fresh ice. Top with ginger ale. Garnish with burnt tangerine zest.

Four Roses

1224 Bonds Mill Road; Lawrenceburg, KY 40342;
(502) 839-3436; fourrosesbourbon.com

F our Roses, both tour and product, appeal to a broad range of people across the spectrum. Master Distiller Jim Rutledge (who plans on retiring in 2015) has produced a terrific product, and with the team from Kirin has resurrected a fine old brand and restored it to quality and prominence. Touring the distillery is pure fun, and the California Mission–style architecture will appeal to a lot of people. If you're planning tours carefully, make sure you take this one—it's a great tour to really give you a sense of what big distillery tours are like.

The Products: Premium Single Barrel Bourbon, Small Batch Bourbon, Yellow Label Bourbon

If you still think about Four Roses, but haven't had it in the past several years, your memories may be clouded by the fact that once upon a time, like, say, until 2002, it wasn't much of a beverage to rave about. The company had been acquired by Seagrams in the 1940s, and in the late 1950s they made the unexpected business decision to sell all the good bourbon overseas and turn the Four Roses brand in the United States into a lower-quality blended whiskey. Until 2002, when the Japanese firm Kirin (of Kirin beer fame) purchased it, that was what you could expect. Kirin, in turn, opted to reintroduce a fine-quality whiskey product back to the US market with Four Roses, and everything changed.

The story goes that Four Roses got its start with owner Paul Jones Jr. in the 1880s. He trademarked the name Four Roses in 1888, and he seems to have been producing whiskey for at least twenty years at that point. By 1922 his company bought out the Franklin Distilling Company— one of the few that operated all the way through Prohibition producing medicinal whiskey—cough, cough—for the market. (You can see some of the Prohibition-era medicine bottles on display behind glass in the Four Roses tasting room.) They sold the family company to Seagrams in 1943.

The distillery is a lovely place. It seems wholly out of place amid the Kentucky landscape, built as it is in the California Mission style of architecture. (I have to admit, I kept picturing Jimmy Stewart and Kim Novak running through at any moment.) Apparently, Paul Jones Jr. made frequent trips to Northern California in the early part of the twentieth century and fell in love with the architectural style he saw there. When he wanted it for his distillery, he consulted a plethora of Kentucky architects, most of whom seemed to have no concept of what he was looking for, but he ultimately found a friend who could translate his vision into reality. The buildings, constructed in 1910, are now on the National Register of Historic Places.

As to the source of the name, the story goes, according to our excellent tour guide, that Mr. Jones courted a lovely Southern belle to whom he proposed a number of times, each time suffering her refusal. Finally she told him that she would think about it, and if she showed up to a forthcoming social event wearing a floral corsage, that meant she would consent to be his bride. When Jones arrived at the event, there was the girl of his dreams, wearing a corsage of four tiny roses. And thus did Four Roses earn its name.

Of note, there is some confusion as to whether Four Roses was in fact tied to an Atlanta family of distillers at the same time named Rose, from whom the name may have come, but the distillery maintains absolutely that Paul Jones is indeed the founder and that the name comes from the story of his romance. I see no reason to doubt that.

Four Roses' visitor center is a gorgeous mix of the modern with hints of period California style—glass, mirrors, and wood everywhere. There lies an abundance of cool ephemera of the sort you expect in the best gift shops, from chotchkes and T-shirts to fine crystal glasses. We arrived on a Saturday afternoon, which turned out to be a very good thing, as we lucked into Heather Boggs as our tour guide. Apparently she only works weekends, but she easily proved one of the very best guides I've ever had on a tour. She knew her product, she loved it, and she was a font of information, able to answer whatever question you asked.

The tour starts with a helpful video, iterating the importance of Four Roses' location along the Salt River, from whence they source their water, and reminding visitors of the stringent guidelines applying to the fabrication of real Kentucky bourbon. When the video finishes, Heather takes over seamlessly, giving us more detail on how whiskey gets made, and the details of what goes on in the process.

Four Roses is a larger-batch producer, and it's more mechanized in its methods than smaller places nearby, but that doesn't mean it's producing a lesser product. One of the noted facts is the use of single-story warehouses to age Four Roses—something that seems to have a specific effect on the aging and flavor. Simply put, in a non-climate-controlled environment, there is a fairly minimal difference in the temperature between the barrels on the bottom row and those on the top, so there's no need to rotate barrels in the aging process. They once had a multistory facility, but sold that to Wild Turkey.

Each one-acre big, single-story warehouse holds approximately 24,000 barrels of bourbon at any given time. As Heather tells us, there are more

barrels of bourbon aging in Kentucky at any given time than there are people and yet, worldwide demand is so high, it gets harder every year for distillers to meet it.

Four Roses' methodology involves crafting ten separate and distinct bourbon recipes, and making use of five different proprietary strains of yeast used on two distinct mash bills of grain: One is 75 percent corn, 20 percent rye, and 5 percent malted barley; the other 60 percent corn, 35 percent rye, and 5 percent malted barley. Each of the yeasts provides a distinct set of notes: delicately fruity, slightly spicy, rich fruit, floral, and herbal. Heather informs us that these same yeast strains have been used since the 1950s, at least on the fine export bourbon being made, and the company owns no less than three hundred proprietary strains of yeast. One thing you learn at distilleries is to take the discussion of yeast and fermentation seriously.

Then we're off to wander the fermenting vats made of old red cypress, then the vast copper stills—first the "beer still" where it's boiled up through twelve layers of metal plates and then into the doubler at 120 proof, from the neck of which it pours out as 140 proof distillate. The red cypress of the vats, Heather tells us, is growing endangered, and eventually they'll have to shift to another neutral wood, like Douglas fir. The average life of a vat, fortunately, is about fifty years.

On the grounds there's a splendid old fountain dating back to 1910, which reminds us just how long this property has been producing bourbon. We see up close the terribly small building where deliveries of grains are made and samples tested—to make sure if something ever goes wrong, they can pinpoint where it happened. They accept deliveries of Danish-grown rye, Wisconsin barley, and Indiana corn regularly. According to Heather, in 2013 only three loads of grain were returned for being substandard. There's a hammer mill on-site to grind the grain.

The company, we learn, pulls and filters about a million gallons of water from the Salt River each day they distill—usually between Labor Day and Memorial Day to mid-June, with little done over the summer to avoid overusing water resources. Four Roses sends about 6,500 gallons of distillate (white dog, white lightning, pick your name) twice a day via tanker truck to Bardstown, where it's barreled and stored. She adds, however, that about three-quarters of that water, thoroughly treated, is returned to the river.

Like its compatriots, Four Roses doesn't reuse its barrels, and also like its fellows, you can purchase a barrel for about $100. They are typically bought by companies making beer, rum, cider, and wine for a second use. "Using a barrel over again is like using a tea bag the second time," says Heather confidently. "There just aren't the flavors and tannins to blend with the distillate and make it into the same thing."

The final part of this adventure is in the tasting room, where a good tour guide is worth her weight in gold. Four Roses makes five different blends of their whiskey, two of which are exported solely to Japan. Heather says those have, respectively, notes of ginger (for the super premium) and of mint, neither of which sounds like a match for the American palate.

What we do try are those readily available here. First is the Four Roses Yellow. As a moderately priced bourbon, this rightfully deserves raves. It's smooth and drinkable, and while it may be the "workaday" bourbon, it's meant to make good cocktails at 80 proof. The nose is spicy and fruity, with caramel and spice on the palate and a mellow finish with a hint of fruitiness. Four Roses Small Batch, at 90 proof, has a charming nose of oak and fruit and a bit of butterscotch, with berries on the tongue and a fruity, smooth, long finish. It's very nice. Finally, the Single Barrel offers some fairly intense flavors—it's your Sunday-go-to-meeting bourbon, per Heather. The nose has maple syrup, spice, and a little cocoa and fruit. On the tongue, it gets quite full, with plum and more oak, then a smooth, creamy finish.

Jim Rutledge is among the most personable people I've had the pleasure to talk with, but then, that's not a terribly uncommon personality trait in his profession, as I've discovered. His fellows have all proven to be a joy in conversation. Perhaps it's the patience required to create a good spirit that does it? He opens up expansively on his subject when given the chance, and he's also played mentor to plenty of other distillers.

Rutledge's story goes something like this: After graduating from the University of Louisville, he got a job offer from Seagrams—then owner of Four Roses—in Research and Development in the Louisville area in 1966. However, he indirectly impacted all the company's brands. As time passed, he moved on to production management and eventually had a hand in almost every area of production for the company, spending eleven years in Louisville before transferring to New York in 1977, where he worked to develop budgets for all Seagrams' US plants.

In the late 1980s he got involved with Four Roses, then an export product, and began campaigning to bring it back to the states in its high-quality form. At the time, Seagrams needed a bourbon, so it seemed like a good deal. When the opportunity to return to work in Louisville presented itself in 1990, Rutledge jumped at the chance. "No one in New York could understand why I'd want to go back and work in a dirty distillery," he says with a rueful laugh. In 1992 he finally returned as administration manager for the Kentucky operations and in 1994 took over as master distiller. At the time, he says, he had a burning passion to get Four Roses back to US markets—the real thing, not the blended whiskey currently appearing under its name over here.

"The United States hadn't seen real Four Roses since 1960," Rutledge says. The company marketed both a blended and a premium whiskey from 1945 on, but at the end of the 1950s, the owners pulled the Kentucky-produced bourbon off the market, turning it into export only (the blended whiskey market generally declined dramatically in the United States during the 1960s, which didn't help matters). Only the blended whiskey remained available over here. He adds that essentially, Seagrams built the brand to what it saw as peak performance, then chose to pull support for it and let it die based on nothing but popularity. Seagrams then changed the blend, making it some 65 percent grain neutral spirits, sourced outside Kentucky.

"From there it became a bottom shelf brand; its reputation was completely destroyed," Rutledge says. The company resisted efforts, even his own, to bring it back, but, he says, "I wasn't at all intimidated by New York." He kept up the fight. Rutledge continued to work in Kentucky for the company, and in 1996 the embargo on the export product was lifted sufficiently that Kentucky employees actually got to *taste* their own product. It was, he says, "a foot in the door, a little bit of progress."

The big change came in 1999, when Seagrams announced they were getting out of the alcohol business, and in 2001 it became official with the majority of liquor brands sold to Diageo and Pernod as Seagrams moved off into the entertainment industry. Four Roses itself got sold to Japanese beer manufacturer Kirin. "It [the export version] was the number one brand of bourbon in Japan at the time, and they didn't want to lose the brand—Kirin had a vision for growing it."

The first week in January of that year, a contingent from Kirin Japan made their way to Kentucky and started asking serious questions of the staff, including Rutledge. He made it clear he felt Kirin ought to kill off the blended whiskey currently borrowing the Four Roses moniker and bring back a true bourbon. It was the right thing at the right time, as the popularity of brown spirits was starting to grow again, and Kirin agreed.

Rutledge says in spite of the decline in the bourbon and whiskey trend from the 1960s onward, the export bourbon's brand sales for Japan had really "shot through the roof" in the late 1980s—their only major global market growth—which meant Seagrams had maintained the Japanese propriety brands.

In the early 2000s, Rutledge needed to seriously reestablish the Four Roses name. "We fought an enormous battle to rebuild the brand in *every single state*," he says. "We had to emphasize that the blended spirit wasn't made by us, but by other distilleries outside Kentucky. One advantage to not really being on the market for so long is that younger audiences picked up on the brand, and people in their twenties and thirties thought it was new. But we had to fight the old blended reputation all the way, even so— even though we'd destroyed all the blended stuff. In terms of marketing and sales, we had to define ourselves as a quality bourbon."

Asked what makes Four Roses special, Rutledge talks about a lot of things, from blending the bourbon to consistency using the ten distinct flavor profiles and their proprietary strains of yeast and the amount of aging. He has, he says, a target recipe here, as he samples each barrel prior to a bottling run and tweaks that recipe with the aim of achieving consistent flavor across the board. Four Roses, he believes, has a strong consistency of taste for consumers.

Single-barrel runs, he says, make for a different experience. The smell and taste of each reads wholly different from each of the others. "An expert couldn't necessarily tell they were from the same distillery," he says. But for many buyers, that's the joy of the single barrel; it's something distinctive.

Next on the list of special qualities, Rutledge harkens back to the early Seagrams days under Sam Bronfman following Prohibition. The company policy required using the finest raw materials, including developing its own strains of grain back in 1960. Following the sale to Kirin, they committed to the same game plan they'd used with the premium export product. The Four Roses corn comes from central Indiana. "Our farmers know the quality of grain we require," he says. "We're using Yellow Corn Number 2; you can check it out in the *Wall Street Journal* commodities section if you like, to see what price it's going for today. We are always willing to pay premium to make sure we get the *best*. The farmers know to maintain that quality for us if they want to be getting more than the *Wall Street Journal* base price."

"It's the distillate that's my focus," says Rutledge with pride. "It must be perfect. Don't fill barrels up with something that's going to make bad bourbon—ever. An off product, something with harshness or mold—you know, it's just not flavorful if the grain itself isn't good."

Four Roses contains a decidedly high rye content—arguably more than any of its competitors. "You get the best rye from cold climates, and back in the late 1990s, we realized the finest was coming from northern Europe, from Sweden, Denmark, or Germany for the most part, and we started buying it. Sourcing and selecting the good stuff pays off.

"In terms of grains, we've also got a long-term relationship with our corn growers; we know what we want. Our corn is 100 percent GMO free. We aren't going to sacrifice on our requirements. Back in the old days with Seagrams, from the Depression to the 1950s, we were number one for a reason. I'll say that we are far better today. We're always striving to get better, and there are a lot of variables, but grain, grain is the key."

Under Rutledge, Heather Boggs's explanation of Four Roses' ten recipes (see above) has come to fruition, further developing the methods that date back to the Seagrams days.

Rutledge isn't aware of any other distillery using so many yeasts (they have over 300 proprietary strains). Long ago, when Four Roses operated five separate distilleries, the company used one specific type of yeast with each of the two mash bills. Even the water sources were different, so the variation was quite distinct. In the late 1960s, four of those distilleries were shuttered, but the additional yeasts were kept active. With now only the Salt River water source, it was impossible to completely duplicate those flavors, but it still provided unique variety.

These days, the bottle with the yellow label—tour guide Heather Boggs's "everyday bourbon"—uses a blend of bourbon crafted from all ten of those recipes. A bottle of single barrel has just one, and small batch contains four. The small batch released each year may contain a blend of any of those ten types in combination.

More than a decade has passed since Four Roses was resurrected from blended oblivion, with Jim Rutledge proudly at the helm as master distiller. In the last three years, the recorded case sales have jumped exponentially from those of previous years. In 2011 they were 42 percent over 2010; in 2012, 58 percent over; in 2013, 71 percent—and it looks like 2014 will see a rise of 70 percent more case sales over 2013. That's something to be proud of, and it suggests that the resurgence of brown spirits—and specifically of American whiskey and bourbon—is a real thing and Four Roses has made a place for itself in the Kentucky firmament, the blended whiskey well forgotten.

If you're buying for the first time, Rutledge says that the high rye content means a little spice on the front. "Expect a highly flavored, slightly spicy drink with real smoothness and mellowness. I just don't think anyone competes with the consistency of our product either. Pick up the yellow label. You'll think 'I can drink this'—no kick, no bite—just good sipping bourbon."

Four Roses Distillery Cocktails

Four Roses Perfect Manhattan

½ ounce sweet vermouth
½ ounce dry vermouth
2 ½ ounces Four Roses Small Batch
  Bourbon
Enough ice cubes to fill a shaker
  three-quarters full
1 twist lemon peel

Combine the vermouths, bourbon, and ice in a mixing glass. Stir gently, don't bruise the spirits and cloud the drink. Strain the mixture into a chilled martini glass. Rub the cut edge of the lemon peel over the rim of the glass and twist it over the drink to release the oils, but don't drop it in. Enjoy.

Four Roses Old-Fashioned

The classic Old-Fashioned was originally created in Louisville, Kentucky, in the 1880s by a bartender at the Pendennis Club.

1 cube sugar (or a splash of simple
  syrup)
2 dashes bitters
2–3 ice cubes
1 ½ ounces Four Roses Small Batch
  Bourbon
1 twist lemon peel for garnish

In an Old-Fashioned glass, place a sugar cube (or use simple syrup as a substitute). Add bitters and just enough water to help dissolve the sugar. Crush or muddle the sugar to coat the bottom of the glass. Add ice cubes and bourbon. Garnish with a twist, or if you'd like, a slice of orange and a cherry.

HEAVEN HILL

1311 Gilkey Run Road, Bardstown, KY
40004; (502) 337-1000; heavenhill.com

Heaven Hill is one of the largest family-owned distilleries nationally and internationally, producing far more than just bourbon. Their well-known products include Evan Williams and Elijah Craig, the company's flagship brands, along with Pikeville Straight Rye, Larceny, Henry McKenna, Fighting Cock, Old Fitzgerald, and Rittenhouse, among others it produces or imports. The company has distribution rights to a wide variety of other spirits, including Burnett's London Dry Gin, HPNOTIQ, and Lunazul Tequlia. The company's Heaven Hill Bernheim distillery in Louisville and its Bardstown facility provide two stops worth making on the Kentucky Bourbon Trail.

Flagship Products: Elijah Craig and Evan Williams

Heaven Hill Products and Imports

Bourbon: Cabin Still Bourbon, Echo Spring Bourbon, Elijah Craig, Evan Williams, Fighting Cock, Heaven Hill, Henry McKenna, J. T. S. Brown, J. W. Dant, Kentucky Supreme, Larceny, Old Fitzgerald, Parkers Heritage, T. W. Samuels, Virgin

Whiskey: Bernheim Original Straight Wheat Whiskey, Georgia Moon Corn Whiskey, Heaven Hill Kentucky Whiskey, Kentucky Deluxe Blended Whiskey, Parker's Heritage Collection, Pikesville Straight Rye Whiskey, Rittenhouse Straight Rye Whiskey, Trybox Series American Whiskey

Other Brand Names: Admiral Nelson's Spiced Rum, Ansac Cognac, Agua Luca Brazilian Rum, Arandas Tequila, Aristocrat (whiskey, vodka, tequila, gin), Blackheart Spiced Rum, Burnett's (gin, vodka), Christian Bros. (brandy, port, sherry), Cinerator Hot Cinnamon, Copa De Oro, Coronet VSQ, Domaine Canton French Ginger Liqueur, Du Bouchett, Dubonnet, Fulton's Harvest Cream Liqueurs, Glen Salen Scotch, High

Rise Vodka, HPNOTIQ Liqueur, Lunazul Tequila, Maripose Agave Nectar, O'Mara's Irish Country Cream, PAMA Pomegranate Liqueur, Ron Leave Rum, Two Fingers Tequila, Whaler's Original Rum

Heaven Hill is a great story to examine: Here is a big producer that still maintains a family ownership and smaller producer style—even though they make or import a phenomenal number of brands. With help from their director of communications, Larry Kass, they provide insight into the economics of the rapidly changing bourbon and whiskey market. Let's be honest, twenty years ago, most people outside the region would have been indifferent to American whiskey—today, we can't get enough of it, and Heaven Hill is one of the larger distilleries leading the charge forward. Evan Williams and Elijah Craig hold up pretty well if you're looking for bourbon to sip, and most of their brands don't present you with overwhelming sticker shock.

The distillery came into being in 1935, early in the Roosevelt era and not long after the end of Prohibition. The Shapira family took a fair amount of risk in opening a distillery—though Prohibition was over, attitudes toward it were still not positive in many places nearby, especially in the religious South. The fledging company had no inventory to speak of and no recognizable brand name. The Depression was still on, and most folks didn't have a lot of cash leftover to purchase bourbon and whiskey. It probably didn't hurt, however, that the company brought in Joseph Beam, a member of *that* Beam family, as master distiller (the Beam family line continues to this day at Heaven Hill, with master distillers Parker and Craig Beam). The company's first bourbon was called Bourbon Falls, one that's gone by the wayside today.

During the Second World War, the distillery was actually shuttered for public production and instead focused on the war effort, but they came roaring back, bringing in Earl Beam as master distiller in 1946. Evan Williams didn't come into existence until the late 1950s, at which point it almost immediately became a best seller for the company. In 1960, the year after current master distiller Parker Beam joined the firm, the company filled its millionth barrel. Parker's son Craig joined up in 1986, and together the pair have been making whiskey ever since. That's also the year Heaven Hill released Elijah Craig 12 Year, the first true "small-batch bourbon," to the market.

By 2004 Heaven Hill had vastly multiplied its empire, expanding from the realm of bourbon and whiskey distilling to importing and distributing a plethora of other products. Awards for their distillery products began to pour in, as the level of national and international whiskey competition continued to grow more serious. That year, they opened the Heaven Hill Distilleries Bourbon Heritage Center. They followed its award-winning success in 2013 by opening the Evan Williams Bourbon Experience in Louisville, on historic Whiskey Row.

For most of the company's history, the focus has been on its own products. Specifically, the best known of those are the Evan Williams and Elijah Craig lines of bourbons and whiskeys, products that have developed solid name recognition and respect in the industry—though newer products like Larceny are fast building a major national reputation.

These days, Heaven Hill is one of the largest makers and holders of distilled spirits in the world, having made some smart decisions about import and acquisition over the past twenty years. Among its import products, the vivid cerulean mix of vodka, cognac, and fruit juice HPNOTIQ (Heaven Hill acquired the import right in 2003), bottled in France, is now easily one of the top ten imported liquor sellers in the United States.

Heaven Hill is also one of the few truly large bourbon makers still locally owned (still by the Shapira family), no small thing in the era of corporate buyouts. It's got as good a historic Kentucky set of bona fides as any of the other big distillers in the region and makes plenty of good product. According to Larry Kass, what makes Heaven Hill particularly special is that while they manage to compete with some of the largest producers and distributors in the world, they also have a very distinctive corporate model that still manages to maintain independence and family-owned status at a time when that's an increasing rarity.

"Our history is actually a particularly interesting case study, when you look at it," says Kass. "At one time, all the distributors in Kentucky were independently owned—often family owned—but since Prohibition there have been very big changes. Obviously, Heaven Hill was founded right after Prohibition specifically as a bourbon company, but over the years we've diversified to the point that we're now the sixth-biggest distilled spirits producer in the United States, and the second-largest bourbon holder in the world. Evan Williams is the second-biggest brand of bourbon out there.

"It's hard not to reflect on the fact that this is a family-owned, independent corporate culture. This is the third generation of the Shapira family, and we've had Beam family members as distillers from the beginning."

Kass speaks well for the distillery and its business, emphasizing the company's two stops on the Bourbon Trail: Bardstown, for more than ten years now, and Louisville, a more recent presence. Bourbon tourism, Kass says, has created a wonderful new sense of bourbon appreciation, and for Heaven Hill, which has more labels than just about any other company, including a plethora of small ones, getting people to visit and see the breadth of what they are doing is a big deal.

Some of those labels, Echo Spring Bourbon for example, have historic resonance for those who keep tabs on product history. For those who don't remember or don't follow American drama, Echo Spring is the reference that Brick, the character in Tennessee Williams's *Cat on a Hot Tin Roof* (played in the film by Paul Newman), makes with regard to his all-too-frequent trips to the liquor cabinet. Clearly, for audiences in the 1950s, the term was synonymous with bourbon. Many of the Heaven Hill brands have that kind of resonance today, just as they and others did in the past.

Kass has a long history with Heaven Hill. He's spent seventeen years with the company, first as a bourbon brand manager and now directing corporate communications. Given the vast scope of Heaven Hill, he's the ideal guy to quiz about the burgeoning renaissance of American bourbon and whiskey, seeing it up close as he does. After all, he promotes a plethora of brands and watches them compete in a liquor market that's also heavily impacted by the company's non-whiskey holdings.

Bourbon, says Kass, wasn't much of a thing when he was growing up in the Northeast. In the 1970s and early 1980s, there was little appreciation, he says, for bourbon or whiskey at all. "If you knew a brand name, it was maybe Jim Beam or Jack Daniel's, if anything. There was just little appreciation, especially outside of Tennessee [and] Kentucky. In the Northeast it was a very different situation. There was no regional affinity for whiskeys then, and it was never marketed particularly well."

Kass's experiences underline the reality that even though the market in the Southeast remained at least solid, the real resurgence of whiskey and bourbon as spirits didn't start until the 1990s. "When I moved to Kentucky about twenty-four years ago, I discovered the tremendous tradition these products had down here. At that time the national demand was less, but that proved to be an untapped equity; there were distilleries, but they had no traction—at the time, there was a lull in interest, and bourbon just wasn't a highly thought of product.

"Over the past ten to twenty years, though, the category has just taken off—it's highly regarded in a way you couldn't have imagined back then. Brown spirits are leading the global charge, I think. There's been a tremendous change in the rate of sales, the way the products are received. Kentucky taps into that—we have an active renaissance of bourbon going on right now in Louisville."

That, according to Kass, has positives and negatives. He admits that the market has led to a bit of befuddlement, especially with the proliferation of non-distilling producers. But in the end, he says proudly, "We have credibility we've made by being completely honest about what we do regardless of the fact that it's a wild and woolly world out here in American whiskey right now." He cites, for example, the Georgia Moon Corn Whiskey that Heaven Hill has produced for thirty years and established as a product at a time when the notion of similar corn whiskeys has gotten trendy and brands are proliferating—not just in Kentucky and Tennessee, but all over.

Heaven Hill, Kass says, is a great example of a company that's large, but it's run "leaner" than the average. The presence of second- and third-generation owners who are hands on and have worked directly to make the business happen is important to the company culture. So is the presence of equally multi-generational distillers from the Beam clan. "I've gotten to see close to twenty years of this, of watching the company expand and make decisions as the industry exploded." he says. "We've had the chance to build a long-term perspective. We understand that culture directly affects sales, so when things happen like the *Moonshiners* reality show, we see a spike in sales of Georgia Moon. When we see ryes starting to take off, and a rise in craft distilling, we recognize that it's a great opportunity to promote our products during what's becoming a pivotal moment."

The explosion in this culture brings more people down to the Bourbon Trail, to explore the distilleries—and that gets people even more excited, Kass says. I feel the need to ask him what the deal is—what's made bourbon so very "hot" in the past decade, and what makes it seem to be growing even faster each year?

"You're not the first person to ask that," Kass says. "There are several reasons. One is premiumization—there's a corollary between price point and growth, because people want a premium product. But I'd also say that craftsmanship plays into it. Right now, the artisan food and beverage culture is really impacting the bourbon industry too, because it plays into the way bourbon is perceived and the way it's made.

"When you can show them that it's an all-natural, traditional process, dependent on grain, yeast, water, and a charred wood barrel—I mean, the nature of bourbon works well with the whole 'slow food' concept, doesn't it? That's what it is. It's on a big scale, but it's the same kind of careful process, when you talk about the tightly regulated effort to make it right. The public consciousness of what it's eating and the making of good bourbon are part of the damn perfect storm.

"You've started to see the first serious whiskey shows and competitions over the past fifteen years or so, the first showing off of master distillers. You have a defined 'place' things come from. We had something like 600,000 people visit last year [2013]. There are a bunch of factors going on—cultural, societal—that all create a new appreciation."

Well, yes, but what about the continued influx of foreign alternatives? Heaven Hill's imports seem to be doing stunningly well too. How, I ask, does bourbon and whiskey made here compete with all that?

Kass laughs. "There's absolutely a thing about American products. We're a younger country, of course. But our own nationalism, national pride helps us at home, and when bigger picture things happen—look at the boycotts of Russian vodka lately, for example, that helps build up our own myth about American products. There's this idea that we've always been looked down on, we're not as important as other country's spirits producers—ditto the California wine industry, right? Now, we're getting some high international praise, and the perception of American whiskey and bourbon is rising. From a pricing standpoint, that also means we can charge more."

He says that the international market, particularly the swelling Asian market, means that bourbon and whiskey producers need to manage their inventories more closely. That stock can be tight because the brands are doing so very well.

"Now the question is how you project demand for whiskey ten, twelve, eighteen years in advance? It's the nature of the beast. The projects look good, we're only beginning to scratch the surface of international markets and we're also trying to meet a high domestic demand. It means you have to plan the way you expand facilities and such. Right now, the Kentucky Department of Revenue tracks bourbon, and there's actually been a slight downtick in production. What does that mean? It means we don't have enough to meet all the export demands. For Heaven Hill it means we're working on growing some of our smaller brands and our big brands both. There are real challenges here—the international potential is *huge*, and we've only just begun to meet it."

For companies like Heaven Hill, given the way they operate, given that there are truly only seven or eight big bourbon distillers, many of those with additional brands of whiskey and scotch, like Jim Beam, will often work in concert. A rising tide, says Kass, raises all boats. "For any number of years, Irish whiskey was on the rise, now the big deal is bourbons. All brown spirits are doing well, in terms of interest and appreciation. The world is a small place, and I think scotch and American whiskey need to work more closely. We've got a commonality of issues to face. The Scots have been looking over here a lot lately too, seeing how we're handling things like tourism."

JIM BEAM

526 Happy Hollow Road, Clermont, KY 40110;
(502) 543-9877; AmericanStillhouse.com

Oldest of the still-operating bourbon producers in Kentucky, Jim Beam traces its history back to the eighteenth century, and its quality hasn't flagged. Everyone knows Jim Beam—the name recognition is universal—and the small batches, including Basil Hayden's and Booker's, just keep raising the bar for good bourbon. The Jim Beam American Stillhouse distillery tour, on gorgeous grounds that include two distillery sites and a cooperage, and that provides abundant historical information, is one you absolutely must make, because it will give you a true sense of just how old and quintessentially American this industry is—and it's a great tour. Jim Beam might be the essence of the industry.

Products: Jim Beam Straight Bourbon Whiskey (White, Choice, Devil's Cut, Seven Year, Black), Jim Beam Harvest Collection, Jim Beam Signature Craft whiskeys, Jim Beam Signature Craft Quarter Cask Bourbon, Jim Beam Rye, Jacob's Ghost (white whiskey), Jim Beam Single Barrel, Beam's Eight Star, Jim Beam Honey, Red Stag by Jim Beam flavored bourbons, Jim Beam Maple, Booker's, Baker's, Basil Hayden's, Knob Creek, Old Grand-dad, Old Crow, Old Overholt Straight Rye Whiskey, Kessler Whiskey (blended)

If there's a granddaddy in the bourbon business in Kentucky, it's Jim Beam. With a brief pause for Prohibition, the brand has been around since 1795, when Jacob Beam (the old family name was Boehm, before they phoneticized it into Beam) started producing barrels of whiskey and selling it under the name "Old Jake Beam" at their distillery called "Old Tub."

A quarter of a century later, his son David took over the business and began its expansion as the Industrial Revolution surged and built up

Photo courtesy of Dan Cohen, Jim Beam

American industry and mercantile culture. He's credited with the switch from pot to column still at the distillery, which produces more whiskey at swifter rates than its predecessor. David's son David M. Beam moved the distillery to Nelson County in 1856, to take advantage of both rail and steamboat shipping. By 1880, when Jim Beam was still a teenager, the family bourbon was already recognized as a national brand.

Jim Beam took over the distillery in 1894. The company still made use of yeast strains he began during the Prohibition years, during which time the company was out of business. Legend has that when Prohibition ended, Beam and his son got the distillery up and running again in just three months, after a fourteen-year hiatus. The brand name didn't change from Old Tub to Jim Beam until World War II, however. Jim Beam passed away in 1947, but his family legacy has continued, as the family's eighth generation starts work with the company.

Today Beam is a subsidiary of Suntory Holdings headquartered in Osaka, Japan, which also owns Maker's Mark as well as a variety of international spirits, including Laphroaig Scotch and the Tyrconnell and Connemara Irish whiskeys. Beam is also one of the few distilleries big enough to have its own cooperage, which you can visit when you tour.

The current master distiller, Fred Noe (Frederick Booker Noe III), is the seventh generation of Beam family distillers. Of note, distillers from the line of Jacob Beam have also served nearly as many generations at Heaven Hill, underlining the family's impact on the industry. The only non-Beam master distiller at Jim Beam, Jerry Dalton, held the title from 1997 to 2008, and before him, Noe's father Frederick Booker Noe. The elder Noe served for more than forty years (he went by "Booker," and the iconic small batch Booker's is named for him).

Beam is a big player, and the company produces some outstanding product. The deal is, almost everyone who drinks bourbon drinks one or more of Beam's products pretty enthusiastically. If you don't believe me, start asking your friends. With two centuries of history behind it, most of us had fathers or grandfathers who drank it too—and frankly, it's possible my ten times great-grandfather in the Blue Ridge Mountains of western Virginia might at some point have had a bit of Old Jake Beam.

The lovely Hannah Pomatto, who gets a mention for being the most helpful PR person I think I've ever dealt with, made the introductions for me with master distiller Fred Noe.

The first thing the affable Noe tells me is that he was born into his role, being as he is the great-grandson of the legendary Mr. Jim Beam

Photo courtesy of Dan Cohen, Jim Beam

himself. His father was Booker Noe, the guy who brought about the advent of Booker's in 1992, the first of the company's signature small-batch collection, an uncut, straight from the barrel offering that was part of the industry's early move toward single barrel. Following his dad's example, he's expanded the distillery's signature options pretty significantly himself.

Noe has spent thirty years on Jim Beam's payroll, but he says it was never assumed that he would naturally follow in his father's footsteps. The elder Noe made sure Fred went to college first. "Actually, Dad always tried to push me away from it," Noe says. "There was absolutely no pressure for me to become the seventh-generation master distiller, and he sort of said, 'don't bank on this.'" For the young Fred growing up, however, the distillery proved a constant lure. Even as a child, the vast grounds provided him with plenty of trucks and trains to watch, lakes to fish in, and places to shoot. "It was a big playground."

The distillery grounds continue to be that kind of lure for tourists—undeniably beautiful, though now undoubtedly more built up to appeal to Bourbon Trail tourists than they were when Noe was a child, but definitely a place you want to walk and observe. You can only imagine the appeal it might have had for a small child who had no interest yet in sipping whiskey.

Things have changed since those days, including the job of the master distiller. "When I was a kid, my Dad worked day and night making whiskey, it was what he did. Now my job has a lot of other aspects that include plenty of marketing and sales aspects. Now you *have* to be able to do some education and marketing too." Part of that, of course, has to do with the growing, thriving market for bourbon and whiskey that's grown up over the past twenty years or so.

"My dad, Elmer T. Lee (of Buffalo Trace), and Jimmy Russell (of Wild Turkey) really promoted Kentucky bourbon in the 1980s. They rekindled the flame and set the stage for us now. They showed the world the versatility of bourbon, got in on the ground floor of the revival of classic cocktails and mixology. For all of us, our forefathers set us up well.

Photo courtesy of Dan Cohen, Jim Beam

"A lot of changes have gone down, especially in the past twenty years or so—extra aging, bottling the bourbon at different strengths than we used to. My Dad's first straight from the barrel, Booker's, was maybe the first time in one hundred years that that kind of thing has been done. Elmer really built on the single-barrel technique, and Jimmy tried his hand at extra aging and higher strengths—the things they tried got people looking at bourbon again." The changes wrought have helped build up markets outside the United States as well, Noe says, as American whiskey battles for its place alongside the traditional Irish and Scottish products with very favorable reception.

"There's a lot of opportunity for us overseas right now," Noe says. "Look at Europe; the fall of the Soviet Union twenty or more years ago opened up a huge market for US products, including ours. Now, Bulgaria of all places loves bourbon—and so do the U.K., Spain, and Germany. There's a lot of opportunity to sell in India now, and China is buying a lot of bourbon. And the thing about that is, we're making today what we'll sell in four to twelve years, so we have to guess about how much we need to lay down."

How, I ask Noe, as I've asked other distillers, do you plan for that? What do you base predictions on? "It's like looking into a crystal ball," he says bluntly. "It's a crap shoot trying to predict for four, nine, twelve years in advance. You look at your sales and project a series of increases based on what's going on now and hope you hit it close. If you're a little bit short, that's ok, because you're still going to sell it all. The industry is doing very well right now; we're having great years." He doesn't see that slowing down or stopping anytime soon. Of course, if American bourbon whiskey wasn't so good, there probably wouldn't be a market like that for it, and for a master distiller like Noe, getting a good product made and out there is critical.

Given Jim Beam's long, successful history, I ask him to explain to me what makes good flavor, what makes good bourbon, from his perspective. "There are a lot of variables," he says. "Lots of people get excited over the mash bill, and that's what you'll hear the most talk about, but it's only a small piece. All of us are using corn, rye, and malted barley, but what affects the flavor are things like the strength of the whiskey at barreling and the amount of rye and barley. Rye gives the bourbon a spiciness. A high rye percentage is much spicier.

"And of course, the amount of time in the barrel, aging, is a big part of what determines what you get. That barrel time accounts for 100 percent of the color and 70 percent of the flavor. The sweetness, the vanilla and toasted nut flavors come from time in the barrel. With all our products, we select based on taste, some lighter, some heavier. For example, with Basil Hayden's, we use a lot more rye. And we age it for seven to eight years and bottle it at 80 proof. That makes it lighter and easier on the palate, and if you're making cocktails, it will give you a lighter Manhattan, for example.

"By contrast, one of my favorites is Knob Creek . . ."

"Oh, mine too," I interrupt.

"Well, then you know we age Knob Creek for nine years, and bottle it at 100 proof," he says. "We developed it in the early 1990s, at a point where my Dad had stepped away from traveling to promote things so much. So he gave the Knob Creek to me. I remember at one point we were traveling around in Alaska and ordering in bars to promote the line, it was us and two other guys. We'd go in, and my dad would order Booker's, I'd order Knob Creek, and the other two would get Booker's and Basil Hayden's."

So how do you find a perfect flavor? There are the usual suspects, starting with the water—the good, limestone water of Kentucky, including the big spring they're on in the Nelson City area and the spring-fed lakes and creeks around the distillery in Clermont. Like Four Roses and many other distilleries, Beam stops production in the summer when the water table drops, usually June to September, but they'll shrink or expand that time based on the water table issues of the moment and the demand levels. While the production is down, the company does maintenance on its equipment.

Noe says real flavor comes, however, by carefully considering the way you age your whiskey in the barrel house. Some distilleries rotate their barrels in the racks—racks allow the barrels to be stored easily six barrels high in a warehouse. Most warehouses are single story, because the heat changes dramatically as you go up.

"The key is not just rotating barrels, but to scatter them in the rackhouse, then mingle the whiskey back together when you bottle it, getting a vertical cross section of the rackhouse. The positions mean they've all aged differently. In the higher barrels, which get warmer in summer, the strength goes up, and you get a 'hotter' flavor. On the bottom, which stays cooler, strength drops, and you have less bite. Those in the middle area are a mix of both. You bring them all together and the finished profile is very consistent. If you want something that has a bigger bite, focus on the barrels that are higher up—my dad taught me all this, of course. He was the sixth generation of the family; I'm the seventh. The learning curve has been passed down along the line since 1795.

"When it comes to what has gone into it since then, we know Jacob Beam's recipe, and it's very similar to what we do today. Jacob, though, was on the frontier with a pot still, making maybe one barrel of whiskey a day

and putting very little age on that. That got it started, and a lot has obviously changed since then. Jacob's grandson David M. Beam moved the distillery [to Nelson County in 1854]. Jim Beam was actually at the distillery through Prohibition. He closed it and he restarted it afterwards, and we're in the same place Jim moved it to after Prohibition today."

Noe continues with family history, including the fact that unlike the handful that stayed open producing medicinal whiskey during the stretch from 1919 to 1933, Beam closed entirely. Jim Beam tried his hand at a number of other businesses in the meantime, including citrus farming, coal mining, and a limestone rock quarry in Clermont, Kentucky. He was seventy years old when he got back into the business after Prohibition was lifted by Franklin Delano Roosevelt.

"My son started working with us a year and a half ago," he tells me in the fall of 2014. "A cousin just started working here too. The eighth generation is learning the whole business—sales, marketing, accounting. They're choosing their fields. My son might decide to become a distiller, but it's his choice." One suspects Fred Noe sounds a lot like his dad Booker did a few decades back, talking to his son.

Given Beam's size and long, long history, I bring up the sudden rise of small craft distillers in Kentucky right now. There's no question there's intense interest building in the industry. Noe has no problem with their arrival on the scene—again reflecting the incredibly welcoming and open attitude the bourbon industry seems to share.

"These craft distillers open the door, and customers are suddenly excited to try more. That opens the door for everyone, as they're looking to try new styles. And the benefit to me is it means I get to develop new products."

Among those products, infused bourbons have proved to be a huge seller for Jim Beam. Noe talks about the Red Stag by Jim Beam line, the black cherry, cider, and cinnamon spice-infused bourbon with natural flavors, and the honey and maple iterations, as well as the wildly popular cinnamon-flavored Kentucky Fire. There's no denying the cinnamon bourbon market has exploded, and Jim Beam's variation is particularly good.

"All of these are bringing more people over to the bourbon category as a whole," Noe says. That includes women, for whom cocktails made with flavored bourbons are a big hit. I hesitate to admit to him that my friend Amy Ripton and I were making cocktails with Red Stag black cherry and Bing Cherry energy drink the previous weekend, and winning over men and women in equal measure. Try it, trust me.

Noe is willing to agree that the bourbon industry neglected women for a long time. "When I first stated promoting our products, there would be nine or ten women at events, and they'd be with their husbands or boyfriends, and at some point in the evening, I'd see a couple of them ease their glasses over to the guys. Now women really enjoy the product. Don't tell a woman she needs a lighter bourbon, ever—bourbon is about acquiring a taste, whoever you are."

He continues with a small lecture on the "right" way to drink, because we do live at a time when a million different cocktail writers like to tell us how to drink our spirits. Noe is refreshingly having none of that.

"I tell people to drink it any damn way you want to, with Coke, with cocktails, neat, on the rocks. The proper way to drink bourbon is the way you like it. I kind of laugh at all the rules—you know, some Scots distillers require men to wear kilts—there are just so many rules about how to drink. I think they can hurt us if we deny that bourbon is versatile. We just take it too seriously. We're just starting to figure out the new cocktail culture. We need to let young consumers discover how they like things on their own."

Noe is fond of cocktail culture. "I like a good, fresh whiskey sour, a good Manhattan, an Old-Fashioned. I'm open to try anything. What I'm seeing now is these mixologists using fresh ingredients, fresh juices, and things you'd never think of . . . I recently had a drink they called Dancing with the Devil, with Devil's Cut, fresh fruit juice and lemon juice, and Tabasco, like a hot whiskey sour. It's a very refreshing drink." The recipe follows.

Noe invites fans to come tour the distillery. "You're welcome to come see bourbon being made from grain to bottle, and participate in the bottling process, and even purchase that bottle yourself." It goes without saying this trip is planned the minute I finish this book, because bottling is fun.

In the not too distant future, if you're a Beam fan new or old, look for more coming from the Signature Craft Series, including the Harvest Blends. Noe says they "thought outside the barrel about eleven years ago" and made whiskey using highly unorthodox ingredients or alternative ingredients, including rolled oats, brown rice, plus creating a high rye and barley content whiskey and a wheated whiskey, all soon to be released. He also promises some quarter cask small-barrel stuff for buyers looking for something completely different. The rising popularity of bourbon has allowed Noe and the folks at Beam some real leeway for creativity, and they are absolutely taking advantage of that.

And Fred . . . I have to confess. Lately, I think Basil Hayden's and Booker's are seriously winning me over.

JIM BEAM COCKTAILS

Dancing with the Devil

1 part Jim Beam Devil's Cut
½ part JDK & Sons O3 Liqueur
 or DeKuyper Triple Sec
1 part fresh lemon sour
1 part passion fruit juice
1–2 dashes Tabasco or Louisiana
 Hot Sauce

Shake all ingredients with ice and
strain into a chilled cocktail glass
or over ice in a double highball
glass. Garnish with a cherry. Video
with instructions at jimbeam.com.

Mountain Summer

*This one was created by my friend Amy
Ripton and myself, because we were looking for fun ways to use Red Stag that no
one else had yet.*

1 part Red Stag cherry bourbon
1 part blueberry puree
2 parts chilled lemonade
Lemon twist for garnish

Option one—Shake with ice, then
strain into a martini glass. Sugar
on rim optional.

Option two—Shake, then serve
in a Collins glass over ice and top
with a little club soda for fizz.

Cherry Moon

As in, you'll reach it with this one.

1 ounce Red Stag cherry bourbon
1 can Bing Cherry energy drink

In an 8-ounce glass, pour Red
Stag and top with ice, stir to chill.
Fill the remainder of the glass
with Bing, or go most of the way
and top with club soda. A dash of
lemon bitters doesn't hurt either.

MAKER'S MARK

3350 Burkes Spring Road, Loretto, KY 40037;
(270) 865-2099; makersmark.com

Maker's Mark, with its romantic post–World War II origin story and its long-term fan base, maintains a special place in the bourbon firmament. It's a slightly mellower, sweeter Kentucky bourbon, one that's terribly easy to sip and enjoy. The company is owned by Beam Suntory these days, but the founding Samuels family and its traditions remain a firm part of the brand. Maker's is a simply beautiful tour, thanks to Margie Samuels' belief in preserving the old Victorian buildings on the site.

The Products: Maker's Mark Kentucky Straight Bourbon Whisky; Maker's Mark Cask Strength; Maker's 46, Maker's Mark White

You've seen the Maker's Mark bottle—extremely distinctive in a world where marketing is increasingly vital. It's nothing new. All its elements are the creation of Margie Samuels, wife of distillery founder Bill Samuels Sr., who created everything from the bottle shape to the typeface on the label—and that utterly distinctive red wax seal. The kind of care and effort that went into creating the bottle also went into the creation of the whiskey, according to master distiller emeritus Bill Samuels Jr. Today, the third generation of the family's master distillers, Rob Samuels, works in the same location his father and grandfather did, all the way back to the 1940s.

That location is just as distinctive as the bottle. The campus is marked by both authentic Victorian buildings that have long stood on the site and by newer buildings built in keeping with the vision of Margie and Bill Sr. During the holidays everything is decked out, and you can even take a tour by candlelight (be aware that while Kentucky may be the South, snow is very much a possibility if you're there in the November through January time frame). It's one of the distilleries where they really go all out to make you feel at home.

Bill Samuels Jr., now retired, tells the story of the distillery and its founding with the kind of love that is notable even among a crop of Kentucky old-school distillers who love, live, and breathe this experience. Although retired in favor of his son Rob, he clearly keeps himself up on the business and also serves as advisor to young distillers who come knocking on his door, another reminder of how close the masters of this profession are—something that sets the bourbon and whiskey industry apart from so much of the larger business world.

When I ask Samuels about his history with the distillery, there's a faint laugh in his voice as he says, "My history goes back to the very beginning." His parents, William T. and Margie Samuels, founded it in 1953, but the story goes back a bit further. "It was my Dad's post–World War II retirement hobby," says Samuels. "During the war, my mom ran the farm, and she continued after he got back. He got underfoot, and she announced to him he'd be getting a job."

Bill Sr. dreamed of buying a distillery, but he dragged his feet about it for six or seven years, according to his son. After Prohibition, many of the old distilleries had not reopened, and of those that had come back, many were shut down during the war or were producing high alcohol content ethanol, mostly used as fuel for machinery for the war effort.

"After the war, the distilleries were closing fast. We were losing one about every three weeks in Kentucky. About sixty of them had restarted following the war, but now they were closing. My dad has always wanted to buy a distillery and with some of them shutting down there was an opportunity—it was a good one, it was cheap, and he wouldn't have to build a new one from scratch."

On June 4, 1953, Bill Sr. purchased the former Burk's Distillery, located in Loretto, Kentucky, with two hundred acres of land and an operating Victorian-era distillery for $35,000. Once he had the property, he began experimenting and reached out to friends to help out, among them people in the distillery industry, including the Motlow family at Jack Daniel's, the Beam family, and Julian "Pappy" Van Winkle himself.

"He learned to make the bourbon he wanted," Samuels says of his father. He adds that at the time, he wasn't into "continuing the legacy." The family had farmed in Kentucky back to 1784, he says, and as a kid he certainly enjoyed roaming the distillery's acreage, but that was as far as it went. He came up in the age of Sputnik, and when he graduated in 1957, his goal was to go to college and become an aerospace engineer.

Meanwhile, as Bill Sr. got the distillery up and running and created a bourbon that met his own demands, a bourbon that tasted good, Margie Samuels went to work developing all the fine details. "She did what today would be considered marketing," says Samuels. She put great time and effort into creating distinctive packaging, and she also went to work preserving the distillery's Victorian buildings, all of which was expensive. She developed the name from looking at symbols on the backs of old English pewter and silver, according to Samuels, and taking note of the way the silversmiths labeled their work.

"My mom was very smart, a little dictatorial; when she had an opinion, it had to happen," says Bill Jr. "She had an absolutely huge impact on how we went to market. There's a reason she's the first woman inducted into the Kentucky Bourbon Hall of Fame . . . at the time, I thought she'd bankrupt Dad. She wanted the high-priced bottle, the wax on it, wanted to save all those old buildings. Dad worried about working capital all the time, but it turned out to be worth it."

Samuels says the development of the bourbon itself involved a great deal of deliberation. "Before Prohibition, it was common that bourbon would burn and be bitter on the tongue, would be very strong, and wouldn't necessarily taste as good as it does today. His father and grandfather had many conversations on the subject, especially since the family had a 170-year-old bourbon recipe that had come down through their family. Of course, original doesn't necessarily mean good—Mike Veach at the Filson County Historical Society is full of stories of early American spirits recipes that used plenty of horrifying ingredients, including a "scotch" that used creosote as a flavor element and many more stories just like it.

Bill Sr. felt that this was a perfect time to reexamine the flavor profile for bourbon, and he began developing the distinctive recipe of Maker's

Mark. When he suggested altering the process to make the bourbon taste really good, Samuels says his grandfather derisively said that "Americans will drink anything." The implication being that especially post-Prohibition, Americans, used to drinking bad bootleg spirits and whatever they could get, would accept spirits that didn't win them with flavor. Bill Sr. disagreed and wanted to market a spirit that people truly enjoyed drinking.

He consulted with his distiller friends and decided what he wanted was a bourbon that finished nicely on the tip of the tongue, rather than on the back. "Never before and never since has this been done," says Samuels. "But I will say our process today is even better than it was in the 1950s, that process of grain to starch to sugar to beer to the maturation process. But I believe that we're the only bourbon in the United States that was ever designed to a specific taste; he spent all this time with those guys trying to create a specific taste profile. It's clear in hindsight that this was likely the first sophisticated bourbon that was handmade like that. That's pretty neat. I think about the craft revolution now, and they've created the bandwagon for that kind of thing."

What Bill Sr. did was to make bourbon without the traditional rye content—the notes that today result in spiciness on the tongue. Instead, he used a blend of red winter wheat and malted barley, making Maker's a truly wheated bourbon. At that point, he did the almost unthinkable and burned the family recipe—and the family never looked back.

During this time, Bill Jr. got himself a couple of engineering degrees and then went on to Vanderbilt law school in Nashville. While he was there, he spent time with the Motlow family of Jack Daniel's, learning something about the whiskey business and how whiskey is made, with his dad's friend Hap Motlow periodically taking him out for a good meal.

When he finished law school and passed the bar exam in 1967, Motlow convinced Samuels that he needed to go home and help his father out for a year. "If it hadn't been for Hap, I wouldn't have gotten through all that. He looked after me for three years. And he was right, it turned out to be a great experience. Dad gave me the opportunity to commercialize his idea. Now forty-plus years later, I've retired and my son runs it."

Samuels pauses then elaborates. "When I came home, my dad was concerned about my domineering personality. I'm a lot like my mother that way. He told me to go out and find customers for the product. I had to figure out a plan for the distillery, essentially soft selling something to people who didn't much care about it. That went on from the late 1960s to the 1980s.

"In 1980 we got lucky. A reporter from the *Wall Street Journal* back at the end of the Jimmy Carter era, when things didn't look great, heard this little distillery in Kentucky was doing really well, and he came down and wrote about us. He filed his report, and that ended up on the front page—and it gave both Maker's and bourbon an instant credibility. Overnight we became this highly respected national brand, and we found ourselves apologizing for not having enough whiskey, because we hadn't planned for this.

"We spent the next thirty years trying to improve and speed up the process without screwing up the whiskey quality. Customers started beating our door down. And during all this time, 90 percent of our effort has been about growing without screwing up the craft. It became real personal, asking ourselves 'How do you do this?' People still ask us about it, and the answer is that we use the same process—if we have people responding to growth by not caring about keeping track of it and making the right changes to meet it, we can go to hell in a hand basket. Hard and fast, the answer is that we won't grow by more than 10 percent per year. All of what we sell is made right here, all of it, and we don't sell for anyone else."

Samuels says that forecasting decided that for them. "It's not even so much about craft as engineering," he says. "And nobody could have forecast what's going on right now. All the brands are hot, and there's no excess supply. I think more need to operate like us . . . it starts for me with my mom's philosophy, which is to make the customers hold their hands up. When choosing who you're going to supply first, for us that choice was the bars rather than the big retailers, spreading the product around rather than filling up cases in big garage retail stores. We're serving our existing customers first, most of whom are inside the United States right now. That's normal for us. We should have more outside the United States—we could do as much as 30 percent of our business there—but we chose to keep it at about 12 percent."

The distillery is no longer strictly family-owned, and I ask Samuels about that. "I should have been able, as a lawyer, to influence that more, but the situation was that when the company was created, they'd simply divided the stock half and half between my mother and father. Right after the *Wall Street Journal* article, my mom got very sick. The estate tax was very high at that point, so we brought in a family-owned company to protect us. We've done that through three sales now, and we still operate like a private business. Obviously, we take the long view of things over the instant gratification of current profit. And I like the new ownership very much; the Suntory family is a third-generation family company, and they seem enamored with the way we do things. Beam Suntory is a good owner."

Those sales were to Hiram Walker in 1982, then to distillery megacompany Allied Domecq about five years later, which in turn sold to Fortune Brands (now Beam Suntory) in 2005. Regardless, Samuels firmly feels that Maker's Mark prospered not by focusing on success, but by keeping the focus directly on product integrity. Looking across the industry right now, he says, "What we have been able to do is totally transform bourbon's image, make it all about craft and content."

I ask him about the rise of bourbon culture, about how Maker's Mark found its audience. "Maker's Mark, remember, was originally aimed at people who didn't much like bourbon, and that included women—and anticipating the cocktail culture, which women are a big part of."

I ask him if his mother drank it herself, and he answers in the affirmative and adds that she drank it with ginger ale especially. "Maker's Mark was created to appeal to people who value a very balanced spirit," he says. Women, he adds, generally came to like it in part through cocktail culture. Existing distillers have been able to craft their products, to move the flavor forward, and remove bitter and sour notes over the past few decades too, giving bourbon a very broad appeal to women.

"I think I saw it start in New York, with the Maker's Mark Manhattan. It turned out that I couldn't go into a bar there without at least one woman coming in and asking for one. Now, I think Old-Fashioneds are becoming the bourbon cocktail of choice. I prefer a Manhattan myself, but my problem is with those Italian vermouths. I don't like them, they're too bitter for me. I recommend you use Dolan's, which is American made. Also, use a small bar spoon—you know the little ones I'm talking about—of cherry juice. That might be my sole contribution to mixology right there. Dolan's is a little harder to find, and make sure you refrigerate it after opening, but you'll like it."

I finish on the note I always do—what do you want people who've never been to your distillery to know before they visit?

"Well," he says. "I think the first thing is that you'll leave excited about bourbon. You're going to have a great time. You can dip your own bottle and buy it. You can taste bourbon. We have really interesting buildings and a National Historic Landmark designation. You get to see every single step of the process. I just want everyone to leave with a smile.

"Maker's drinkers come to Mecca, as it were, and aren't disappointed. Or kids, too—there are lots of agendas, and we have an outstanding visitor's staff who'll find out what you're interested in. We want you to enjoy your tours, but we try to keep tour groups under thirty people. We carve out the trade groups. We've got 130,000 people coming through a year, and we try to make a big impact—we want you to leave thinking this is a great place to go to work."

Interestingly enough, Maker's Mark was the first of the bourbon distilleries to instigate a visitor's program, back in 1967. "My sister and my dad liked the idea of city people coming down and oohing and aahing over what a nice place to work we were," says Samuels.

As I write this, Rob Samuels, now the master distiller, is overseeing some big restoration and renovation plans, including creating a huge glass atrium "like the one at the Victoria and Albert Museum in London" at the back of a three-story Victorian house. The distillery is working to make the campus itself largely truck and automobile free in keeping with the history and spirit of the distillery. Rob is also working on bringing in an exhibit of the work of glass artist Dale Chihuly in 2015. "He's got vision," says Bill Jr. of his son. Clearly it runs in the family.

MAKER'S MARK DISTILLERY COCKTAILS

Fancy Bourbon Punch

(by mixologist Matt Wallace)
This is an all-occasion punch for any party, particularly summertime gatherings.

1 cup granulated sugar
Peels of 3 lemons and 1 orange
1 liter strong tea (preferably green tea)
Juice of peeled fruit
1 liter Maker's Mark Bourbon
250 ml sparkling wine (club soda can be used for a less fancy version)
Freshly grated nutmeg*

Combine sugar and citrus peels in the bottom of a punch bowl. Muddle together until sugar starts to clump. Let sit for about two hours (while not necessary, this does add a little complexity). Brew the tea for about thirty minutes, remove loose tea or tea bags, and allow to cool. Add the juice of the peeled fruit, tea, and bourbon. Stir. Top with sparkling wine just before serving and stir gently. Top with freshly grated nutmeg and serve.

*If you can't grate fresh nutmeg, don't use the prepackaged powdered stuff. It will turn your punch into a paste. If fresh isn't possible, garnish with citrus wheels or fresh fruit.

OLD POGUE

716 West Second Street, Maysville, KY 41056; oldpogue.com

The Pogue family distillery dates back to 1876, and its family of distillers had a fine reputation in Kentucky and beyond. The original distillery closed during World War II (except for production of fuel-grade ethanol), and in 2005 John Pogue and his family took steps to bring it back and build up excitement about the brand again. Since then the Pogue family of small-batch products has been steadily building interest from bourbon lovers across the country. The distillery tour includes the historic family home-place—which you can rent out for weddings and events—and the charming craft distillery. Besides the bourbon, the less aged Five Fathers Rye is a product really worth tasting.

Products: Old Pogue, Old Pogue Master's Select, Five Fathers Pure Rye Malt Whiskey, Limestone Landing Rye White Whiskey

The Old Pogue distillery in Maysville only officially began producing its own whiskey again in early 2012. Before that, the distillery had been defunct since World War II, though the descendants of the original Pogue family had been working steadily to bring the product back to the market since 2004, when they started sharing the idea for public knowledge; according to John Pogue, master distiller, the family has been working on the project since at least the mid-1990s. At the beginning of the project, like many distilleries including Woodford Reserve in the early days, Old Pogue sourced their whiskey, in this case via the nearby Heaven Hill. Today they're proudly laying down their own.

The twenty-first-century version of Old Pogue has gotten rave reviews so far, and there's no good reason not to look forward to the product they're aging right now. The family has put a great deal of time and effort into learning how to do things right, in tribute to their family history, and their genuine commitment is admirable. Plenty of the bourbon lovers I know in the Louisville area favor Pogue in the extreme—and its growing reputation as a premium bourbon seems to increase each year.

The Old Pogue distillery tour serves as a good contrast to some of the larger, more industrialized experiences. I'm a firm believer that when you make a distillery tour, you need to look at every possible size and shape, to get a feeling for the differences and really appreciate the fact that great bourbons are truly coming from everything from huge mechanized plants to tiny craft distillers.

Photo courtesy of John Pogue, Old Pogue Distillery

John Pogue, distiller and sixth-generation member of the Pogue family, stresses the history of the distillery and of Maysville generally. Maysville was indeed part of the old "Bourbon County, Virginia," back in the days when Kentucky was still a territory and the first distillers made their way into the area and discovered the Ohio River made an ideal mode of transport for their goods—including barrels of spirits.

The original site of H. E. Pogue's distillery, started in 1876, was near the Limestone Landing area where the first distilleries in the region started in the eighteenth century. John's father is the fifth H. E. Pogue to bear the name. The elder H. E. started manufacturing Old Pogue Kentucky Straight Bourbon Whiskey, according to John Pogue, producing about fifty barrels a day with a staff totaling perhaps one hundred people prior to the advent of the Volstead Act in 1919.

During that stretch of Prohibition from 1919 to 1933, the Pogue family—headed by H. E. Pogue III—produced medicinal whiskey, using the brand name "Old Jordan," and actually purchased two other out-of-state distilleries and served, like some others, as a bonded whiskey warehouse for the government. When Prohibition was repealed, however, Pogue's enthusiasm appears to have waned a bit, worn down by his recent past, and he eventually sold the company to the Rose Distillery in Chicago.

"I don't blame him; he'd been through a lot at that point," says John Pogue. "He'd been in World War I, and his dad [H. E. Pogue II] died in a distillery accident while he was overseas. He came home and here he was, twenty-two years old and head of a distillery. When he finally did sell out, he was actually hired by the Rose Distillery to make spirits. Schenley bought the distillery a few years later, during World War II, and they had a massive fuel grade ethanol contract that lasted until 1963 or so. When that contract dried up, the company packed up and moved back to Chicago, leaving the distillery buildings empty. They burned in a big fire in 1973, and that was the end of it for a while."

John Pogue says that the family kept the memory of the distillery and the whiskey going, however. "At some point back in the 1990s, my dad, my grandfather, my cousins, and I all got together, and we had this basement full of memorabilia that we needed to decide what to do with. Do we sell it? Keep passing it down through the family? Just put it back where it came from? Eventually we came back to the idea of putting it back where it belonged and starting to make bourbon again. At that point, I have to say, we really didn't imagine the bourbon renaissance that was about to take off. I left my work in geology and started learning to make bourbon."

The Pogue family distillery was about to come back, thanks to the same family that started it more than a century before.

Photo courtesy of John Pogue, Old Pogue Distillery

How, I ask him, did he decide to be a distiller, in spite of his family history?

"Well, I studied with the aim of ending up in the oil industry. I was educated to understand how to refine that oil to make gas or kerosene, so distilling isn't really that far from where I was at the time. My cousin Paul Pogue is really our head distiller—he started out as an oral surgeon. We were at different points in our understanding of how to make bourbon. He was at a better point than me. We had to learn a lot, though; some aspects of it

Photo courtesy of John Pogue, Old Pogue Distillery

didn't add up at first for us. That's one of the reasons we were sourcing at the beginning. You really have two avenues to get into the spirits business—one is to source and the other is to start making unaged spirits, and we opted to go with sourcing. But I think our advantage is both our unique history and our approach to the business, which is frankly a lot of fun."

The release of their very small-batch, limited-edition Five Fathers Rye in 2013 marked the point that their own first product hit the market, and the reception by the public was more than cordial. At 100 proof, the rye whiskey has distinct notes of honey, nutmeg, clove, sweet orange, vanilla, and caramel—a very smooth product that ends on a spicy note with a mix of toffee, pepper, citrus, and tobacco. The product was so eagerly anticipated that buyers had to sign up with the distillery if they wished to purchase a bottle the day of the release. The reviews were excellent, with Robert Parker awarding it a 95/100. Paul and John Pogue had proved their abilities with the first release.

Since then the Limestone Landing clear whiskey has also hit the market with a very favorable response and high rankings from reviewers. Now

we're just waiting for the time when their own bourbon is released in quantity after the full aging period.

As we talk, John launches into a paean to whiskey tasting, starting with a description of Old Pogue as it stands right now. "What we've got is a nicely balanced seven- to nine-year spirit at 91 proof, and it's got a pretty good rye-pepper note in it, the spiciness rye gives you, and then a sweeter note on the finish. We generally want it to be very even, easy to drink, and when it's even across the top it tends to be easy drinking. A bottle from 1902 actually inspired our choices.

"Bourbon," he says, "is complex when you analyze all the aspects of it. I'm fascinated by the complex chemistry that happens while it's in the barrel, because you just can't duplicate all of that in the laboratory. It's exciting to delve into what people can taste in a bourbon—some of the notes are very faint, but with enough practice you can learn to identify them.

"I read a paper a couple of months ago on the subject of taste bud density in humans, and it turns out that less than 1 percent of people can identify some of these concentrations. There are over 4,000—4,000!—such compounds in a whiskey and there are 460 aromatic compounds, and believe it or not, the tongue can pick up things that all our fine equipment cannot. You can't imitate it. You know, if we could make bourbon up in a lab, we would, but we simply can't duplicate this process." Pogue's excitement is palpable, and it's cool to talk to a distiller who's also a scientist capable of cheerfully geeking out on his subject matter.

"It's just not possible to copy it," he says again. "Ok, some of that might be fiscal—if you spared no expense, then maybe, but still, with thousands of compounds, even with a huge budget it would be incredibly difficult. Which brings us back to the fact that the old is the right way; we simply can't make it faster and cheaper than we already do, and we ascribe value to that."

I ask him why, in particular, he thinks bourbon's time has come—and his own bourbon's time has come. "I think some of that starts with the craft brewing industry," he says. "I think right now, the craft brewing industry is ahead of craft spirits by ten to twenty years, honestly. But they've shown us the potential. I've made beer, but now I distill it and put it in a barrel, which is a more complicated process. But nationally, and then internationally, you saw the rise of an appreciation for craft beers, and I think now you're seeing an appreciation really grow for craft spirits.

"Internationally, more is being consumed than ever before. Asia has opened up for all sorts of brands, and there's a limited supply. People took notice, and the Chinese and Japanese interest is huge, so there's the potential for so much industry growth there. And the truth is, a lot of scotch customers are branching out in their tastes, and that's been dominant in the Asian market—there's a Mitsubishi plant down the street from us, and the CEO tries to buy up the place. It's an insatiable new market; they're excited."

With all the demand for bourbon, what makes Old Pogue stand out, I ask. What's driving your customers to buy?

"I think people like the flavor profile, which is what I'd mostly refer to as being very consistent and balanced, as I said earlier. There's vanilla, honey oak. It's even. But I think the intangibles count too, our story, our family history that interests people. We've got six family members who are fifth and sixth generation. We're basing it on the original product, trying to

Photo courtesy of John Pogue, Old Pogue Distillery

retrace the steps of our great-grandparents and great-great-grandparents. That's endearing to people, on top of good products. Don't get me wrong on old recipes. I mean, some of the stuff made back then was awful, or it was trial and error in process.

"We know how to get it right these days. And we're unconventional for a distillery, but I think we get surprisingly good results. We aren't making a super historic product, I mean, I'm using a modern yeast strain from a yeast bank, and obviously biochemistry has come a long, long way. I really embrace that fact. But with the family recipe, there's interplay of old and new. The new things can't be ignored—biochemistry of the kind we have wasn't available in the nineteenth century. And with yeast, you've got a very important flavor note, you have to make adjustments—it's interesting learning, and I use several strains depending on the whiskey I'm making.

"We've got three products out right now, our bourbon, then the Lime-stone Landing, which is an unaged white spirit, and the Five Fathers, an aged two years, single malt rye. We started with an old recipe, dating to 1792, which predates us. We didn't get our start until 1876. But it's an old class of whiskey, something we were curious about, somewhere between a scotch and a bourbon, very distinct. There's an interesting window with this product, the much older stuff tends to get ethery, too fruity. There's a scotch aroma to this, and we've still got iterations of it sitting. It's like scotch with some additional sweetness with the malted grain.

"I don't know many others that make anything remotely like this. It's a 1700s idea of rye whiskey. That's what Scotland did with scotch. They're making single malt barley whiskey. But corn grows best here, and this is a transition spirit between scotch and bourbon, and it's 110 proof, so it's hotter."

You should know before you come and visit the distillery that you've got a good chance of doing the tour with John Pogue himself. Tours are scheduled Wednesday through Sunday only, and you need to schedule your tour online in advance and show up promptly. Pogue says to be aware that the entrance to the distillery is on Germantown Road, and you'll pass over a hillside before you get there (yes, it's really pretty). The driveway, he says, "is a little intense, there's a drop-off that looks intimidating, so use caution." The schedule works that way, Pogue says, because they're a distillery first and a tourism destination second, but nonetheless, the tour feedback is incredibly positive and Pogue is a treasury of family history.

The Pogue family gives a lot of applause to Maysville and its support of their endeavor. "I believe Maysville really is the heart of the area where bourbon got started," says John Pogue. "It was a shipping port down the Ohio for everything: corn, furniture, bourbon, everything produced nearby. Really, this might be the beginning place for bourbon. We were shipping white dog down to the French in New Orleans in oak barrels, and when we started putting it in the charred barrels, they wanted more because it reminded them of brandy, which was their preferred spirit. You start to see the first advertisements for 'bourbon whiskey' from Maysville merchants about 1821. It's been here a long time."

VENDOME COPPER AND BRASS WORKS

Though a few of the distilleries in Tennessee and Kentucky purchase stills from Europe, the vast majority of the ones you see come from Vendome Copper and Brass in Louisville, Kentucky. The company has a long history of still production, dating back to the 1920s when founder W. Elmore Sherman bought the Hoffman Ahlers brass- and coppersmithing firm where he'd been bookkeeper, renamed it, and continued its reputation for excellence in brewing and distilling equipment. He passed it on through the generations; today his grandsons Tom and Dick Sherman own and operate Vendome.

Over the decades, Vendome has been challenged to make other products during the stretch of Prohibition (1919–1932), survived the massive Louisville flood of 1937, and manufactured equipment for distilled alcohol to support the war effort during World War II. By the 1950s Vendome had expanded its focus to include stainless steel technologies for its products, as well as the more traditional copper and brass. They also began to expand to other food- and beverage-related industries, as well as chemical and manufacturing concerns. During the 1970s and 1980s, the world market for fuel alcohol distillation also broke wide open, and Vendome answered those needs as well.

The boom of the spirits business by the 1980s meant that Vendome's audience for spirits distillation equipment expanded, as well as the international market. Today they continue to produce distillation equipment for all these industries, and for the vast majority of US distillers and brew works, Vendome is the first place you call when you need a still, a tub, a kettle, or any one of a number of crucial pieces of equipment they produce. That includes custom designs for distilleries or breweries that need particular sizes, shapes, and so on.

If you're touring in Tennessee or Kentucky, look for the plate on the equipment that says Vendome—most of the time, you'll see it right there. Without Vendome, the industry might never have reached its current level of success.

OLD POGUE DISTILLERY COCKTAILS

Newport Sinner

1 ½ ounces Five Fathers Rye
  Whiskey
¾ ounce Carpano Antica
  vermouth
½ ounce Bluecoat American Dry
  Gin
½ ounce Luxardo Maraschino
  Liqueur
6 dashes Angostura Bitters
Lemon twist for garnish

Combine all ingredients except
lemon twist in a cocktail shaker
with ice and shake until thoroughly
mixed. Pour over ice and garnish
with a lemon twist.

Kentucky Punch

12 ounces frozen orange juice
  concentrate (thawed)
12 ounces frozen lemonade
  concentrate (thawed)
1 cup lemon juice
1 liter Old Pogue Bourbon
2 liters lemon-lime soda, such as
  Sprite or 7Up

Combine all ingredients except
soda in a large container and chill.
Pour over block of ice and stir in
soda. Serves thirty-two people.

Kentucky Blizzard

1 ½ ounces Old Pogue Bourbon
1 ½ ounces cranberry juice
½ ounce lime juice
½ ounce grenadine
1 teaspoon sugar

Shake all ingredients with cracked
ice. Strain into a martini glass.

Bourbon Slush

7 cups water
2 cups sugar
2 cups Old Pogue Bourbon
2 cups strong tea (use four tea bags)
12 ounces frozen lemonade
  concentrate
12 ounces frozen orange juice
  concentrate

Bring 7 cups water and 2 cups
sugar to a full boil until dissolved.
Mix all ingredients together and
freeze at least twenty-four hours in
small plastic containers. To serve,
put two scoops of slush in a glass
and top up with 7Up or Sprite
(if you want to cut down on the
sweetness, you can use club soda
instead of 7Up or Sprite). You
can, of course, add more bourbon
according to your taste!

TOWN BRANCH

Alltech Lexington Brewing and Distilling Company,
401 Cross Street, Lexington, KY 40508;
(859) 255-2337; kentuckyale.com

Alltech may indeed be the new kid on the block in many ways, but their founder, Dr. Pearse Lyons, knows his way around both brewing and distilling, having been trained, among other places, at Guinness in Ireland. The distillery's beautiful new Lexington campus is not only a destination but a lovely example of the potential for urban distilleries in a state known for sprawling, rural campuses. Town Branch may not yet be on your radar, but it will be, not only for the bourbon but also for their increasingly popular Kentucky Bourbon Barrel Ale. Town Branch was one of my very first visits when I began this book, and it's a tour worth taking.

The Products: Town Branch Bourbon, Town Branch Rye, Pearse Lyons Reserve, Bluegrass Sundown, Kentucky Bourbon Barrel Ale, Kentucky Bourbon Barrel Stout, Kentucky Ale, Kentucky Kolsch, Kentucky IPA, assorted seasonal products

Alltech's gorgeous brewing and distilling facility in downtown Lexington proved a revelation to me. Its urban location, in a historic part of the city no less, seems incongruous at first. The distillery, however, is absolutely lovely—a combination of old and new styles of architecture, some of which harken back to Alltech founder Dr. Pearse Lyons's Irish heritage, some to the history of the city itself, and some purely contemporary.

The first thing to know is that Town Branch comprises both brewery and distillery, and they also produce some mighty fine beer. The details go something like this: Pearse Lyons, the first Irishman to be accepted at the British School of Malting and Brewing, was granted a master's in brewing

and a doctorate in yeast fermentation. Degrees in hand, Lyons accepted a job as a biochemist at Irish Distillers, which in turn led him to Kentucky to work in brewing and distilling. Lyons said he soon realized that his knowledge of yeast fermentation could help the livestock and poultry industry, which provided the opportunity to form the company Alltech in 1980.

On a larger scale, Lyons's company's goal is ". . . to improve the health and performance of people, animals, and plants through natural nutrition and scientific innovation. Alltech improves health and performance through its innovative use of yeast fermentation. Alltech is guided by the 'ACE' principle, our promise that in doing business we have a positive impact on the **a**nimal, the **c**onsumer, and the **e**nvironment." With regard to the company's business, that means work with animal feeds and the like, but it also goes back to Lyons's love of good whiskey and good beer. Even so, it makes for a very different business perspective than is typical of the state's many longtime, family-owned distilleries with their histories dating back to Prohibition and before.

Alltech purchased the old Lexington Brewing Company downtown in 1999, and there began its first experiments in producing good craft beer

Microbrewing at Town Branch

Visiting a brewstillery means you get to explore craft beer and craft bourbon in one place. Here are the beers to watch for, either when you visit or at your favorite local craft beer depot.

Kentucky Ale—A hybrid English Pale-Irish Red ale style that got the brewing side started. Light amber color, great body, and rich flavor, thanks in part to the native Kentucky water. Smooth and epically drinkable.

Kentucky Kolsch—For all your friends who swear by mediocre lighter American beers, here's a truly *good* beer they'll take to heart. The light pilsner made in the Cologne style makes use of Alltech's specialized yeast, pale malts, and malted white wheat for one of the smoothest-drinking beers you've had in a good long while.

Kentucky Bourbon Barrel Stout—Brewed and aged with Alltech's Café Citadelle Haitian Coffee, then aged in bourbon barrels, this is a solid stout, complex and rich in flavor. Dark roasted malts, with notes of coffee and vanilla, the true stout lover will gravitate this way.

with their Kentucky Ale. LBC had been in operation since 1794, one of the very first brew houses along the Town Branch of the Elkhorn River, from which the new bourbon made by Alltech now proudly takes its moniker. Lyons hoped at the time to save a historic site and preserve some of this city's brewing history. Meanwhile, he also had the genius idea to make use of his ample brewing knowledge to promote other facets of his company.

According to Lyons, they started brewing Kentucky Ale as a way to have beer at trade shows as a tangible showcase of the company's core competency in yeast fermentation. What happened, unsurprisingly, is that those people at the trade shows, and in the larger community, liked it so much they wanted to know where and how to buy it. The beers were so popular, it made sense to market them well beyond trade shows, so they did just that. In 2012 the distillery side of the business opened, introducing

Kentucky Bourbon Barrel Ale—Aged up to six weeks in freshly decanted bourbon barrels, you'll taste the delicate but true notes of vanilla and oak in this one. Smooth, robust, and delicious, this can be enjoyed on its own, served with a meal, or enjoyed as an after-dinner drink.

Kentucky IPA—A lovely, citrusy India Pale Ale in the American style, it's mild and not too hoppy. If you like IPA, you'll like this, and if you're more neutral on hops, you'll still appreciate it. I loved it.

Town Branch also produces barrel-aged seasonal offerings. When I visited last, it was a spring Kentucky Peach Barrel Wheat Ale, with an 8 percent alcohol content and delicate peach flavors. I suspect I could pour it in champagne flutes and fool any Southern ladies luncheon into thinking it was anything but beer. There's a different specialty beer each quarter, including a Christmas Ale and Pumpkin Barrel-Aged Ale.

You can also find taprooms for tasting at Bluegrass Airport in Lexington, Whitaker Bank Ballpark in Lexington, and the KFC Yum! Center in Louisville. Get more information at kentuckyale.com.

Town Branch bourbon and other products to the public. Of course, the name is borrowed directly from the Town Branch, the water that helped start it all in the city more than two centuries before.

The tour is designed so that you get both sides—bourbon and beer, and when you visit, plan on spending the time to explore and sample both. The craft beers in particular are excellent (see the "Microbrewing at Town Branch" sidebar), and their presence makes this a perfect stop when you have a mixed group of beer and whiskey drinkers, to say the least. They refer to themselves as a "brewstillery," and that works just fine.

Though urban, the environment at Town Branch celebrates urban gardening in a lovely manner. Dr. Lyons's wife, Deirdre, the director of corporate image, is responsible for the elegant landscaping that adds character and gives the place a warm and green sensibility. Aside from geraniums and roses, one of the visitor favorites is the Hops Garden, lovingly cultivated along one distillery wall. Hops are notoriously hard to grow, but for most of us, who know only whether we like our beer hoppy (like an IPA) or not hoppy (like a pilsner), the charming growing vines also provide a lesson in how beer gets its taste.

Photo courtesy of Josh Meredith, Original Makers Club

When touring, you'll pass the hops on your way from the visitor center and beer tasting room to the distillery. Town Branch is decidedly craft and small batch—here you won't see the number of fermenters or stills, or the volume of fermenting product, that you will at larger locations, but the experience is very similar as you move through the yeasty-scented cypress fermenting vats to the copper stills. Town Branch makes use of a double-pot still, more in the Irish and British Isle traditions than the continuous stills used by larger distillers in Kentucky.

Indeed, as you taste Town Branch products, you may be struck by how much their traditional bourbon drinks like an Irish whiskey. I am happy to admit just how enjoyable this tasting was and recommend it as a staple on your home bar as an alternative to more traditional Kentucky bourbons. (It is also perhaps no coincidence that Alltech opened a distillery in County Carlow, Ireland, almost at the same time Town Branch was opened, producing malt whiskey.)

Mark Coffman, director of Engineering and Projects at Alltech, and the guy behind making all this happen on a day-to-day basis, helps to tour us around when we visit. The genial Coffman is the sort of person you imagine having spent a life devoted to making great beer and whiskey, but he came to it from the engineering side of things, having spent twenty years with the company. He says he learned the brewing and distilling aspects of his job by trial and error; after spending plenty of time working for a company focused on yeast-based products, it made logical sense. "Alltech really has a number of things that interrelate because of the fermentation aspect, from fuel and ethanol production to beverages," says Coffman.

He transitions into his role as brewer and distiller. "Everyone is so busy," he says. "You learn a lot of different areas because you need to, and by taking certain steps move into those roles with the company—in this case, it fell into my lap." While he may damn himself with faint praise, one thing abundantly obvious at Alltech is just how devoted its employees are to the company, and how willingly they learn skills and make things happen. Coffman is the epitome of this aesthetic.

He explains that especially because of their small-batch size and their location, they don't use the traditional cook system you might find at larger distilleries, in part because they didn't have space for a cooker for grains when they moved into their downtown location. Likewise, they chose other options, though still within the stringent regulations for Kentucky bourbon, and they're very pleased with the outcome.

Temperature and proofing are critical. The pot still at Town Branch only takes the mixture up to about 135–138 proof, where the larger continuous stills reach 160 proof. "We rely on distillation and cuts to balance things out, and the selection of barrel wood and the aging process has a lot to do with it," says Coffman.

Town Branch stores and ages their barrels in a shared facility in Bardstown, Kentucky. It's a non-climate-controlled space, and they keep their barrels on the second and third levels only, to maintain a consistency of heating and cooling and therefore a uniform flavor, based on the spirits' expansion and contraction in the charred oak barrels. The barrels are aged from four to six years.

"In terms of being a craft distiller, we're on the large side, but nothing like bigger distilleries. We may deal with 10.5 barrels in twenty-four hours as we're bottling. The large distilleries go through more than one hundred in the same time, and the really small craft houses, maybe three or four," says Coffman. For consistency they may blend ten batches together, to maintain equilibrium and a consistency of flavor when they bottle. "Even if you're tasting three barrels from one batch, if you're tasting day one versus day ten, you'll get some variation. And the character of the wood itself, the barrels, the magic of that wood can't be underestimated in this process."

Coffman says, "There's a truly scientific craft and artistry to reproduce that flavor consistently. We strive to keep that consistency."

He tells me they go with about a quarter of an inch of char on the interior of their white oak barrels, leaving plenty of surface area for the extracts, and that also acts as a carbon filter, bringing out the character in the whiskey—it does a bit of the same thing as Tennessee's famed Lincoln County method (saving the fact that Tennessee's method involves a separate filtration through maple charcoal), except this process is long and slow by comparison.

When the barrels are emptied, they go to a good cause—brewing Alltech's excellent Kentucky Bourbon Barrel Ale. This whole process creates an exceptionally sippable, drinkable bourbon. I'll be honest, if I have to choose a Kentucky bourbon to sip on, this would be one of my first—and a new discovery rapidly becoming a go-to can only be a good thing. What you get is a light spicy note on the first taste, with a little bit of a wood note and some light caramel to follow. For me it was instantly smooth, and the taste rich but not overwhelming, with notes of pecan, caramel, and brown sugar. As we're tasting, Coffman says if you want to open this one with water, use room temperature—either still or fizzy to your taste—not chilled.

Photo courtesy of Josh Meredith, Original Makers Club

Like many distilleries they're more active on the bourbon creation between fall and spring, with summer more heavily focused on beer. Coffman says they're looking at new expansions now, including a potential facility in Pikeville, Kentucky, geared toward making whiskey rather than beer, and perhaps a white lightning–type product to reflect the area's traditional culture. There's also, he says, the relocation of the Dublin, Ireland, distillery to an old church that makes for a terrific touring experience. "The need to expand, well, that's a good problem to have," says Coffman with a grin.

Town Branch earned gold at the 2012 Whiskey USA and the World Spirits Competition in Germany—impressive for a brand-new entry.

If you visit now, look for some new product. Of note, look for Pearse Lyons Reserve, which is a true single malt whiskey though they don't call it that; since they're aging in second-generation barrels from bourbon production, the barrels are never allowed to dry out. The notes are brown sugar, nutmeg, and a hint of molasses, and it makes splendid cocktails as well as good sipping whiskey. The favorite cocktail take involves blending it with Ale 8, a locally produced ginger ale. My personal take is blending with Birmingham, Alabama's Buffalo Rock ginger ale, which is more like a particularly strong ginger beer, but this is one I tend to skip blending and drink neat. There's also a robust true rye whiskey, with a lovely malted flavor that comes from a blend of 55 percent rye and 30 percent corn. Consider drinking this one with a touch of ice to emphasize the spiciness.

The drink that won everyone over in my friend circle was the Bluegrass Sundown. This is what happens when you blend dark-roast coffee with bourbon and sugar. It's like immediate Irish coffee gratification. If you want the perfect brunch cocktail, add to it two parts boiling water and a fine layer of heavy cream on top. Sip while hot. "Heavenly" is about the only proper descriptive reflecting just how good this actually is to drink. (You can pick up the tempered glasses ideal for serving this cocktail on the kentuckyale.com website, and thus not worry about the glass shattering while offering a proper visual display of this beverage to your guests.)

TOWN BRANCH COCKTAIL

Bluegrass Sundown Coffee

Town Branch sells specialty glasses for this purpose, but a regular coffee mug or a glass Irish coffee mug works in a pinch.

Shake your bottle of Bluegrass Sundown well. Fill your glass one-third full of Bluegrass Sundown. Add ⅔ cup boiling water. Float a tablespoon of heavy cream on top. Cool to drinkability and sip.

WILD TURKEY

1417 Versailles Road, Lawrenceburg, KY 40342;
(502) 839-2182; wildturkeybourbon.com

Wild Turkey is the stuff of legends—even if you don't drink bourbon, you've heard of Wild Turkey. And if you're a bourbon drinker, you certainly don't mind a sip of it every now and then. The master distiller, Jimmy Russell, now eighty, is himself a legend in the business with a story dating back to 1954. Though he shares the job with his son these days, Jimmy's reputation for creating fine bourbon, and his willingness to serve as mentor and guide to any number of younger distillers, has helped build the brand even further.

Products: 101 Bourbon (the original), 81 Bourbon, 81 Rye, 101 Rye, Wild Turkey Diamond, Wild Turkey Forgiven, Spiced, Rare Breed, Kentucky Spirit, Russell's Reserve

Wild Turkey is one of those legendary bourbons, the kind that's been referenced in hundreds of movies, TV shows, books, and pieces of music, from twangy country to heavy metal. It needs no introduction, because it's recognized in nearly every corner of the world, with major US distribution plus emerging markets in Asia and Australia. Long before people really appreciated bourbon the way they've come to in the past couple of decades, Wild Turkey was a spirit to be reckoned with, always holding its own.

It doesn't hurt that the brand has 150 years of history, going back to 1855 when a small company, Austin Nichols, set up as a grocer and started selling wine and spirits—of course, his company would later purchase the distillery. That part didn't come along until the Ripy Brothers started it in 1869. The brothers came to Kentucky from County Tyrone in Ireland, first building up their own grocery business, then starting a distillery that eventually made large quantities of spirits, sold well beyond the borders of Kentucky.

Photo courtesy of DeLeon + Primmer Architecture Workshop

By 1893 the Ripy bourbon had such a fine reputation that it was selected over hundreds of other Kentucky bourbons as the state's entry for the World's Exposition that year. The business, still known as the Ripy Distillery, continued to thrive until Prohibition came along in 1919. During that era they sold their product in small, "medicinal" amounts, like many other Kentucky distilleries, and it was the aforementioned Austin Nichols doing the selling. When the new Roosevelt administration repealed Prohibition in 1933, the distillery got back to work for real, owned by Austin Nichols—with the company solely focused on spirits instead of the grocery industry.

In the early 1940s, while hunting wild turkeys in South Carolina, an Austin Nichols executive named Thomas McCarthy brought along some of the undiluted 101 proof bourbon he'd acquired at their warehouse. His buddies liked it so much, they began asking him to bring along "some of that wild turkey bourbon" to other things, making reference to the trip. McCarthy liked the name, and the company began marketing the product as Wild Turkey Bourbon.

Wild Turkey has expanded its product line since then, but the original bourbon recipe remains as it was in 1940. The distillery is now owned by the Campari Group, but the bourbon tradition it established continues. Since 1954 master distiller Jimmy Russell has been at the helm, and he is uncompromising in his devotion to the product. His son Eddie is now part of the crew as associate distiller; he came on board in 1981, which may seem like a long time, except that his father's been here since 1954.

Thanks to my friend Ben Palos, I was lucky enough to secure an interview with Jimmy Russell. Trust me, he is every bit as gracious, thoughtful, and modest as all the stories make him out to be. He's a delight to speak with. Possessed of a soft, pleasant Kentucky drawl, he's easy to follow, but his acute wit shows through in every aspect of conversation.

Russell may very well be the longest-serving master distiller in the world at this point, and he tells me he grew up in the Lawrenceburg area, and most of his family was employed by distilleries. His dad worked at Wild Turkey, so he knew a good bit about the business before he became part of it all. His wife, Joretta, also worked there, and it was her influence that brought him to the company. "I started on September 10, 1954," he says with pride. "I've been at the same place for sixty years."

I first ask him about the changes he's seen in the industry in recent years. "There are a lot more small distilleries turning up," he says. "There used to be small, family-owned distilleries, of course, and a lot of those old ones have been bought up and consolidated, but now there are the new 'microdistilleries' as they're called, you see the small ones starting up again. I've tried to be involved all I can across the industry. Get the word out; if anybody needs me, I'll be glad to help them out."

That seems to be the essence of Jimmy Russell, and nearly every small distiller I've talked with has done nothing but sing his praises—many of them have gone to Lawrenceburg to work with him over the years, or to seek out his advice. He says the many bourbon distillers along the Bourbon Trail all help each other out. "The bourbon business is better for that cooperation, and we all live within an hour or so of each other. We all meet up at the Bardstown Festival in September."

This attitude underlines what I've seen so often in this industry—there really aren't great insider secrets—distillers aid one another, and most of the time genuinely like each other and enjoy the company of their fellows.

It's clear they feel their interaction makes the quality of everyone's work go up, even when they have strong opinions about what makes things right.

Russell tells his own origin story like a man who gets asked to tell it often—perhaps because so many people are intrigued about a man who at eighty still loves his work enough to keep excelling as Russell does. "I started out in quality control," Russell says of his history with Wild Turkey. "I took grain samples to test. I'd unload the trucks. Nowadays, a lot of what I did is considered lab analysis, but in those days we did a little bit of everything."

He says the master distiller at the time, Bill Hughes, took him under his wing. "He was particular with everything, and let me tell you, he worked every day. Everything we did was on-the-job training in our industry. You learned from experience. Then it was the same as it is now. You make sure you have good grain, the best water, good yeast; it was the same day in and day out for consistency."

He talks a bit about the fact that most bourbon distilleries are essentially doing the same thing. The ingredients and formulas are regulated by law to a great extent, he points out. "But it's like cooking, a lot of people can make the same dish, but they all do something a little bit different to get a different taste, a different flavor.

"We tried to keep it the same with every batch over the years. We have much better equipment now, and we have our own strain of yeast we're using every single day, and it's at least fifty-nine years old. All of it matters in getting the product we put out. In 1954 when I started, the Wild Turkey 101 Proof was the only thing we put out. Over the years we've added a number of products, but everything here is still Wild Turkey, and we do not buy or sell anything else. We do everything for ourselves."

That's a matter of pride at a point in time when the issue of rectified spirits has come up for debate again in the world at large, but for Russell it's of no matter. The concern is clearly doing everything in his corner of the world himself, making Wild Turkey the way he sees fit, from good ingredients—something he stresses over and over.

"I'll tell you our mash bill is lighter on corn than some, with more barley malt and rye. We distill at a low proof, 120, not 160, and double

Photo courtesy of DeLeon + Primmer Architecture Workshop

distill. We barrel at 110 proof. We age for longer than most. It all makes for consistency. As to the lower temperatures, well, we like the results. You can cook a good steak to well done, and in my opinion it just won't have as much flavor. We haven't changed our formula one bit."

I ask him about the history of bourbon, how he thinks it got to be such a dominant industry in this part of the country. His response is meditative, focused, and you get the sense he thinks about it quite a bit. From his perspective, the land was just made for it.

"The main thing is that bourbon started right here, in Bourbon County, Kentucky. We had everything you needed to make it, the water, the weather—we had hot summers and cold winters, which is important—the whiskey in the barrels, it's like it's breathing in and out of the wood as it expands and contracts with the temperature, and that makes for good flavor. You add to that, we had good limestone water here. The minerals make flavor too. We had the grain or could source it, and again, the temperatures were important."

One thing I feel I have to ask someone like Jimmy Russell is how the culture has evolved—after all, bourbon's role in the market today is quite different than it was twenty years ago, let alone sixty. I want to know, does this mean it's finally come into its own?

"There are some big things, no question," Russell says. "Back when I started, people thought of bourbon as a gentleman's drink, you understand. It was what got ordered in their favorite bars, and it was part of the culture—you'd have a cigar after dinner and a glass of bourbon, and you'd play cards. It didn't have the worldwide following yet—now it's huge in Japan and Australia, huge. And the ladies just didn't drink it then. It wasn't allowed, really. Now, when I do seminars, the majority of the people coming are women."

Are we having any impact on the industry now that we're buying more? Russell laughs and says, "Let me tell you, the first thing that happened is that the labels started to look much, much better. And the ladies read those labels more than men did, too. But bourbon is appealing to a lot more people than it used to, period. It's not just the drink of the Southern gentleman anymore. I think some of the switch away from bourbon used to come from younger men trying to be different from their dads, because the drinkers used to be just older men. Now, anyone twenty-one and up is a potential bourbon drinker." In Russell's eyes that's a good thing, because it gives him a chance to share some fine spirits.

Shifting gears, I go back to the bourbon itself. So does a bottle of bourbon get better, like a bottle of fine wine? "When you take that bourbon out of the charred oak barrel," says Russell seriously, "it stops the aging process. It stays eight years old like it was then, even if you've had that bottle on the shelf for years. But as long as it doesn't change color, you're fine. It's still the same bourbon it was when it was bottled. But if it goes all murky now, the color goes wrong or gets muddy, you don't want to drink it. I've got bottles dating all the way back to Prohibition in my office."

The reference to Prohibition brings up a number of questions about the current market, especially since Wild Turkey now sells so many different iterations of its product.

Russell points out that bourbon is outstandingly popular as the local drink in Kentucky, any laws on the books notwithstanding. "The state of Kentucky is actually still dry in most counties, it's still in Prohibition as far as that goes," he says. "Other states, well, Virginia and South Carolina, are control states with regard to our products—everything goes through

TASTE PROFILES

Wild Turkey 81 Bourbon—classic Wild Turkey spicy finish, but a mellower counterpart to Wild Turkey 81 Rye.

Wild Turkey 101—flavors of almonds, honey, and blackberries.

Wild Turkey 101 Bourbon—Toasted oak and caramel flavors with notes of honey, brown sugar, oranges, and a hint of tobacco. Its high proof contributes to its bolder flavor.

Wild Turkey 81 Rye—rich aromas and flavors of vanilla and big, broad spice. Less sweet than bourbon, it has subtle hints of rye toast with a light smokiness.

Wild Turkey 101 Rye—peppery, bold flavor that rye bourbons are known for with hints of honey and citrus. The finish is zesty with a touch of sweetness.

Wild Turkey Diamond—mingling of thirteen- and sixteen-year whiskeys that yield tantalizing notes of caramel and vanilla, complete with a spicy oak finish.

Wild Turkey Forgiven—six-year-old bourbon mixed with four-year-old rye. The whiskey opens bold and finishes smooth, with tasting notes of creamy vanilla and oak, and a peppery, cinnamon finish.

Wild Turkey Spiced—combines classic bourbon flavor with island spices. Akin to a spiced rum, this bourbon offers notes of vanilla, caramel, and cloves.

Wild Turkey Rare Breed—remarkably smooth flavor considering its high alcohol content (112.4 proof), with hints of light oranges, mint, and tones of sweet tobacco.

Wild Turkey Kentucky Spirit—single-barrel bourbon that is full-bodied with rich vanilla flavors and a hint of sweetness. It's a complex bourbon with layers of almonds, honey, blackberries, and leather. The finish is long and dark, lingering well after each sip.

the state's liquor regulations, and you can't buy all our products. When it comes down to it, we have to comply with federal laws first, then local, and all the states have different laws—there's no single guideline."

And what happens in the market next? "More and more foreign markets will open up. Last week, we had a group in from South Korea—other cultures are getting more and more into American bourbon and whiskey, some even moving away from scotch, and that's huge . . . it's huge." Indeed, it's hard not to be aware that the European and Asian markets are knocking on the door here, and Russell reiterates especially the Japanese market for Wild Turkey, where it's well distributed already.

I ask, so how does someone new to bourbon properly taste it, whether they're Japanese or Australian, or an American who's grown up around it but never drunk it? "Taste for balance," he says with assurance. "Find the notes of caramel and vanilla, the sweetness in the bourbon. For myself, I'm looking for aroma first, then the taste, the flavor; I'm looking for something I want to sit around and sip."

Finally, I bring up the subject of bourbon tourism. After all, I want readers to make their way down here and have the same experiences I've had. "The whole Kentucky Bourbon Trail, the marketing, is working wonders. Last year, I think we had 80,000 visitors from all over the world tour through our distillery. We see a lot of future for that. I think the total is something like 100 million people through all the facilities in the past six years all together. It absolutely makes us look to the future."

The expanding market, he adds, means he's got to look at what he needs to produce to meet the rising demand. As of right now, he says, Wild Turkey has some half million barrels in storage, knowing they won't be ready for eight to ten years. "We put a lot in storage," he adds mildly. Of course, with his son Eddie Russell as associate distiller, that storage will stay in the family, even if Jimmy decides to retire one day. Like many of the distilleries in Kentucky, there is a long, multi-generational tradition that runs through Wild Turkey.

He finishes up by reminding me to come and visit again. Wild Turkey has a gorgeous new visitor center, and guests can walk through and see the whole operation.

Wild Turkey Cocktails

Boulevardier Swizzle
(created by Naren Young)

1 ounce Wild Turkey 101 Bourbon
1 ounce Cinzano Rosso
1 ounce Campari
3 dashes orange bitters

Build over crushed ice. Swizzle and add more crushed ice. Garnish with an orange twist.

Chamomile Old-Fashioned
(created by Naren Young)

2 ounces Russell's Reserve 6 Year Old Rye
¼ ounce chamomile syrup
3 dashes chamomile tincture

Stir with ice and strain on fresh ice in a rocks glass. Spray with chamomile tincture.

Jimmy Walbanger
(created by Sean Hoard)

2 ounces Wild Turkey 101 Bourbon
½ ounce Galliano
½ ounce orange juice
¼ ounce lemon juice
¼ ounce Grade B maple syrup
1 dash absinthe
1 ½ ounces club soda

Shake first six ingredients with ice, strain into a Collins glass, and top with club soda.

Archer Homestead

2 ounces Wild Turkey 101 Rye
¾ ounce lemon juice
½ ounce Lairds Apple Brandy
¼ ounce honey syrup
1 bottle Strongbow Hard Cider

Shake first four ingredients over ice and strain over fresh ice into a 12-ounce glass. Top with Strongbow Cider and garnish with an apple slice or lemon peel.

Leap of Faith

(served at Honor in San Francisco)

1 ½ ounces Wild Turkey 81 Rye
¾ ounce Cocchi Rosa
½ ounce pür•likör spice
½ ounce lemon juice
½ ounce gum syrup
Splash clove bitters

Combine all ingredients in a shaker with ice and shake. Serve over fresh ice.

The Old and The New

(created by Justin August Fairweather of Evelyn)

2 ounces Wild Turkey 101 Rye

To make a Wild Turkey 101 Rye Old-Fashioned Jelly Orange wedge:
1 teaspoon sugar
1 splash water
2 dashes Angostura Bitters
2 ounces Wild Turkey 101 Rye
1 teaspoon powdered unflavored gelatin
1 orange, cut in half

Mix sugar, water, Angostura Bitters, and Wild Turkey 101 Rye in an Old-Fashioned glass filled with ice and stir. Mix with gelatin and pour into a hollowed orange skin to set.

Cut out a Jelly Orange wedge and serve with Wild Turkey 101 Rye.

Note: Wild Turkey 101 Rye is hard to find, so this could also work with the more readily available Wild Turkey 81 Rye.

WILLETT

Kentucky Bourbon Distillers, 1869 Loretto Road,
Bardstown, KY 40004; (502) 348-0899

illett, a private, family-owned company—better known in the past as Kentucky Bourbon Distillers—produces a wide variety of bourbon and spirits, but the Willett brand specifically has become a very desirable one in recent years—receiving superb reviews from professionals and ordinary fans alike. The Willett tour, part of the Kentucky Bourbon Trail Craft Tour, is delightful, full of wonderfully restored buildings, many dating to the 1930s when the distillery reopened after Prohibition. A bed and breakfast on the grounds is forthcoming. What's very appealing about the brand is its family ties and its commitment to spreading its reputation through word of mouth, rather than relying on big advertising campaigns.

Products: Willett, Johnny Drum, Kentucky Pride, Kentucky Vintage, Noah's Mill, Pure Kentucky Old Bardstown, Rowan Creek

Willett is a lengthy family saga about bourbon, so let's start at the beginning, shall we?

The Willett family has a long and detailed history in the liquor industry, back to the colonial era and beyond. The family's influence extends beyond their own family's distillery—the Barton distillery also has ties back to the Willett family.

The family traces its presence on this continent back to one Edward Willett, born in Herefordshire, England, in 1657 and brought to the colonies as a young boy. As a teenager he was sent back to England, this time to London, to learn the pewter trade from a cousin, and he adopted a family tradition, a bird over a crown, as his maker's mark (the particular bird is

known as a "willett" for its distinctive cry), its ties said to be to the English family's coat of arms.

Edward Willett returned to Maryland to settle, making a name for himself as a pewter smith. His son William followed him into the trade, and the family eventually supplied a good deal of the pewter ware intended for the Kentucky territory. His son, William Jr., opened a tavern offering lodging to travelers. In 1792 he moved from Maryland to Kentucky, and it was his grandson, John David Willett, born in 1841, who would begin the family tradition of distilling.

After the Civil War, John Willett became a partner and master distiller at the Moore, Willett and Frenke Distillery in Bardstown. It's said that because of failing eyesight he eventually sold the distillery to his brothers-in-law, Ben F. Mattingly and Tom Moore (from which would branch the Tom Moore Distillery that would become Barton); however, he went on to work at no less than five additional distilleries, three in Bardstown and two in Louisville, developing mash bills the Willett Distilling Company would later use.

His own son, Lambert, grew up learning from his father and worked heavily in the industry, including as part owner of the Clear Springs

Distillery bought from Jim Beam, until Prohibition, at which point he chose to raise hogs and cattle at his farm. When Prohibition ended, Lambert became the superintendent at the Max Selliger & Co. Distillery (better known as the Bernheim Distillery), a company where he'd been involved extensively before Prohibition.

Lambert's son Thompson joined his father at Bernheim as assistant superintendent at just twenty-five, right after the end of Prohibition. Two years later he and his brother Johnny, an engineer, founded the Willett Distilling Company on the family farm. They completed their first batch of whiskey there—thirty barrels—on March 17, 1937. The new whiskey was stored in the traditional metal-clad warehouses that still stand today—built on high ground to make sure the breezes aid the whiskey as it ages. In 1942 the elder Willett retired from Bernheim and returned to Bardstown to manage the family farm and help with the running of the family distillery.

After World War II, Thompson and Johnny's brother Paul Willett was enlisted to run the bottling, and they hired an experienced master distiller, Charlie Thomason. Eventually brother Robert Willett, a lawyer, came into the business, and another brother, Charlie, built up a wholesale business distributing Willett and other products.

In 1972 Even G. Kulsveen married Thompson's daughter Martha (who'd long been involved in the running of the family business and currently serves as the company's president). In 1981 he purchased the property and started Kentucky Bourbon Distillers, Ltd., which continues to operate. Even's son Drew came on board in 2004 after graduating from college, and Britt Kulsveen Chavanne,

Photo courtesy of Britt K. Chavanne, Willett Distillery

Even's daughter, and her husband, Hunter Chavanne, joined the business toward the end of 2005, after Hurricane Katrina sent them from their home in Baton Rouge. Drew's wife, Janelle, eventually came in to run the distillery gift shop and visitor center.

Between the early 1980s and 2012, KBD/Willett operated primarily as a bottling and packaging facility providing custom contract bottling for a number of major brands, as well as continuing to bottle the reserves aging in the distillery's warehouses, but in 2012 the family and their dynamic and talented small group of employees began cooking mash again. The first barrels went into storage on January 27, 2012, which would have been the 103rd birthday of Thompson Willett.

In recent years the family has worked extremely hard to restore and revitalize the property, and that effort has seen tremendous return. It's one of the things that makes the visit to the Willett Distillery truly worthwhile. The presence of buildings and even the original still from 1936 make the place distinctive among many of the newer, larger, and more updated facilities.

Today Kentucky Bourbon Distillers produces a number of brands of premium bourbon, aged anywhere between four and twenty years. The Willett bourbon is made using the original mash bills that Thompson Willett used, along with a few Drew Kulsveen developed on his own. With very small-batch, hands-on efforts, they worry more about quality than anything else. As of October 2014 they'd filled 10,000 barrels, which are now aging in the warehouses dating back to the distillery's founding. Like most of the area's distilleries, they close in July and August for maintenance, resuming in September.

Britt Kulsveen Chavanne, who took the time to discuss the operations with me, says they keep those mash bills a family secret. I ask her what makes the Willett brand distinctive. "The greatest distinction between our products and others in the market stems from the extremely small size of our operation and how hands-on we truly still are," she says. "Our small-batch bottlings are a mingling of twenty to twenty-two barrels at a time.

"There is no official regulation or definition of the term 'small batch'; one distillery's small batch could be five hundred barrels, another's could be ten. In addition, a number of our products are bottled at cask strength/ barrel proof or are very minimally reduced in strength. This allows the consumer to taste the whiskey raw and captures the flavor straight from the barrel, or very close to it, and gives them the opportunity to reduce it down to a proof of their liking. Another great distinction overall is that we are truly a family operation in every sense of the word and use the most traditional of methods to this day. We have always done things in a manner to produce the highest quality we possibly can and have never focused on quantity, sometimes at a cost to the overall efficiency of our operations."

When I ask her how the company blends for the perfect flavor, Chavanne bristles at the term *blend* in reference to mingling the barrel contents, lest we confuse the distillery's product with a "blended" bourbon—a distinctly inferior option. "There are blended whiskeys in the market, but a blended whiskey is a mixture of both whiskey and neutral grain spirits (essentially vodka) and allows the addition of flavoring and coloring materials. This could not be more opposite from our products."

Photo courtesy of Britt K. Chavanne, Willett Distillery

She's dead right, of course, and that underlines the important message of Kentucky bourbon itself—that it is an additive-free product. Bear in mind, this is about grain, yeast, limestone water (theirs comes from the property), and charred oak barrels, put through an aging process. If you remember nothing else about Kentucky bourbon, remember that.

Britt Chavanne continues, "We do take an assortment of barrels which range in age and proof, and comingle those together to achieve our desired flavor profile. Some of our products, such as our Willett Family Estate Small Batch Rye, do comingle barrels using two different mash bills: one that is an original used by our grandfather and a more current mash bill developed by my brother Drew."

Chavanne, raised in a distilling family, has some choice words to say about aging too. "All of our bourbon products currently available in the market use whiskey that is a minimum of four years old. We do have a rye whiskey that is a minimum of two years old [a more typical base for rye products]. You're required to state the age of the whiskey being used if it's less than four years old, but not required to state an age if the whiskey is older than that. You're also required to state the age of the youngest whiskey used. I mention this because age statements don't necessarily disclose as much as you might expect. If someone has a product in which they comingle barrels that are four, six, eight, and fifteen years of age, if an age is claimed, you would have to state that it's four years old, even though much older whiskeys have been used."

When it comes to the sources for their ingredients, they focus on local where possible and high quality. Chavanne's brother Drew Kulsveen says they source their corn from nearby Caldwell Farms, keeping the grain source local.

Britt says, "We don't disclose the particulars of any of our mash bills; they're considered both family recipes and trade secrets. However, we do have a total of six that we use (four bourbon and two rye). In general, we use a higher content of malted barley than most traditional mash bills. Our corn and wheat are locally sourced, and our rye comes from the upper Midwest. Our malted barley comes from Wisconsin. Our water is sourced on our property by spring-fed lakes. Our barrels are manufactured by Kentucky Cooperage (also known as Independent Stave)." She also mentions that after the barrels have been used, they're often sold to local craft brewers for further use.

Willett also has a very word-of-mouth viewpoint when it comes to marketing and advertising. That's a big deal when the larger companies have the budgets and the advantage of high-budget advertising, but the growing word-of-mouth on Willett is outstanding. My friend Paul Koonz, who has been my de facto bourbon adviser throughout this book, lists Willett as a top choice, and so do many of the serious Kentucky bourbon lovers I've met, the people who take their drink of choice very seriously indeed.

"We are a family operation through and through, and we're extremely passionate about it. That shows through in both our products and our distillery, and the property in general," says Chavanne, referencing the incredible effort they've put into the distillery's restoration over the past several years. "We don't use any formal marketing or advertising—all our products are of very limited production and strictly allocated. Our marketing—a very loose use of the term—is more of a grassroots approach: We don't have any brand ambassadors for our outside sales force; all of our tastings

Photo courtesy of Britt K. Chavanne, Willett Distillery

and events are conducted by a member of our family. We still do things the traditional, old-fashioned and old-school way, in that we are extremely hands on and not an automated operation. This pertains to our distilling and bottling operations, as well as the way we conduct business in general."

Willett has a long history, so how does that affect the choices you make as the folks who've truly revived the brand, I ask. The long family history is deep, and obviously drives Chavanne, her brother, and the rest of the crew to make good things happen.

"At the end of the day, long family history withstanding or not, we are passionate about what we do—to the point of downright stubbornness really—and will always do our best to preserve our family's name and reputation in all that we do. Between my father's side of the family, which is Norwegian, and my mother's side of the family, which is Irish, our passion is furious. I hope that they are able to taste this."

How is the sudden rebirth of the American craft whiskey industry affecting your choices about the distillery and growth?

"We have always made decisions for the benefit of our distillery and family business, and what makes sense for us," she says. "I honestly don't believe we're like any other operation, and as such, we've never made decisions or choices by comparing our operation to others or considering what others are doing. We don't conduct market research. We make decisions as a family collaboration. In short, I suppose that we don't see this business as a competition but as a way of life. Our production is based on what we are operationally set up to do, and we do the best we can with the very limited size of our production capabilities and small staff. There are growing pains to be sure—an industry-wide shortage of aging inventory and all sorts of challenges—but we love it."

I ask Chavanne what she wants visitors to know about the distillery and its tour, before they find their way to the property. She makes it clear she hasn't spent a lot of time at other distilleries, but she knows what she expects from her own, joking that she has a little bias when it comes to Willett. But her family pride and her strong commitment to the business are evident in everything she says.

"I can tell you that we offer a very exclusive and authentic experience, and our property is simply charming," Chavanne tells me. "All of our tour guides are extremely passionate and enthusiastic, and most importantly, they are friendly, highly knowledgeable, and take pride in representing our family. We provide tourists with a full hands-on experience, intimate and personal, from tasting the mash out of the fermenting tanks to filling barrels and hammering the bungs into those barrels. Even though all distilleries are only allowed to pour two one-ounce samples, we do provide tourists the opportunity to choose what they want to sample." As an aside, she adds, "We have approximately fifteen or more selections to choose from, including our Single Barrel Cask Strength bottlings that are rare and up to twenty-five years old."

If you're coming for the tour, she reminds guests that "Our tours are on the hour, and we will conduct the tour even if only one person arrives. I would highly recommend touring our family's distillery and a larger distillery that is on the Kentucky Bourbon Trail, on the non-Craft tour, to see both ends of the spectrum." This is a tour I haven't done yet, but it's high on the list of things I'm looking forward to experiencing.

WILLETT DISTILLERY COCKTAILS

Kentucky Peach Tea

A few slices fresh ginger
1 large slice peach
Mint leaves
2 ounces Willett Pot Still Reserve
½ ounce Dolin Rouge
½ ounce ginger ale
An additional peach slice and
   ginger slice for garnish

Muddle the ginger and peach thoroughly in the bottom of an Old-Fashioned glass. Next add the mint and muddle lightly. Place a few ice cubes in the glass and pour in the Willett Pot Still Reserve and Dolin Rouge. Stir well and add a splash of ginger ale on top. Garnish with a peach slice and a ginger slice.

Blackberry Bourbon Martini

1 teaspoon brown sugar
2 dashes Angostura Bitters
Water
6 blackberries
2 ounces Noah's Mill

In a cocktail shaker, add brown sugar and pour bitters on top. Add one tablespoon water and stir thoroughly. Next, drop in three blackberries and muddle. Drop in ice cubes and the Noah's Mill. Stir for a few seconds and strain into a martini glass. **Note:** You may have to strain more than once. Garnish with the remaining three blackberries on a toothpick.

The Darjeeling Express

8 ounces vanilla chai tea
1 tablespoon Willett Pot Still
   Reserve
1 teaspoon natural cane turbinado
   sugar
1 teaspoon half-and-half
Cinnamon stick
Dash ground nutmeg

After steeping tea for five minutes, add Willett Pot Still Reserve, sugar, half-and-half, and cinnamon stick. Stir for a few seconds using the cinnamon stick and top it off with a dash of nutmeg.

WOODFORD RESERVE

7855 McCracken Pike, Versailles, KY 40383;
(859) 879-1812; woodfordreserve.com

Woodford is a favorite tourist destination, not just for the beautiful rolling hills that surround it, but for its historic locale and the attention it gives the whole tourism experience with its elegant, streamlined visitor center. Woodford is also a highly drinkable bourbon that appeals both to fans of the alcohol genre and to new drinkers alike.

The Products: Woodford Reserve Bourbon, Woodford Reserve Double Oaked, Woodford Reserve Rye Whiskey, specialty limited releases

Woodford Reserve, owned by Brown-Forman, remains one of the most beautiful distilleries in Kentucky. The drive from Lexington or Versailles takes you through back roads of lushly green rolling hills and past myriad pastures in pristine condition, marked off by stone or wooden fencing. You'll see barns that look like massive estates, gorgeous horses exercising, and abundant old-growth trees defining boundaries. Woodford County is stunning, and the horse culture and picturesque towns that have grown up there are worth sightseeing themselves. Woodford happens to be the first bourbon distillery I ever visited, well before I knew I'd write a book on the topic someday. For many bourbon drinkers, Woodford is a mecca—the source of one of their very favorites. It's one of mine, too, quite aside from my sentimental fondness for the place itself.

The distillery tour is designed to be incredibly user-friendly. I have to admit, I miss the old days when you got to walk down the hill to the distilling and barrel storage facilities, but the newest updates definitely make it appealing for all ages, and no less gorgeous.

The smallest of the major distillers in the area, Woodford Reserve definitely qualifies as a small-batch bourbon, and its popularity among serious bourbon lovers is not to be questioned. My friend Paul Koontz introduced me to Woodford back in the days before I was remotely a bourbon drinker, and it was easy to love the stuff. The Distiller's Select is most Woodford lovers' product of choice: It starts out with warm notes of maple and pecan at first, then the second taste brings in notes of spice and fruit. If, like me, you're prone to add a single ice cube, then you'll find it opens up; it gets a "skooch" sweeter and the fruit expands on your palate.

The Double Oaked is lovely, but distinctly sweeter, with butterscotch on its nose, and caramel and spice as the first notes. As Paul says, "I really want to poach pears in this." The distillery releases a select, limited-edition Master's Collection each fall as well, varying in style. They've been doing this since 2005, and there are aficionados lining up to grab each iteration as it becomes available.

"It was our intention to respond to the challenge of making something special occasion with this one," says Master Distiller Chris Morris. "It's aimed at the folks who enjoy something special, perhaps as an after-dinner drink in the mode of Grand Marnier or cognac. And it's so many people's drink of choice in that category now. The Master's Collection varies quite a bit each year, and it's fun for us to experiment. It could be malt, it could be rye—it's innovative whiskey, and it's not always a bourbon. It's aimed at Woodford fans, whiskey collectors, or whiskey geeks—there's a wide range out there."

Like me, he loves Distiller's Select best. "That's the heart of the family," he says when I admit to him how much I love the stuff. "It was Mr. Owsley's intention that be so. Honestly, I never find anyone who doesn't like Woodford. You can go global. It'll be the one everyone likes: 'I don't really like bourbon, but I like Woodford' kind of thing. It's the core of our business."

Woodford as distillery and a product sometimes seems to be the refined essence of what people outside the region and the industry romantically imagine the world of bourbon making to be—and bourbon itself to be. First, the distillery grounds themselves have a magical quality. The first time my husband and I toured, I was writing a magazine piece and we were lucky enough to get a tour with production manager Conor

O'Driscoll, whose encyclopedic knowledge of the distillery's history and culture, as well as his expounding on the minutiae of production, made the experience wholly extraordinary.

When I went back to visit for this book, things had changed a bit—the general tour was distinctly more tourist-focused and less personal than my other experience had been—the young woman who gave the tour had plenty of knowledge, but perhaps lacked the grand passion we loved with O'Driscoll. Even so, the busy crowd touring with us very much enjoyed the whole thing, even with electronic devices to carry the tour guide's words, and travel around the grounds dependent on small buses, rather than feet.

Woodford lies on a site where distilling has been going on almost continuously since the eighteenth century, and the history of that has sunk into the land almost as surely as at other sites of historic pilgrimage. If the Bourbon Trail is a pilgrimage, this is one of its chief shrines. The first distilling done here probably began about 1780, and the first of the still-standing buildings dates to the 1830s. Elijah Pepper started his first distillery here, and it bore the name of his son and successor, Oscar Pepper. Dr. James Crow, a Scottish immigrant who worked with Oscar for decades, is credited with the invention of the sour mash process used to this day to create bourbon and whiskey across the region. By then, the place was known as the Oscar Pepper Distillery.

The Pepper family sold it to Leopold Labrot and James Graham in 1878, and their families kept it going, with a pause for Prohibition in 1919, up until World War II, at which point it was sold directly to the current owners, Brown-Forman. In the late 1960s Brown-Forman opted to close the operation and sell it off a few years later. In a wise decision, they repurchased the land in 1993 and started over, opening officially in March 1996.

"Ever since then we've been progressively improving processes at the distillery," says Master Distiller Chris Morris. "Everything is evolving for Woodford; we're not a giant, we're small batch, but we're not a small brand. We're steadily increasing the number of barrels per batch to meet demand. Our cooperage has steadily improved. We've got much better barrels.

"We make a better product today than ever. Last month we might have 150 barrels of bourbon that make up a batch, this month, 130—our first batches were five barrels, back in the 1990s. That made it difficult. With so few, there was more potential for inconsistency. Having 130 barrels makes it easier. Each barrel plays an ever smaller role, and you don't have to carefully taste all of them; you can only taste so many. You can simply sample barrels from each day of production. We have maybe ten days of production in a batch. One might be fruity, one grainy, one malty—we're looking at about five areas of flavor—then we can carefully put the batch together, reduce to proof, taste, and if we need to bring in more barrels for the right flavor, we can do that. And these days, we're bottling every day. It's a well-oiled machine."

Morris himself is one of the best things about Woodford Reserve, a joy to talk to every time. He's just the second distiller at Woodford since the reopening, and he trained under his predecessor. His father spent forty-one years at Brown-Forman and brought him to the company. His parents met and got married while working for Brown-Forman, and he started working for the company at eighteen, in the lab, setting up samples for a master

Brown–Forman

The Brown-Forman company owns Woodford Reserve, as well as Jack Daniel's Tennessee whiskey and a wide variety of other fine spirits brands. The company, founded in 1870 by Louisville businessman George Garvin Brown, started Old Forester Kentucky Straight Bourbon Whiskey, still made by the company today. The current board chairman, George Garvin Brown IV, comes from the fifth generation of the Brown family. In Louisville alone the company employs more than 1,000 people.

Brown-Forman's global brands of wine and spirits include Canadian Mist whiskeys, Chambord Liqueur, Collingwood Canadian Whiskey, Don Eduardo Tequila, Early Times, el Jimador, Finlandia, Gentleman Jack and Jack Daniel's, Herradura, Korbel, Maximus, Old Forester, Pepe Lopez, Sonoma Cutrer, Southern Comfort, Tuaca, and Woodford Reserve.

distiller even before he could legally taste them. "That was thirty-eight years ago, and I listened the whole time. I was being trained from day one," says Morris.

Woodford Reserve, Morris tells me, evolved from the challenges developing across the beverage industry in the 1980s and 1990s, when super-premium single malt scotches started to take off across the industry, and when red wines from California and the craft beer movement both experienced their first push of major growth worldwide. "The late 1980s was about a return to flavor," Morris says. "And Brown-Forman's CEO Owsley Brown II wanted a new bourbon to compete in that market, a bourbon that would have its own home-place, and would be of the utmost quality and craftsmanship."

The company repurchased and restored the old Pepper Distillery, and aimed to make the vision come to life, using old-school methods from around the world to make a new product. The name of the new bourbon came from Woodford County. "But," says Morris, "though it's a neat home-place, the history starts with us. It's new. We create it for you today. The brand is still growing. It's just tremendous. Woodford became a catalyst in the industry quickly. Other craft distillers visited, and the brand has been emulated."

There's good reason for that emulation. As I said above, it's just excellent product, whether you're drinking it straight, on ice, or in a cocktail. For the record, Morris likes an Old-Fashioned in a very old-school method, just sugar, water, Woodford, bitters, and a twist of citrus. "I'm not so much for the muddled fruit," he says. I couldn't agree more.

Thus we return full circle to that distillery tour. The visitor center itself, where you arrive and explore first, is large, gracious, and absolutely up-to-date, with current design elements that include wood flooring, a splendid glassed gas fireplace, comfortable couches, and coffee tables made of wood recycled from old mash fermenters. It's charming. I have to say, I miss some of the older variation, but there is no denying its comfort, appeal, and welcoming nature.

Once you arrive at the visitor center, you purchase tour tickets and receive a transmitter with ear bud, ensuring you will hear your tour guide.

Groups make their way out to the veranda, where you'll hop on a small, cozy tour bus and travel the short distance around and down the hill to the distillery proper. The buildings of stone and whitewashed board harken instantly back to another time, anachronous with the electronic listening devices. Again, whether sunny or overcast, the green and beauty of the place just overwhelms. No wonder people want to work here.

Inside the distillery proper, you're treated to the sight of the huge cypress fermenters and the yeasty smell of the mash, a mix of 72 percent corn, 18 percent rye, and 10 percent malted barley. We learn that the wells on the property provide the Kentucky limestone-filtered water, a crucial ingredient, rich in calcium and magnesium but free of iron. The yeast is a proprietary strain, as is that of each and every distiller it seems, this one created in 1929.

From there you're led to views of the copper stills in which the whiskey is thrice distilled before being put into charred oak barrels for maturation, through which the whiskey will acquire both color and flavor. Woodford's American oak barrels come from their very own cooperage in Louisville. The charred oak's tannins, your tour guide will remind you, bring all those honey, vanilla, maple syrup, butterscotch, and caramel notes to your bourbon (not unlike what oak does for wine). The barrels, once filled, are bunged with native Kentucky yellow poplar, because the wood forms a tight seal.

I love the barrel storage house, lightly climate controlled to trick Mother Nature a few times during winter. Heat causes the maturing bourbon to swell, seeping into the wood to absorb its flavors, cool temperatures allow it to contract again. The climate control makes the taste such that it seems the bourbon aged longer. The smell of the barrel storage is wondrous, redolent of the "angels' share" that evaporates from the barrels over the course of aging. On this visit in 2014, I caught my last glimpse of Elijah, the eighteen-year-old white-furred mouser who'd apparently retired from his mouse-killing days. Being a cat lover I was quite thrilled with Elijah, who lounged comfortably under the barrel house signs on my last visit. He passed away just a few months later, and while there is no doubt a new mouser to take his place, it's hard not to have soft spot for the old guy.

Your last glimpses of the distilling process, if you're lucky, will end with a chance to witness the tasting and bottling procedure right there. Woodford sells off its used barrels to distillers making other product, including craft beer and other spirits, like rum. The rules of the Kentucky method, as you remember, stipulate no reuse of the barrels for new bourbon.

Then it's back up the hill on the bus to the tasting room, which is a terrific experience. The guided tasting allows you to truly get a sense of what flavors are supposed to be. I particularly enjoyed the option to taste first neat, then with an ice cube or water. It turns out I really like my bourbon with a single ice cube. My husband and my friend Paul voted neat. Paul's lovely wife, Anne, seemed to be on my side, not that it was girls against boys or anything.

Dee Ford, who heads up tourism at the Woodford home-place and visitor center, says, "I think Woodford provides a truly complete immersive experience. It takes the maker's world to the drinker's world and explains the process very thoroughly. You get a sense of the craftsmanship, the details, the aesthetics—really the authenticity. All the Woodford there is bottled in that space, and it's very labor intensive.

"Everyone's on their own journey with bourbon. Some people who come here are serious lovers of the drink; some are totally new to it. I like that we provide something for everyone along that path. Some are going to like it straight; some are going to want cocktails. We just want to say we're happy if you choose ours. We want you to know, though, that hospitality is another piece of what you get here when you come to visit."

WOODFORD RESERVE DISTILLERY COCKTAIL

Woodford Mule

Like the Moscow Mule, but with bourbon.

1 ounce Woodford Reserve
1 can ginger beer
Lime wheel to garnish

Pour your Woodford over ice and
stir to chill, then add the chilled
ginger beer. We usually have these
not in a copper mug, but in a
ceramic one.

TENNESSEE

Tennessee has a long and distinguished distilling tradition, but for the better part of the twentieth century we tried to wipe it from the public eye, as though we were somehow embarrassed that once upon a time we produced very fine whiskey across the state. Outside of celebrating the culture in Lynchburg on occasion, we still seemed, for the longest time, to brush off the fact that Jack Daniel's has continued to produce huge quantities of Tennessee whiskey and helped define our state across the world as an exceptional producer. Statistically, Jack accounts for almost all the whiskey produced by the state, even when balanced against the second-largest long-term producer, George Dickel, and all the small distilleries that have popped up combined together. And, of course, with those two distilleries have come jobs, tax revenue, and a host of other benefits to the state as a whole.

Here in the South, in what's popularly referred to as the "buckle of the Bible Belt" (I think there are at least five states vying for that title, frankly, but Tennessee tends to claim it loudest), popular conversation always comes down to the old canard about the "bootleggers and the teetotaling Baptists" being in cahoots for their own benefits, but the cultural question is larger than that. Yes, we have a number of conservative religious sects in Tennessee that eschew alcohol consumption, and yes, we have a lengthy tradition, especially in East Tennessee, of illegal whiskey production. But it still doesn't explain wholly the reality that Tennessee has generally overlooked its potential to create very fine spirits for the better part of a century. Fortuitously, we seem to have suddenly resurrected our spirits making potential in the past few years.

Like Kentucky, we have everything needed to make a good whiskey. We have limestone-fed springs that provide perfect water. We have four distinct seasons that allow the aging casks to absorb the whiskey into the charred wood in the heat, and contract in the cold, forcing it back out. We have access to outstanding corn to make that whiskey from, and we have the wide spaces to build distilleries and warehouses. Only now are we rediscovering the drive to do that outside the hollows around Lynchburg and Tullahoma, from where outstanding whiskey has been pouring regardless of state attitudes since the 1930s and back before Prohibition.

Mike Veach of the Filson County Historical Society in Kentucky opines that the rise of local distillers in Tennessee seems to have been very similar to that phenomenon in Kentucky, with the biggest difference being due to the fact that the Ohio River provided the kind of transportation that inspired the use of the earliest charred oak barrels to begin with. Because of the massive trade along the Ohio, you saw more distilleries emerge faster in Kentucky. Likewise, he says, it took Tennessee much longer to develop a reputation for its products as well, and Tennessee was generally slower to adopt the use of barrels for aging than Kentucky, where it was the absolute norm by 1850. Certainly, by the time Daniel, Dickel, and Nelson truly established themselves as purveyors of good whiskey in the last quarter of the nineteenth century, barrel aging was the norm, and Tennessee whiskey had built itself a reputation.

Unlike Kentucky, Tennessee's traditions didn't rebound following Prohibition. For one thing we started earlier and lasted far longer than Prohibition nationally. With a law passed in 1909, Tennessee went officially dry by 1910 and didn't truly lift that until 1937 (nationally, the 18th Amendment passed in 1919 and went into effect in 1920, and the 21st Amendment lifted Prohibition in 1933, shortly after the election of Franklin Delano Roosevelt). By 1938 two distilleries were coming back on line, George Dickel (originally Cascade Springs) and Jack Daniel's, and most of the rest of the state's long and detailed distilling history was erased until the 1990s.

Tennessee distillers, like Kentucky's, started making and aging liquor as early as they started settling the area. The earliest distillery on record seems to have existed by 1771 in Shelby County in West Tennessee, but East and Middle Tennessee filled up as time went on. Exact numbers vary, depending upon whom you talk to, but according to Eric Byford, the filmmaker responsible for *Straight Up, Tennessee Whiskey*, there were some 170 licensed distilleries in the state prior to the onset of Prohibition, which works out to an average of two distilleries for each county. Of course, they were more realistically concentrated in high-density population areas. Nevertheless, the reality is that none of them except Jack and George managed to recover after nearly twenty years of state-enforced shuttered doors. Some distilleries moved out of the state in 1910 in an attempt to keep operating, but when the Volstead Act passed, they vanished regardless.

With a longer period of Prohibition, it's perhaps less surprising that by the time it had finished, many distillers had moved on to other opportunities or retired, but it's worth noting that only three counties actually continued to allow distilling within their borders afterwards: Moore, Lincoln, and Coffee. It wouldn't be until 2009, when a group of dedicated would-be craft distillers decided they were ready to bring the industry back, before things really took off again. In just five years, amazing things have begun to happen, and bigger plans are already in play.

It's not fair to say that nothing happened between 1938 and 2009, because Phil Prichard did start the ball rolling in the late 1990s by starting his craft distillery in Kelso, Tennessee, in one of the few legal counties in the state at that time. The real change, however, came about when Mike Williams (Collier and McKeel), Darek Bell and Andrew Webber (Corsair Artisan Distillery), and others, many of whom are discussed in the following chapters, dared to take on the state legislature and win.

Counties and municipalities are now able to vote on the issue of craft distilleries within their boundaries, and since that happened the state is gradually becoming aware of their presence and potential. As of this writing, there are more than thirty registered distilleries in the state of Tennessee, though some of them are truly fledgling companies and others are currently bottling and packaging, rather than producing their own product as of yet. As these distilleries rise, you also see a growing presence of additional products beyond the expected brown whiskey.

First, there's an interest in the revival of the state's illegal whiskey production, so expect to hear a great deal in the spirits news in the immediate future about the nature of just what "moonshine" is. Right now, while a number of alcohol products on the market are designated "moonshine," there's no legal definition for what that term means.

If you ask Billy Kaufman at Short Mountain Distillery in Woodbury or Travis Hixon at Popcorn Sutton in Newport, they'll tell you in no uncertain terms about the old recipes used by wildcatters to make illegal shines back in the woods. They've talked to the old-timers. They know how it got made and they know how it was made. They're both working from recipes that were once made and sold illegally. For guys with that kind of historical focus and interest in making a genuine product, the only way something gets called shine is if it actually is one.

In your neighborhood liquor store, you'll likely see unaged white whiskeys labeled as "moonshine," and that isn't quite right. That's not to say an unaged corn whiskey is bad—quite the contrary, many of them are excellent—but they probably need to be called "white whiskey" or "white dog" rather than moonshine. Of course, you'll also find plenty of "moonshine" that's a closer cousin to the flavored vodkas out there—essentially, neutral grain spirits, tweaked to have a bit of flavor or heavily flavored with artificial fruity things. Again, some of these products are pretty good, but they aren't, technically speaking, moonshine. They're probably better referred to as flavored vodka themselves, but there is kitsch to using the term "moonshine" when you're in the heart of Tennessee, and those brands are marketed like that.

I very much hope the chapters that follow, as much as they let you know about great places to visit, will give you an overview of the philosophies on moonshine and white whiskey. At least until the laws decide to regulate the terminology and ingredients for a shine versus a white dog versus a flavored neutral grain spirit, you can be aware. Let it inform you as you visit, try, and taste. One thing I learned from Billy Kaufman is that the old recipe from his retired wildcatters is smooth and delicious, not the nasty, burning stuff you get in the movies.

As these new distillers present themselves, you see more than whiskey on the tasting lists. That's quite simply because whiskey requires age,

Tennessee Distilleries

The rapid rise of distilleries in Tennessee since the law changed means the number of distilleries seems to grow every day. I suspect there will be three or four more by the publication date of this book, and even more a year or so later. Statistically, Jack Daniel's makes Tennessee whiskey almost exclusively, given its volume of production, followed by George Dickel and then all the microdistilleries that have sprung up, none of which measure up when you start talking about real volume. They do matter in terms of style, quality, and access though. Having now visited nearly every one of these places, I have to tell you, you need to try the little distilleries. Their original products are what make Tennessee really interesting.

That's not to criticize Jack and George; they've been making good product for a long, long time. There's a reason why people keep buying. By the time this book is published, there may be a new distillery starting up in Memphis, and one or two more in the Nashville area, including Leiper's Fork and Thompson's Station, just south of Nashville in Williamson County. There are also several bottlers and packagers, companies that are aiming to start producing their own product in the near future.

Beechtree Distillery—Nashville
Corsair Artisan—Nashville
Chattanooga Whiskey—Chattanooga
Cumberland Cask—Nashville
George Dickel—Cascade Hollow (Tullahoma)
H Clark Distillery—Thompson's Station
Jack Daniel's—Lynchburg
Nelson's Greenbrier—Nashville
Ole Smokey—Gatlinburg
Speakeasy Spirits/ Pennington's—Nashville
Popcorn Sutton Distilling—Cocke County
Prichard's—Kelso and Nashville
Short Mountain—Woodbury
Tenn South—Lynnville

generally, and making it is a pricey investment. So all these young distilleries need product they can make without a long-term commitment to aging, which is why you see so many producing vodka, gin, and rum, as well as Tennessee's more traditional brown whiskey.

Indeed, the shelves are starting to explode with good locally made products. Corsair's gin holds its own over many of the bigger names, and the vodka that Tenn South is turning out is every bit as good as the more well-known nationals. Whisper Creek Tennessee Sipping Cream can kick the ass of most of the so-called Irish creams on the shelf. The arrival of these products has fueled the "buy local" cultural trend enormously, and that's been a huge positive. I could doubtless mention something made by nearly every single distillery operating right now as a must-try product—and feel pretty good about doing so. They're bringing new ideas to the table every day, and as we start to embrace them for the revenue and job impact they provide, we should also celebrate the creativity they've brought to the industry. It all comes back to Tennessee whiskey, though, because on some level, almost all the new distillers and the old are focused on making whiskey; it's this state's legacy. That includes many distilleries that are doing very well with other products right now.

Master distillers Jeff Arnett at Jack Daniel's and Allisa Henley and formerly John Lunn at George Dickel (Lunn has recently moved to Popcorn Sutton) set a very high bar for the Tennessee whiskey being made in this state, and they have the force of the companies' history and recipes behind them. For clarity's sake, like most large distillers, the companies have larger owners: Jack is owned by Brown-Forman and George by Diageo.

Tennessee whiskey, by definition, doesn't much differ in recipe from Kentucky bourbon. To make Tennessee whiskey you have to follow all the Kentucky bourbon rules: It must be 51 percent corn, aged in brand-new charred oak barrels, distilled to no more than 160 proof, and barreled at no more than 125 proof. The resulting product should be bottled at 80 proof or greater. To be called "Tennessee whiskey" or "Tennessee sour mash whiskey," it must also be produced in Tennessee, not simply bottled here from something produced elsewhere.

Of course, then there is the Lincoln County Process. The whole reason that Tennessee whiskey has a smoothness, a mellowness, and indeed, some sweetness, comes down to the Lincoln County Process. While this was something officially codified after Prohibition, the Lincoln County Process predates that era.

James Hensley, the general manager these days at Nelson's Greenbrier Distillery in Nashville, and also one of the area's best-known liquor historians, says the process was common among nineteenth-century makers and that, at least unofficially, Jack Daniel himself, George Dickel, and Charles Nelson all agreed on the importance of the procedure well before the turn of the twentieth century and actually pressured the legislature to require the process at the time.

Simply put, the Lincoln County Process requires that the distillate that comes off the still be filtered through layers of sugar maple charcoal to remove impurities before it is barreled and aged. "Lincoln County Process" took its name from Lincoln County, where Jack Daniel's in Lynchburg was located, before a shift in county borders put it in Moore County instead. (Lincoln, Moore, and Coffee Counties were the only ones allowing distilling prior to the 2009 law change.) Today, if you see the words "Tennessee Whiskey" on the label, you should know that it's made following these very specific rules, including the Lincoln County Process. Of note, the one exception is Prichard's, which was grandfathered when the law was enacted in 2013.

So Tennessee, a longtime source of an iconic product, is in a huge phase of transition as young distilleries take off and begin maturing. It's hard even to list all the distilleries, because new ones are appearing with astonishing frequency. In my home, Williamson County, Lee Kennedy has just broken ground for his new Leiper's Creek Distillery as I'm writing, and H Clark has opened its doors in Thompson's Station down the road from me. Popular white whiskey producer Ole Smokey in Gatlinburg just sold for over $60 million, as it continues to draw in stunningly large tourist crowds. Beechtree Distillery in Nashville is laying down whiskey to age, after making moonshine in the owner's native Fernvale. Cumberland Cask is resurrecting another old family company in the Nashville area;

Chattanooga Whiskey Company is finally building its new distillery space; and half a dozen newer companies are touting white whiskey products. I can't wait to see where we are in 2019, a decade after we let go of the restrictions of the past and started down this new path.

Within this chapter you'll find the bigger and older distilleries, Jack and George, of course, and the admiration for the work that Jeff Arnett, John Lunn, and Allisa Henley do. You'll also discover the newer kids on the block, including the efforts of Phil Prichard, who dared to take some significant risks back in the 1990s. The story of this state's changes can't be told without Billy Kaufman, Darek Bell, Andrew Webber, Mike Williams, Jeff and Jenny Pennington, and some of the other newcomers to the stage. In a few years, they'll all be elder statesmen guiding the next generation of young distillers along, even as they're still pretty young themselves. Lastly a special mention to Troy and Sons, a company that's technically in North Carolina, but with a Nashville heart and a deep tie to Tennessee traditions.

Corsair Artisan Distillery

1200 Clinton St #110, Nashville, TN 37203;
(615) 200-0320; corsairartisan.com

C orsair Artisan, one of the first microdistilleries in operation in Tennessee after the laws changed, is known for its unusual spirits and small-batch runs of intriguing smoked and unusual grain content whiskeys (like the exciting Quinoa they have out at this writing), a red absinthe, a smashing vanilla vodka, and a dashing spiced rum, as well as a true ginhead's juniper- and citrus-forward gin. They've also got a smooth bourbon made at their Bowling Green location, so they can maintain its Kentucky bona fides. The addition of a sleek tasting room, plus a warm and convivial taproom where local and regional beers are always on draft, makes Corsair a great tourism bet. If you like to be challenged by some of the most original variations on whiskey out there, then Corsair is a brilliant option.

The Products: Triple Smoked Whiskey, Ryemageddon, Quinoa Whiskey, Artisan Gin, Red Absinthe, Vanilla Bean Vodka, Spiced Rum, seasonal and experimental products including Genever, Wry Moon, Pumpkin Spice Moonshine, Grainiac Whiskey, Cherrywood Smoke Whiskey

Darek Bell and Andrew Webber, the owner and president of Corsair, respectively, got in on the ground floor of the microdistillery movement in the region. Nashville native Bell spent plenty of time in New York, along with his wife, Amy Lee Bell, watched the trend in micro-spirits develop there and on the West Coast, and wanted to be a part of it. He saw the potential for small-scale, creative distilling in his home state, but arcane state laws at the time prohibited his opening a distillery in the Nashville area. Knowing what he wanted to do, in 2009 Bell teamed with other would-be distillers, including a former Franklin legislator-turned-lobbyist named Mike Williams (founder of Collier and McKeel) and set about getting the law changed. It was no easy task.

"The law change was brutal," Bell says frankly, as we sit in the Corsair taproom at Marathon Motor Works on a 95 degree day, enjoying blessed shade and cool stone.

If you don't know Darek, he's a dapper dresser—he has style. His waistcoat in subtle, subdued violet and cream plaid and his proper wingtips harken back to the 1940s and add to the whole outlier vibe Corsair has cultivated. They're named for pirates, after all.

Photo courtesy of Darek Bell, Corsair Distillery

"There was this great moment in one of the state senator's offices. I said 'I hope you'll vote in favor of this law, Senator.' And he said, 'Son, wine's good, Jesus drank wine; but beer and whiskey are right out.'"

He reminds me that after Prohibition, only three counties in Tennessee—Lincoln, Moore and Coffee—allowed for distilling, but none of the rest. Nashville, where he hoped to open, didn't permit it. So Darek and Andrew found themselves a site in Bowling Green, Kentucky, and started making spirits anyway.

Darek says that when Mike Williams proposed the new bill, it focused on Waverly and Davidson Counties specifically—and it looked like the bill would be killed. "The session was very fire and brimstone," he tells me, full of the old-school religious fervor Tennessee is known for, for good or ill. "Then this old, grizzled farmer type stands up at the back of the room and asks, 'Will this bill help my farmers sell more of their corn? If it does, then I'm all for it . . . ' I mean, I thought *STFU*. I thought it was dead. Dead . . . Then it passed. I was stunned—and that's an understatement."

What had felt to Mike and Darek like a very long shot sailed right through with the promise of potential help to the state's agriculture—its number one source of revenue (the second, of course, is tourism). Even so, there was still a bit of an issue in Davidson County, and it had to be worked through with Mayor Karl Dean. The presence of Yazoo and its success had already built up the profile of microbreweries, and they were going great guns, but a distillery was, as Darek says, "a distinctly different beast." They still needed to change the local ordinances in order to do things like open a tasting room, but still, metro Davidson was far easier to deal with than the state.

"It took us a year of working with the legislature to get the state law changed, and nine months on the local . . . that was one long startup period," he says, noting that meanwhile, Bowling Green was already in operation. After nearly two and a half years of work, Corsair finally opened in Music City.

The advantage of having Bowling Green product also meant that with a newly opened larger premises, Darek and Andrew already knew what they were doing when it came to the act of distilling. The pair had started out together, and they've built the business together, with Darek as owner and distiller, and Andrew as president and distiller.

"Andrew is one of my oldest friends. I met him in middle school by insulting his argyle socks—for which he has never forgiven me. Andrew's family made wine in the summer, so he grew up around wine making. We used to make beer and wine together, then we got into making biodiesel for an old junker diesel Mercedes I owned. One day while working on smelly biodiesel in the brutal heat, he said, 'I wish we were making whiskey.' And we switched to distilling. He was getting a Vanderbilt MBA to get a nice respectable job, and I pitched him on starting a distillery and joining a small risky venture with little chance of success. Somehow, I totally convinced him to start the company with me."

Darek studied at the Siebel Brewing Institute and graduated from Scotland's legendary Bruichladdich Distilling Academy. The study of Scotch as well as American whiskey gave him new perspectives and helped encourage the pair on their merry way toward the more experimental end

of the spectrum when it came to production. In the process Darek wrote two well-respected volumes, *Alt Whiskeys* and the very recent *Fire Water: Experimental Smoked Whiskeys*, both about creating alternative whiskeys.

Their experimental philosophy sets Corsair apart from the usual distillery startup, and part of that is economic. As has been pointed out in these pages, aged spirits take years to become marketable, and young distilleries have few options to get cash flow going. The first is to source whiskey and hope that after you start selling your own formulation, it works for the people who've already bought into your brand. The second is to create unaged products and start selling them. That's the option Corsair chose.

It was a good one. Corsair's gin hooked me long before I even tried the whiskey. (Ok, Darek sent a bottle with me to a gin-loving friend's house party, and that was all she wrote. We all drank nothing but Corsair gin and tonics all night and were converted as though on the road to Damascus.)

"From the beginning our goal was to make our own whiskey, to be honest with our customers about what we were doing, and to distill all the time and seriously learn the craft," Darek says.

He'd had experience with friends sourcing whiskey while learning the craft, and when the friends' own product came out, the customers didn't

Photos courtesy of Darek Bell, Corsair Distillery

favor it over the sourced and had to be won over. Darek and Andrew didn't want to find themselves in that position.

"It was important to us; it was about our own ethos. This way we were allowed from the beginning to do things you just can't source. I mean, you can't source a smoked amaranth whiskey, and it doesn't take much to make an alt whiskey—which is what we wanted to do."

He waxes on about early experiences in competitions across the country, noting that things like Scotch are traditionally judged based on age—but if you point out to the judges that the product you've got is say, cherrywood smoked, then you'll get judged on that quality. Likewise, they found themselves scoring highly against other young whiskeys. "It's important people know, we're not trying to be the same Tennessee whiskey; that was important to us early on."

Darek, Andrew, Darek's wife, Amy Lee, and the rest of the staff are aware that Corsair has a certain cult status as a distillery, and they covet that reputation. "We're kind of like the cult wineries in California," he says. "We try interesting new stuff; we keep pushing the boundaries. If you're a strict traditionalist, you might not like everything we do, but we keep pushing ourselves and our whiskeys to new places."

CORSAIR ARTISAN DISTILLERY *125*

At this writing, Corsair is looking to expand in Nashville. They've acquired two new buildings in southeast Nashville, not far from where the old Nashville Sounds Stadium was located, for use in both barrel storage and distilling (counting the output from both Bowling Green and Nashville, they should produce some 16,000 cases this year). They've also got a three hundred-acre farm and malting facility in the Bells Bend community north of the city, where they'll be malting their own grains, the workhorse for beer and whiskey both. They have the powerhouse aid of distiller Andrea Clodfelter on board, and they've also just brought on master brewer Karen Bohannon Lassiter, late of Bosco's, whose creative vibe and skill set very much match their innovative, freethinking style. Lassiter is making the exceptional brews they serve in the Nashville taproom, including a heady, hop-forward IPA and an intriguing archaeological exploration or two: Viking Ale (with juniper and heather) and an ancient Egyptian brew too. (And yes, that means there is a female master distiller and female brewmaster too.)

Corsair tries some one hundred new whiskey recipes annually, some only in tiny batches, but they pay off. The best of those winds up in competitions, and the winners among them are brought into production, at least as limited runs. The company is smoking all their own barrels, using assorted woods. There's plenty of new product development going on here, and the end results are always intriguing, always worth tasting—and buying if alt whiskeys are to your tastes.

As I finish this interview, Darek takes me on a tour, letting me go back and sniff bottles of whiskey smoked with a variety of woods, from the more expected maple to alder and fruitwoods like pear, macadamia wood, and so on. "With our triple-smoked whiskey, what you get is three woods, creating three different notes. The judges loved it. And we discover unexpected things—like maple smoke gives a sweet note on the finish, so you maybe want to pair that with something that gives it a great nose. That's kind of how we'd reverse engineer a recipe—we put lots of our money into R&D, not so much into marketing. The question is always 'where can whiskey go, and where can we take it?' Smoked whiskeys are one way US distillers haven't really been creative yet—we're more inspired by craft beers and the risks they've been taking in that direction." He grins, "Creativity is free."

That creativity is expanding hugely, as Corsair also gets ready to knock it out of the park with cider, perry, and an apple brandy. Tennessee is not necessarily a great wine state; our terroir doesn't welcome a lot of grapes, but we do apples brilliantly—pears too. Corsair gets that, and they're both buying and planting apples these days (up at their Bells Bend farm).

Corsair has experienced a massive increase in tourism in both locations in the past year or so. In Nashville part of that is owed to the expanding popularity of Marathon Motor Works as a location, but in tracking online ticket sales, visitors from Chicago, Detroit, Indy, and Atlanta all outnumber local guests.

That's to be expected. Prior to the change in distilling laws, Nashville was a little behind the curve in craft beer culture and didn't really have a cocktail culture. In the ensuing years, it's taken off like wildfire, and some of that is the proliferation of new local spirits. Tourists sometimes catch on before the locals do.

"When we first opened, the West Coast was more than 90 percent of our market," Darek Bell tells me. "I could still easily ship it all to California—but I don't. I really like where we've come the last couple of years." And he wants Nashville to be part of it.

If you visit to tour and taste, be aware that the Nashville facility offers both a taproom full of local craft beers and the liquor tasting room in a separate part of the building. In between lies the distillery itself, with bold copper stills boiling away.

Corsair is well worth the effort to taste the product—you'll not find anything similar in the region.

CORSAIR ARTISAN DISTILLERY COCKTAILS

Cranberry and Jalapeño Daiquiri

1 ½ ounces Corsair Spiced Rum
1 tablespoon cranberry sauce
2 tablespoons jalapeño simple syrup*
1 lime, juiced
1 ounce cranberry juice
1 cup ice
Cranberries and jalapeño slice for garnish

In a shaker add rum, cranberry sauce, jalapeño simple syrup, lime, cranberry juice, and ice. Shake mixture until chilled. Strain mixture into serving glass. Garnish with cranberries and jalapeño slices.

Pomegranate and Rye Mule

1 ½ ounces Corsair Ryemageddon
1 pomegranate, squeezed to release juice (about 3 ounces) and seeds
½ lime, juiced
1 cup ice
Ginger beer
Rosemary sprigs for garnish

Fill a cocktail shaker with Corsair Ryemageddon, pomegranate juice, lime, and ice. Shake mixture then pour into a mason jar. Top off with ginger beer. Garnish with a rosemary sprig.

*Jalapeño simple syrup

1 cup water
1 cup sugar
1 jalapeño, roughly chopped

In a saucepan combine sugar, water, and jalapeño. Let boil until sugar dissolves. Strain mixture and let cool. Extra syrup may be stored in a glass container for up to a week.

Cranberry and Black Pepper Gin and Tonic

3 ounces Corsair Gin
4 tablespoons cranberry and black peppercorn simple syrup*
1 lime, juiced
½ cup of ice
Tonic water
Slice of lime with cracked pepper and cranberries for garnish

Fill a cocktail shaker with gin, simple syrup, lime, and ice. Shake mixture then pour into serving glass. Top with tonic water. Garnish with a slice of lime with cracked pepper and cranberries.

Yields: 2 servings

*Cranberry and black peppercorn simple syrup

1 cup water
1 cup sugar
15 black peppercorns
8 cranberries

In a saucepan combine sugar, water, peppercorns, and cranberries. Let boil until sugar dissolves. Strain mixture and let cool. Extra syrup may be stored in a glass container for up to a week.

GEORGE DICKEL

1950 Cascade Hollow Road, Tullahoma, TN
37388; (931) 857-4110; georgedickel.com

George Dickel is the second name people think of when it comes to Tennessee whiskey, and the Diageo-owned company puts out excellent products and is deserving of consideration when you're looking for a Tennessee whiskey. Cascade Hollow isn't far from Lynchburg, so you can make both tours in a weekend, and I heartily recommend doing so. The grounds are stunning, showcasing the cascade spring that gave the distillery its earliest name, the staff is personable, and the whiskey deserves tasting.

The Products: George Dickel Sour Mash Whisky #8, George Dickel Sour Mash Whisky #12, George Dickel Rye, George Dickel White Corn Whisky, George Dickel Barrel Select

Cascade Hollow is a lovely place in all seasons: There's a creek flowing between the visitor center and the distillery proper carrying the same limestone water that goes into your "whisky," and the nearby hills and trees are pretty even when they're bare for winter. The visitor center has a nice rustic feel and plenty of merchandising, like all the big distilleries, but it's also completely charming.

If you've just noticed the products above spell whiskey "whisky"—it's because that's the way Dickel spells it, and George Dickel himself opted to use that spelling way back in the nineteenth century. It's the spelling you find in Scotland, used to refer to scotch, and Mr. Dickel felt his "whisky" compared to the finest stuff Scotland produced at the time.

But without digressing further into fun with foodies, the point is that there are too many people who forget there's a second big distillery in Tennessee, and that's a shame—in part because Dickel's history goes back

well into the nineteenth century, before Prohibition threw its long-reaching wrench into Tennessee's distilling culture.

German-born immigrant George Dickel came to the United States in the 1840s, settled in the Nashville area, and like many of his fellow future distillery owners, made his living first as a merchant who sold liquor. He was a typical wholesale buyer of the time—purchasing from distillers and filling his own jugs with it. It is perhaps not at all surprising that Mr. Dickel sold whiskey that was produced in Cascade Hollow, near Tullahoma, among other products. He and his wife founded George Dickel and Company in 1870.

In the late 1860s, so the story goes, George Dickel and his wife, Augusta, visited the Tullahoma area for the first time and were so taken with it that within a few years they decided to settle there and produce whiskey. The original Cascade Distillery, founded by John F. Brown and F. E. Cunningham, took its name from the area where they'd settled.

In 1888 Dickel's brother-in-law and business partner Victor Schwab acquired a controlling interest in Cascade Distillery along with the exclusive right to bottle and sell what was then called "Cascade Tennessee Whisky." The distillery officially came under the control of Dickel and Schwab.

As they experimented—according to current master distiller Allisa Henley—Dickel determined that "whisky" made during the winter months was preferable to that made in the summer. It was, he believed, much smoother. The result of this realization brought about the cold-mellowing process for which Dickel is distinctive among Tennessee whiskey makers today.

Like most distillers of his time, George Dickel agreed that charcoal mellowing via the Lincoln County Process was a vital part of making good, smooth whiskey. But Dickel took it a step further personally, choosing to chill the whiskey made at every period during the year before running it through the sugar maple charcoal filter.

The product continued to be called Cascade Tennessee Whisky, even after the purchase by Dickel and Schwab. Only after he passed away in 1894 after several years of declining health did the name change to George Dickel to honor the late owner and distiller.

When Tennessee's prohibition took effect, ten years before national Prohibition, Schwab moved the company to Louisville, where it remained even as Tennessee maintained its prohibition well past the end of the national period. In 1937 Schenley Distilling Company purchased the company and, twenty years later, in 1958, decided to return it to its original location. After nearly fifty years, George Dickel's had come back to Tennessee. The current distillery was built about half a mile from the original location when the company moved back to Tullahoma.

Production began almost immediately, using the original recipe from Dickel's Cascade Distillery, and in 1964, with some age on the product, the very first bottles made their way back to the shelves, where they've been a prominent name ever since.

In 1987 Schenley sold the company to British distillery multi-brand giant Guinness & Co. (under their United Distillers spirits division umbrella), and in 1997 Guinness merged its holding with Grand Metropolitan, another sizable multinational, to become Diageo, which also controls interest in Johnnie Walker scotch, J&B, Bailey's Irish Cream, Smirnoff, and many others, including beers and wines.

But when it comes down to it, the Tennessee whiskey made at George Dickel today is the same old-fashioned style it always has been, created at the hands of Allisa Henley. (When I wrote the draft of this book, Henley was the assistant to master distiller John Lunn, who moved on to Popcorn Sutton in early 2015).

I met Allisa and John Lunn on that fateful first tour, but I was lucky enough to talk with Allisa again this year in preparation for this volume. Quite aside from her dedication and talent, Allisa is, like Troy Ball at Troy and Sons and Andrea Clodfelter at Corsair Artisan, a reminder that the old-school and old-guard world of male-only distillers is also starting to fade, especially as culture and the artisan cocktail movement vastly expand the interest in brown spirits worldwide. You can no longer assume your whiskey is made by just men.

"I've been here over ten years," says Henley. "I've really been given good opportunities; I've worked in almost every aspect of the business, including marketing, finance, PR, and now distillation—I've learned everything hands on."

Henley, a Tullahoma native who grew up here, got her MBA and started with the company in marketing and tourism. As she progressed, she visited the distillery daily, learned the technical aspects of distilling as a matter of course, both from master distiller John Lunn and from the workers in all aspects of product, whom she dealt with constantly.

"We say Dickel is 'handmade the hard way,'" she says. "It's true and I learned each step in the process by getting my hands dirty. I've been involved for years."

She's been officially a distiller only since 2014; prior to that she served as marketing director (the capacity in which I first met her). "I think it's very much my role, more than marketing and seminars, tours and tastings—there's so much love here, so much passion behind it—the touch, the smell, the experience. As I was teaching people about it, more and more I wanted to do it myself."

Henley says the Dickel mash bill runs to 84 percent corn, 8 percent rye, and 8 percent malted barley. That's a very high corn content, and she believes it adds to the fundamental sweetness of the product.

The other critical process is the cold filtering. "When the distillate comes off our still, we chill it before it ever hits the charcoal—we have since George Dickel's days—and the change in temperature also changes what gets filtered out of the raw whiskey. I think that's where our very smooth finish comes from. Historically, we are the only cold-mellower in Tennessee. One of the things about Tennessee is that we have four very distinct seasons down here, which you need for whiskey production, and George Dickel believed the whiskey made in the winter was just better than in the summer.

"We have different variants, of course, as everyone does, but the finish is always consistent on our whiskey. That has to do with the charcoal process. We also only age in single-story warehouses, and I think that's unique to the Tennessee industry. The higher whiskey is stored, the faster it ages, so as you can imagine there's a big temperature change from the top of the storage to the bottom, 1 to 2 degrees, so a single story lets us better keep the aging process consistent."

She talks about the company's products, because Dickel is more than the well-known No. 8 whiskey.

The No. 1 White Corn Whisky never sees a barrel, she says. "It's right off the cold-mellow, and it has a sweet smell that reminds me of buttered popcorn."

The No. 8 Black Label product, a more typical aged product, she says, "has a little grain taste, and a little maple, some smoke on the back end. Scotch drinkers tend to like that, even though it's not the peaty flavor of Scotch that's going on; it's a subtle smoke but it's there."

The No. 12 is easily the most popular of the whiskeys, at least among the Tennessee whiskey drinkers I know. "It's got the best of both worlds," says Henley. "There are great vanilla and caramel notes coming through, and the oak also comes through. And it's got a nice balance, none of it is too heavy.

The numbers actually don't pertain to the amount of aging a product gets. The No. 8 is aged five to seven years and is sold at 80 proof, while the No. 12 is aged seven to nine years and is 90 proof. "I don't know where the numbers come from historically, possibly from taste profiles or recipe numbers," says Henley.

The oldest product, the Barrel Select, gets ten-plus years of aging. "We hand select each of these, and it's so smooth, you get a really nice oak."

The hugely popular George Dickel Rye is a great example of how the many distillers who purchase product from companies like MGP can customize something to meet their own needs and make it distinctly their own. In this case, the rye may be purchased, but it is put through the cold-mellow charcoal filter process before aging so that it maintains Dickel's signature finish, something that none of the other companies do and, according to Henley, makes that product special and uniquely theirs. Dickel is far from unusual in sourcing a rye product; it's something that happens across the industry—what makes it theirs is that cold-mellowing.

"For me, rye is spicy and peppery," says Henley. "It's very up front and in your face. With the cold process, ours is fruity on the front end, more subtle. You still get that nice pepper on the back, and a nice, dry finish." They age the rye for about two years.

"I think people are really surprised about cold filtration generally—not just in the rye. Most know about the Lincoln County Process, but not about the difference the cold makes."

Diageo has their own Scottish cooperage, but Dickel frequently sends their used barrels to Scotland for scotch and other product aging, since scotch doesn't require the use of a new barrel (the industry there also uses other types of wood besides the de rigueur oak of the Americans).

I ask Henley how it feels to find herself in the distiller's seat at this stage of her career with Dickel.

"I was born in Tullahoma, five miles from the distillery. It's a pretty typical small town—I still live there today. There's a lot of pride and passion about what we do here. As to being a distiller, honestly, to have that job—it's a *huge* honor to be entrusted with this legend, just huge. This is a great company to work with."

Ok, I want to know which of the company's products she favors.

"I go more for the No. 12, with just a couple of ice cubes. But I love a Manhattan made with the rye, and the 8 makes a terrific whiskey sour. It's all very versatile."

What do you want someone who's come down to take the tour to know?

"We have a tradition that dates back to the 1870s, and we take pride in that. Also, you need to know that this is truly handmade, handcrafted. There's a person at every single step, and it really is as hands-on as you can make it. There's someone working and smelling and tasting at every turn.

"If your experience is mostly Kentucky, the big difference is our charcoal filtration. Both places have traditionally had a big distillery culture because of the limestone water, and the limestone is indigenous to the region—the pure spring water is just vital; you have to have a good water source. We have so many springs in such a small area. But it's the Lincoln County Process that sets us apart."

George Dickel Cocktails

The Back Forty

1 ½ ounces George Dickel #12
½ ounce maple syrup
1 ounce fresh lemon juice

Add all to a cocktail shaker filled with cracked ice, shake vigorously, and pour into a rocks glass. Garnish with lemon twist.

Cascade Cooler

Allisa told me this is one of her favorites. After trying it, I have to add it to my list too.

1 ¼ ounces George Dickel Cascade
  Hollow Batch Recipe
1 ½ ounces cranberry juice
½ ounce lime juice
1 teaspoon sugar
1 cup crushed ice
1 lemon wedge for garnish

Add George Dickel, cranberry juice, lime juice, sugar, and crushed ice in blender. Blend on slow speed for 15 to 30 seconds, or until mixture appears frozen, and pour into a 12-ounce glass. Garnish with lemon.

Dickel Drop

1 ½ ounces George Dickel #8
2 ounces lemon-lime soda

Add George Dickel and lemon-lime soda in a cracked-ice-filled glass and stir.

Dr. Dickel

1 ½ ounces George Dickel #12
3 ounces Dr. Pepper soda

Build in a highball glass over ice, stir, and serve. As Southern as it gets.

Brown Derby Cocktail

2 ounces George Dickel #12
½ ounce grapefruit juice
½ ounce honey

Shake with ice and strain into a cocktail glass.

Old Hickory

2 ounces bacon-infused George
  Dickel #12*
3 dashes Angostura Bitters
¼ ounce maple syrup
Bacon and sage for garnish

Shake ingredients over ice and
pour into tumbler. Garnish with
bacon and sage.

*Pour 3 ounces of liquid bacon fat into a
container with contents of one bottle of
Dickel #12. Cool for six to eight hours
in the refrigerator, then strain off fat and
pour whiskey back into the bottle.

Slippery Dickel

1 ½ ounces George Dickel
  Tennessee Whisky
¾ ounce orange liqueur
¾ ounce lime juice
1 teaspoon grenadine syrup

Shake ingredients over broken ice
and strain into an Old-Fashioned
glass over ice. Garnish with an
orange wheel.

Eric Byford—Beardforce Films and Straight Up, Tennessee Whiskey

Filmmaker Eric Byford came by his passion via a long road, but his short film *Straight Up, Tennessee Whiskey* and his forthcoming Kentucky bourbon–based follow-up make for one of the best introductions to the business and its history for novices out there, and they're worth plenty of enjoyment to longtime fans as well. Since the release of *Straight Up* in 2013, Byford has made the rounds of the festival circuit, garnering awards and laurels, and spreading the whiskey gospel. He's now working on a companion film, *Straight Up, Kentucky Bourbon*.

Eric started out studying film at the University of Tennessee-Knoxville in the 1990s, in a curriculum that required him to create five-minute "news stories" twice weekly. He quickly found himself playing cameraman and editor for classmates' projects and enjoying the process, even as he worked as a DJ and ran a bar as well, by the time he was twenty-two. Time passed as he followed the bar and nightclub route. He says he woke one morning in his late thirties, about to become a parent for the third time, and asked himself what he wanted to do with the rest of his life.

The possibility of following his film dreams was an itch he "still needed to scratch," and he quickly found himself enrolled in a crash film course at the Nashville Film Institute. The first film, *Straight Up*, was intended to be a five-minute project, but it became a nearly thirty-eight-minute documentary on Tennessee whiskey.

Originally, the goal was to make something on the history of whiskey in the state, focusing on moonshiners, but as he sat writing the film outline at the bar in Mickey Roo's in Franklin in 2013, he realized it needed to be bigger. With the help of his crew, Caleb Watson, Matthew Voss, Zach Montanari, and Thax Christianson, he set out to make a movie. His odyssey led him to talk with the movers and shakers who changed the Tennessee laws, like

Murfreesboro's Senator Bill Ketron, and to visit Napa and Sonoma in California and see for himself what the wine industry had done for the state. He came away ultimately with a vision of the impact the whiskey industry has had on the country as a whole and wanted to tell the story of Kentucky as well. At this writing, he's filming, as he makes efforts to crowdfund its production to finance it—the first film was a student project; this is independent.

"This has been a crazy ride," he says. "People just don't realize that when you're talking about the history of whiskey, you're really talking about the history of this country. Alcohol has played a huge role in all of it. A whiskey tax funded almost every war we've fought, up until Prohibition, and when that began they had to institute a national income tax to offset the loss of revenue. Prohibition was a terrible financial decision.

"Even through Prohibition there were still six licensed whiskey distilleries producing it for medicinal purposes, and the others did things like make neoprene, penicillin. Bourbon, whiskey, it's a mainstay, a huge supplier of jobs, of tax base—you support your local distillery, you support your country. George Washington had three distilleries; it dates back that long. Bourbon was the first product ever designated as a United States Native Product by Congress in 1964. The Food and Drug Act came about in the early twentieth century in large part because rectifiers were making neutral grain spirits, putting in additives and color, and calling it bourbon. The distillers objected and you got legislation and regulation. So it financed the country and it inspired us to enact responsible food and safety laws, and consumer's rights laws were born largely from that. The impact has been huge!

"Whiskey, bourbon, most people don't know the backstory. It's been really misunderstood and it's been integral to our society from day one. Kentucky produces about 98 percent of the bourbon made, and it's created a whole culture. If you visit, you'll be blown away by the food and other culture that's grown up around it. The distillery industry kept putting people to work through the recession in 2008, and kept the state going." The fact that whiskey is made of the cleanest of ingredients—water, grain, yeast, charred oak barrels—that too has a huge impact. "It's not full of chemicals and additives and dyes," he says forcefully.

Byford is glad to see Tennessee finally following Kentucky's example. "Prior to 2009, there were only three distilleries operating in the state," he says. "Before Prohibition, there were about 170 distilleries here, and even given the fact that Jack Daniel's pretty much keeps the entire population of Lynchburg and Moore County employed, it used to seem like we were embarrassed by that because it was whiskey. Now I think things are starting to change. Since the laws changed, there are new startup distilleries everywhere. We're taking more pride in it than we used to."

Byford is unapologetic in his excitement to see Tennessee start to return to its whiskey heritage, and he hopes we become as supportive as Kentucky has been to our distillery industry. "Whether you live in Kentucky or Tennessee, when you go into a bar, just ask to see the local whiskey list. Even if you don't order it, your requests will make the bar and restaurant owners consider carrying more of the products, and that in turn can lead to more jobs for your neighbors, more money for schools and roads. It will have a big impact."

Ultimately, Byford says what he wants people to remember is that there is something special about these two states, with their four seasons and their limestone water that makes distilling and aging whiskey effective like few other places nationally. "It's important to me to educate people," he says. "When you support these distillers, you support your neighbor, you support your country, and you know what you're drinking."

When he finishes work on the Kentucky documentary, Byford's dream is to explore the world's other indigenous alcohols, from Russian vodka to scotch to saki. His passion is evident, and he's happy to share it. You can order a copy of *Straight Up, Tennessee Whiskey* at Eric's website, beardforcefilms.com.

JACK DANIEL'S OLD NUMBER 7 BRAND

182 Lynchburg Highway, Lynchburg, TN 37352;
(931) 759-6357; jackdaniels.com

When you measure production, statistically just about all the whiskey coming out of Tennessee is Jack Daniel's. Set in the beautiful hollows of legendarily dry Lynchburg, Jack Daniel's is an impressive experience as a distillery tour—and the entire town pretty much exists because of Jack's presence. The distillery has been running steadily since the mid-nineteenth century with time off for Prohibition, and the company is synonymous with the words "Tennessee whiskey" for most consumers worldwide.

The Products: Jack Daniel's Old No. 7 Tennessee Whiskey, Gentleman Jack, Jack Daniel's Single Barrel, Tennessee Honey, Tennessee Fire, Rested Tennessee Rye Whiskey, Jack Daniel's Number 27 Gold Tennessee Whiskey, Winter Jack Tennessee Cider, Unaged Tennessee Rye, Jack Daniel's Sinatra Select, assorted special editions and Master Distiller Limited Edition Series.

Jack Daniel's is probably the first name that comes to mind when you bring up the topic of Tennessee whiskey. If you live in Tennessee, it's impossible to be unaware of Jack Daniel's. I knew the name long before I moved here, and the name "Lynchburg, Tennessee," holds a special reverence for drinkers worldwide. For a very long time, most people who mentioned "Tennessee whiskey" may very well not have been aware there was any other kind of whiskey—because for close to a century, Jack has had that kind of market dominance.

As we know well, however, there are other Tennessee whiskeys, and there are other types of whiskey made in Tennessee ("Tennessee whiskey" is a special thing, and not the same as any old whiskey made in Tennessee). But for a very long time, Jack Daniel's has had pride of place in this state, especially after Prohibition, when, unlike Kentucky, Tennessee didn't do all that much to build up its distilling industry again. Only Jack and George made it through to continue the traditions and the name.

Photo courtesy of Jack Daniel's Distillery

That's changing now, and new distilleries producing whiskey and other spirits are popping up everywhere, but Jack Daniel's still maintains a very special place in the hearts of Tennesseans—and under master distiller Jeff Arnett, still is producing excellent whiskey.

The founder, Jack Daniel, was born somewhere between 1846 and 1850, depending on whose records you read, and grew up as a farmer's son in Moore County, Tennessee, until the age of ten when he entered into an apprenticeship with a storekeeper. During his tenure he learned how to make one of the store's most popular products, corn whiskey.

According to the story, young Jack came to understand the approved methods of the time, including the sour mash process, and also to filter his product using what's referred to as the "Lincoln County Process" in Tennessee whiskey production, filtering your distillate through layers of hard sugar maple charcoal prior to barreling. The state histories tell us this was already a well-used technique in the state by the early 1860s.

Fortuitously for Daniel, his age kept him from the nearby battles of the raging Civil War. Jack's teacher, the Reverend Dan Call, was pressured by evangelists to either give up his distilling in the early 1860s or give up his additional profession as minister. The teenaged Jack bought him out. He opted to move the distillery to a hollow with a limestone cave spring in Lynchburg, and you know the rest. Daniel prospered as a distiller, one among many in that post–Civil War era that would include the Dickel and the Nelson families as well. Daniel's has the honor of being the oldest "registered" distillery in the United States, registering meaning that they paid some of the

Photo courtesy of Jack Daniel's Distillery

taxes that helped get the country out of its huge Civil War debt burden— wars are never cheap.

Daniel, a man of minor stature, adopted as an adult a black frock coat and tidy planter's hat that are now recognizable to everyone. His skill in marketing matched his zeal as a producer, early on being recognized for concepts like commemorative bottles and exciting promotions (including hot air balloons). In the early twentieth century, he brought his young cousin, Lemuel "Lem" Motlow, in and began teaching him the business as sales grew well beyond the boundaries of Tennessee and indeed, outside the United States

It was Motlow who encouraged Daniel to take the risk of entering their whiskey in the 1904 St. Louis World's Exposition (the same world fair later featured in the musical *Meet Me in St. Louis*) whiskey competition, where it won a gold medal as best whiskey, and it repeated that trick in 1905 (this time in Europe), adding to its reputation.

In 1906 a special decanter was designed for use only in the Oak Bar at the famed Maxwell House Hotel in Nashville. At about the same time, while visiting this very hotel, Theodore Roosevelt got a taste of the signature house coffee and proclaimed it "good to the last drop." It was a watershed moment for Tennessee libations, and the world has come to know both well in the following hundred years.

In 1911, shortly after prohibition had already hit Tennessee (yes, we started early, in 1909, instead of waiting for the Volstead Act a decade later), Jack Daniel passed away as the result of an infection following a broken toe he'd never had set or treated, perhaps as early as 1906. Legend says the broken toe came after he heartily kicked the old office safe. Nelson Eddy, brand historian for Jack Daniel's today, says the story passed down is that gangrene set in and a doctor had to amputate the injured digit. Sadly, it wasn't caught soon enough and the gangrene spread, resulting in a series of amputations and Jack's eventual demise. Eddy says some wonder now whether Jack was diabetic and if poor circulation to his extremities might have contributed to the complications, but a century later we don't know with any certainty.

He never gave away the reasoning behind his name choice, and "Old Number 7" remains a mystery. There are many guesses, from the idea that it's the recipe number, to the number of attractive young ladies the confirmed bachelor courted, but no one knows for sure.

After Jack's passing, Lem Motlow took over the business in full, which the unmarried Jack had deeded to him in 1910, and moved the offices briefly to St. Louis, prior to the onset of national Prohibition in 1919. During this St. Louis exile period, the whiskey kept winning medals, in Ghent, Belgium, London, England, and even a much-coveted Certificate of Institute of Hygiene in London. The world was responding well. With the introduction of Prohibition after World War I, Motlow got out of the whiskey business and focused on mule trading for the duration.

In 1930, three years before even national Prohibition was ended, a fire destroyed the distillery, and Lem Motlow was forced to rebuild it completely in 1938, after legal distilling and aging whiskey in both the state and Moore County was allowed to resume. With the end of Prohibition in Tennessee, he dove straight back into making whiskey, after spending time as a state senator trying to get the law repealed himself. Few others among Tennessee's many distilleries followed suit. Moore County, where Lynchburg sits, remained dry.

In 1939 Lem Motlow introduced the Green Label as an additional product.

The distillery closed during World War II as part of the war effort, but reopened and began production again in 1947. Motlow passed away that year, but the Motlow family kept the Jack Daniel's company and tradition going.

Jack Daniel's was purchased by Brown-Forman in 1956, but the Motlow family, including Lem's son "Hap" (Daniel Evans) Motlow (who in turn mentored Bill Samuels up at Maker's Mark) continued to operate the distillery. Over the years, Jack made its name in the hands of everyone from Frank Sinatra to William Faulkner to the punk, metal, and even country musicians of the 1970s to the 2000s.

Jeff Arnett came to Jack Daniel's some seven years ago, a lucky number for him, since he also happens to be the seventh master distiller in the "old Number 7" company's history. "I'm the first one not born in Lynchburg," he says. "I'm from Jackson, and I went to college to be an engineer, not believing I was destined to be a distiller."

Out of college, he got an MBA and then took a job with Procter & Gamble in the food and beverage industry, with an eye toward quality control aspects. He worked for P & G with Folger's Coffee in New Orleans, then with Sunny Delight juice drink in Texas, and finally came back to Jackson, Tennessee, with the company's Pringles potato chip brand.

All this time he was a huge fan of Jack Daniel's, a member of the Jack Daniel's Squires Association, created in the 1950s to celebrate the brand and honor loyal consumers.

In 2000 Arnett heard P & G was considering making changes to or selling its Pringles division, and he sent a resume off to a Nashville headhunter. The headhunter had a contract with Jack Daniel's to help fill a quality control position, and Arnett soon found himself interviewing for what he says "most Squires would consider their absolute dream job."

He says, "Procter & Gamble was a great company, don't get me wrong, but nothing inspires the kind of passion that something like the

Photo courtesy of Jack Daniel's Distillery

opportunity to work for Jack Daniel's does. To this day, fourteen years in, I'm learning something new every day. That's very satisfying."

Working for quality control at Jack Daniel's taught him a lot about what a master distiller needs to know. It started, he says, with things like monitoring the vital cave spring water for quality, including checking the mineral content and doing metals analysis. "The water is one of the real reasons why this distillery is here; it's crucial to the whiskey quality," says Arnett.

Then there was the matter of checking grain samples and determining what was acceptable, and why those parameters that had been set mattered. Arnett's job took him all over the distillery itself—the warehouse, barrel storage, and packaging—checking for the small details that make all the difference. He tasted fermenter samples and beer samples: "I learned what a healthy fermenter smells like," he says. He came to understand the importance of the yeast that goes into the mash.

"The propriety yeast strain we use comes from right here, that's why it's important. It's the same yeast we've been using since Prohibition, propagated in this hollow. You can't steal it, actually, because if you did, once you got too far away from here, it would start interacting with other cultures and start to change. We've got a guy with a master's in microbiology whose whole job is to care for the yeast. It's got to overpower what comes in on the grain that otherwise might alter the flavor—and you might get something good or something terrible with those bacterias, and obviously you don't want that . . . there are all sorts of things you can have happen with yeast; if you let it go, yeast can create so much heat it kills itself, so you've got to manage the cooling water, for example. Quality control involves a lot of aspects you wouldn't think about necessarily to begin with . . . even making sure thermometers are properly calibrated; the product is only as consistent as the temperature."

He continues with a list of the requirements a quality control specialist needs to deal with in a distillery, and you get a strong sense of just how much attention to detail is required to make good whiskey. While a pot still may be a thing of beauty, a column still does a better job, and that copper from which the still is constructed helps remove carcinogens and elements that are sulfury on the nose, among other things.

"You learn the distillate has a distinct character before it's run through the sugar maple charcoal filter, and a different one afterwards," Arnett says. "You learn all these discerning techniques, but of course, no technology you're using can tell you what the end product is going to taste like. We have a hundred tasters we rely on throughout the whole process. I train those tasters, so they can recognize and communicate any issues at any given part of the process."

Arnett talks at length about the "heart" of what he does: the melding of the science behind the creation of whiskey with the need to create what he calls an interesting product. Jack Daniel's has eighty-six warehouses for barrel storage right now. The company keeps a detailed history of how each barrel develops in each location in the warehouses, taking samples from perhaps 1,500 to 2,000 barrels each month, especially when things are unusual, like atypical seasonal temperatures, which can influence the aging whiskey.

"What we find is that those warehouse locations hold up in terms of what they typically produce," he says. "The barrels at the top have a darker,

Photo courtesy of Jack Daniel's Distillery

richer color, a greater angel's share; the ones on the ground floor are much lighter. Hot air rises, and the heat drives the whiskey into the barrel wood, and when it's cold, it leeches back out. With our Jack Daniel's Black Label, we take a couple of hundred barrels to put together that taste, similar to what one barrel, if it were moved from spot to spot progressively through the aging process, would look and taste like, and you get that characteristic sweetness and the oak note.

"For the Green Label we stick to the ground floor, so it's lighter; our Single Barrel comes from the top floors, it's darker and has more barrel flavor. We use a toasted barrel with deep grooves that effectively double the inside surface to create the Sinatra Select, giving it more oak. Gentleman Jack gets double charcoal filtered, to make it especially mellow. It's fun, all of this—and thirteen years pass in the blink of an eye."

I ask Arnett about the thing that makes Tennessee whiskey Tennessee. That is, of course, specifically the Lincoln County Process, without which we're really just bourbon—with the percentages of corn and the toasted barrels (corporate owner Brown-Forman has its own cooperage, of course). To reiterate, that's the passing of the distillate through a filter of sugar maple charcoal before it goes into the barrel, which mellows the product and makes it sweeter. It doesn't taste like Kentucky bourbon whiskey, as Arnett reminds me.

Part of that is because historically, Jack and its Tennessee compatriots have a lower rye content, so there's less bold spiciness than in Kentucky, where the bourbons include two to three times more rye.

Prior to Tennessee's prohibition beginning in 1909, there was an alliance of the state's distillers who expressed a desire for "perfection through clarification" of Tennessee whiskey. "They talk about removing the 'hog track' in the old papers," says Arnett. "What they mean by that is the graininess in the flavor. Remember, corn is what hogs eat, so it's the 'hog track.' Not just Jack, but George Dickel, Nelson's Greenbrier, several of the big players at the time held hands on this, and it resulted in some of the best whiskey in the world at that time. It's the reason Jack Daniel's won gold at the World's Fair in the early twentieth century.

"They believed in the Lincoln County Process. But after Prohibition, many of them just didn't come back. Jack Daniel's carried the torch until recently. Without the process, it's bourbon. We've got an affirmation letter on the subject from the federal government, from the Alcohol Bureau, dated 1941, and the Motlow family fought for that distinction, even after Jack had died.

"When we take the distillate off the still, it's still bourbon; it's very different post charcoal mellowing than it is beforehand. This is the state's heritage. Kind of like the Scots take malted barley, and smoked and peated and all the rest, it makes scotch; it's the process that gives it all those interesting characteristics that make it what it is. The Lincoln County Process is what makes Tennessee whiskey what it is in the same way. It's distinct, and it says something about the product you're getting, like a wine label says 'Merlot' or 'Chardonnay' and you know what you're getting, and it should have those characteristics you know are Merlot or Chardonnay. That doesn't mean all of them are identical, but that it should have certain characteristics. Dickel tastes distinctly different from Jack, but it has the true characteristics of Tennessee whiskey."

What the name does, at a point in time when there are contentions over standards, says Arnett, is hold the product to a particular standard.

"It's good for the consumer—the 'Tennessee whiskey' on the label tells the consumer it went through this process, that no corners were cut. It's good business for everyone, and Tennessee continues to benefit from the global renown our whiskey has built up. That extra step, I'd argue, is a premium process."

In arguing for that premium nature, Arnett says we first have to consider that bourbon at its base is a quality product; its ingredients are all natural: limestone water, good grain, yeast, a charred barrel. There are, he adds, no additives. Back in the nineteenth century, it wasn't unusual to see young whiskey colored artificially or flavored; today, aside from the deliberately flavored products, like the cinnamon whiskeys, that doesn't happen.

"Educate yourself when it comes to the labels on the bottle, especially when it comes to something that says 'blended whiskey,' because in most cases 'blending' is cheapening the product."

In the current climate, as lawmakers try to decide the long-term ramifications of designations like "Tennessee whiskey," Arnett praises the models that have preceded this one. "Scotch laws have made scotch revered, there are clearly defined tenets for it, and now when they're having to combat products from elsewhere that say 'scotch' on them, they can say that isn't scotch. Consumers should know what something is when they read the label; it should tell you the value of your product. The California wine label has become like that in recent years, because they have certain standards that make California wine excellent; they produce fantastic wines, and they've had the foresight to be protective of that.

"So when we talk about the reputation of Tennessee whiskey, we need to keep it real and keep it honest; having 'Tennessee whiskey' on the label, that's our state's heritage."

Having Brown-Forman as a parent company, one which has a number of heritage brands under its umbrella, Arnett says, helps underline the value that history places on a product. "Loyal patrons are very emotionally tied to that history; they get fired up about it. It's why they choose those brands," says Arnett. "We want to maintain that passion."

So in the end, I ask, what do you want people to know about Jack Daniel's?

"I want them first to know it's an all-natural product, like bourbon. I want them to know there's an art behind creating it. When you drink it, resist the urge to shoot it, and sip it slowly," he says. "When you do that, think about the flavors, the sweetness and oak balance are very unique in Jack Daniel's. You don't have to be a fan to appreciate that uniqueness. It's like scotch—there's an artistry to how they take their grain base and create a complex flavor system."

Arnett maintains that Jack has a robust flavor, more so than others. "It's got a strong sense of place—as I said, the water, the grain, our proprietary yeast make it what it is, things it wouldn't be made elsewhere."

If you're going to start tasting, he recommends beginning with Gentleman Jack, saying that while it's not necessarily a "beginner's whiskey," the product dating to 1988 has a softer finish and prominent sweetness, which draws new fans in. After that the next choice is the Black Label, the best known of the products. "When people try it blindfolded, this is the product they choose; it's very good." says Arnett.

Moving beyond, Arnett recommends the Single Barrel. "It's got a very rock and roll reputation," he says. "It's a robust, aromatic expression of whiskey, very flavorful and a good value for its complexity."

When people are introduced to whiskey generally, Arnett adds, they start out with a cocktail—something like a classic Jack and Coke. It's perhaps two to three parts whiskey to Coke or something like that. After a while it's more Jack and less Coke, and eventually the new whiskey lover is gently sipping Jack on the rocks without a mixer as their cocktail of choice.

"As long as they're enjoying it, and drinking responsibly, then let them drink the way they like," he says. "And mixed drinks and cocktail culture are pretty wonderful."

JACK DANIEL'S DISTILLERY COCKTAILS

Jack and Ginger

3 ounces ginger ale
1 ounce Jack Daniel's Black Label

Serve over rocks in a Collins glass.
Garnish with a lime twist.

The Iroquois Gentleman

1 ½ ounces Gentleman Jack
½ ounce Chambord
3 ½ ounces lemonade
1 ½ ounces lemon-lime soda such
   as 7Up or Sprite

Shake Gentleman Jack, Chambord, and lemonade in an ice-filled
shaker. Strain into a glass, with or
without ice. Add the lemon-lime
soda. Garnish with a lemon twist.

Velvet Elvis

1 ½ ounces Jack Daniel's Old No. 7
½ ounce Chambord
3 ½ ounces sweet and sour mix
1 ½ ounces lemon-lime soda such
   as 7Up or Sprite

Shake in an ice-filled shaker. Strain
into a glass, with or without ice.
Add lemon-lime soda. Garnish
with a lemon wedge.

NELSON'S GREENBRIER DISTILLERY

1414 Clinton Street, Nashville, TN 37203;
(615) 913-8800; greenbrierdistillery.com

Nelson's is a labor of love, by a pair of heirs, several generations removed, to one of the oldest and most established distillers in the state of Tennessee. Brothers Andy and Charlie Nelson have committed themselves to reviving the family business and began by bringing in general manager James Hensley and producing an exceptionally solid rectified product, Belle Meade Bourbon, while learning the business of distilling and beginning their own production in the Nashville area. Look for their newer products, including the Belle Meade Bourbon Sherry Cask Finish, house-made Nelson's Greenbrier Tennessee White Whiskey, and more to come available in 2015 and beyond.

The Products: Belle Meade Sour Mash Straight Bourbon, Nelson's Greenbrier Handmade White Whiskey, Belle Meade Sherry Cask Finished Bourbon

Clinton Street in Nashville, just slightly to the south and west of Germantown, flourishes these days with the expansion and growth at Marathon Motor Works, where Corsair Artisan has its Nashville distillery space, and where a plethora of other exciting businesses have also decided to locate, among them Mike Wolfe's (of *American Pickers* fame) Antique Archaeology and local sweet-making favorite Bang Candy Company. As this book was being written, just down the street at 1414 Clinton—an easy two-block walk—Charlie and Andy Nelson were beginning the build-out on their new version of the old family business—Nelson's Greenbrier Distillery. Their Belle Meade Bourbon, inspired by a brand once produced by their three times great-grandfather, Charles Nelson, has been on the shelves for several years now.

Charlie and Andy, along with their general manager, James Hensley, made a very distinct choice when they decided to open a distillery. Amid the controversy over the issue of sourcing bourbon, they opted to create a single product by bottling the sourced whiskey—the aforementioned Belle Meade Bourbon—even as they started studying and learning to distill the old-fashioned way on their own.

It's not revealing any industry secret to acknowledge that sourcing is very common in the microdistillery culture, but as has been said earlier in this book, young distilleries need moneymaking products early on. There are two options: Start by making a product yourself that doesn't require aging and using that to fund the bourbon you need to age for years before selling, or source your whiskey temporarily while your own is sitting in casks. The latter is a tough decision, because it means you build a reputation for a taste profile that may or may not match what you produce later on your own, and customers have already built particular expectations. Happily for the Nelsons, they truly understand how that works, and have new names and new products to pair with their self-made whiskey. With James Henley's sound advice on board, they have a solid future ahead of them.

Meanwhile, Belle Meade Bourbon has gotten a lot of positive national and regional press, ranging from *Saveur* to *Garden & Gun*. The small-batch (they use four carefully selected barrels per batch), high rye content bourbon comes in at just over 90 proof. With a label and marketing imagery evocative of the labels used by the original Charles Nelson, the product takes its name from Belle Meade Plantation in West Nashville.

Still standing and open to the public for tours, Belle Meade is best known as a central point in horse racing history in the South. Many of today's Kentucky Derby winners can trace their line back to Bonnie Scotland, one of Belle Meade's finest. He's even pictured on the label, along with another of the Harding family's prize racers.

"We were going to put the horses' names on the label itself, to promote the history," says Charlie Nelson with a grin. "The horse on the left is Bonnie Scotland, and he had a daughter called something like 'Bourbon Belle,' which is great. But the horse on the right was called, unfortunately, Brown Dick . . . so, you know, we decided it might not be the best idea."

While James Hensley has been a powerhouse name in Nashville's mixology culture for a number of years now, the Nelson brothers never intended to be distillers. This fact is important, because, as Charlie says, they firmly believe that the job came to them. Given the family history, that's not an unreasonable supposition.

On the sweltering, asphalt-blistering August day I visit the distillery build-out to do this interview, Charlie and James are holed up inside a blessedly air-conditioned trailer inside the back part of the distillery. They've already got mash cooking and the stills fired up so they can lay down their new product to age, even if the crew is still putting up walls and finishing ceilings around them. Workers are focused on getting the front of the building closed off, and the construction on what will be tasting room, reception area, and gift shop finished.

(Happily, they completed construction in November 2014, and what you will see now is a rather wonderful facility, tailor-made for tourists as well as distillers.)

Even in the trailer there's evidence of the old, old history of the family's distilling in the area scattered about: old bottles, labels, and calendars they've accumulated in the quest for Charles Nelson's nineteenth-century business.

I interrupt Charlie and James at lunch, but luckily for me they love telling their story. "I didn't know anything about my family history in this industry until about eight years ago," Charlie begins meditatively. "I was finishing up college, and my dad called. He and my mom had bought a whole cow from a farmer, and he invited Andy and me to go with him to pick up the meat at the butcher. This was up off Interstate 65 north of Nashville at Green Brier, and we pulled off at the exit and stopped at what was a Citgo station then. There was a historical marker there, commemorating Nelson's Greenbrier Distillery and Charles Nelson, the distiller. I mean, it was 'Holy crap, that's my name!'"

When they got to the butcher's, they asked both him and their dad, Bill, more and learned the details: The area by the Citgo had once held a barrel house, the nearby spring had provided the distillery's water, and Charles Nelson had once been the Nashville area's premier distiller, even before Jack Daniel's and George Dickel were truly big names.

The butcher—whose business sat there on Distillery Street—pointed out the nearby location of the original warehouse and still-flowing spring of limestone-filtered water. From there they made their way to the local historical society, where they saw two bottles of Nelson's product. The family had had stories, of course, but here was the physical evidence of everything they'd been told.

"We went home and started working on a business plan," says Charlie Nelson. "We learned the history and the ins and outs of the industry. It turns out most of the big guys knew all about Nelson's, and that helped open doors for us."

They began raising money, absolutely the toughest part, Charlie says ruefully, echoing so many young distillers across the region. The original plan was to lay down barrels of whiskey and just let it sit, but that clearly brought no revenue.

"It felt like we were banging our heads against the wall," he admits. "We're not lucky enough to have the luxury of just waiting for money to roll in, but honestly, I wouldn't rather be doing anything else. I've put absolutely everything I have into this. And I want to be true to the original; it was very important to get our own distillery going."

The family knew by now that Charles Nelson had produced any number of products and had solid ideas about the details. For example, they knew the original version of Belle Meade Bourbon, made in conjunction with the Sperry Wade Company in Nashville, was a high rye content bourbon. "At that point, we put up all we had for a loan, started building a brand, and sourced the best whiskey we could. Then it was a matter of building a space of our own, laying down whiskey we made ourselves. We started bottling and making Belle Meade Bourbon available two years ago, and two weeks ago we started laying down our own. We didn't really so much decide to do this as it found us. I never expected us to make it this far really; it's been a matter of serendipity for eight years, and we're finally really making our whiskey."

Without their great, great, great-grandfather, Charles Nelson, the founder, it is unlikely Charlie and Andy would be distillers at all. "It all starts with him," says Charlie.

Charles the elder was born July 4, 1835, in Hagenow, in northern Germany. His father was in the soap and candle business, with a fair amount of success. In 1850 he decided to move his family to the United States.

"They sold the business and all their possessions, converted the money to gold, and had special clothes made, sewing all the gold into hidden pockets for the trip," says Charlie. "They boarded the *Helena Sloman*, which it turns out is a fairly famous ship—I actually learned about it on the History Channel. The *Helena Sloman* made three or so voyages from Hamburg to New York and had many famous passengers, including members of the Heinz family (that's now Heinz ketchup and all that). On this voyage, they sailed through a very severe storm, which washed a number of passengers overboard—including Charles's father in his suit filled with gold coins, which dragged him straight down."

The family and other passengers were rescued by an English ship, the *Devonshire*, and the Nelsons quickly found themselves in New York, without

Photo courtesy of Charles Nelson, Nelson's Greenbrier Distillery

their paterfamilias or the lost fortune. Charles, just fifteen, found work in the soap and candle business to support the family; by age seventeen he and a brother had saved enough money to pack the Nelson clan up for Cincinnati, where he entered the meat trade as a butcher.

"Cincinnati was kind of 'pork-opolis' back then, and there were a lot of breweries and distilleries," says Charlie Nelson. The reason the two thrived side by side was that the spent grains from the mash used in beer and liquor making were often sold off as feed for hogs and cattle. Likewise, the now-butcher Charles Nelson learned a great deal about alcohol production as a matter of course.

Young Charles married, had a son, and was widowed in rapid succession during this time, and at some point before 1860, he moved again, this time to Nashville, where he got into the wholesale grocery business. He dealt, Charlie says, with coffee, meat, and whiskey, and his customers included Joel Cheek (of Maxwell House Hotel and coffee fame) and early supermarket founder H. G. Hill. He became one of the very first merchants to sell whiskey in bottles, rather than jugs or barrels, eventually

NELSON'S GREENBRIER DISTILLERY *159*

buying the local distillery producing that whiskey. Bourbon historian Mike Veach provided Charlie and Andy with an 1860s trademark example belonging to Charles Nelson from the Filson Archives.

Nelson also received a patent for improved distillation methods that expanded production capacity early in his distilling tenure. His distillery certainly predated Jack Daniel's and was designated Distillery #5 in Tennessee at the time—along with Daniel's and Cascade (later George Dickel), he had one of the few large producing distilleries in a state with hundreds in operation.

Eventually Nelson's grew to produce more than thirty different labels, some in conjunction with other businesses, including whiskey, rye, bourbon, brandy, gin, and "angelica wine." Among them was Green Brier Tennessee Whiskey. The company notably produced Belle Meade Bourbon in partnership with Sperry Wade & Company of Nashville, and a malt whiskey called "Old Yanisse" with B. J. Sims of Memphis. Records exist of Nelson's selling not only across the United States, as far as San Francisco and New York, but also exporting to Spain, France, Russia, and even the Philippines (this last about the time of the Spanish American War).

By 1885 Charlie Nelson says his ancestor produced about 380,000 gallons of liquor a year (the next largest distiller, Jack Daniel's, was producing just upwards of 20,000 gallons at the time). In 1889 Nelson founded the Nashville Trust Company and helped start the city's first musical union about the same time.

When Charles Nelson died in 1891, his wife, Louisa, took over the business, one of the first women in American history to run a major

Photo courtesy of Charles Nelson, Nelson's Greenbrier Distillery

distilling company, nearly thirty years before she and her daughters would be granted the right to vote. "It was absolutely a male-dominated industry at the time," says Charlie. "We're really proud of her." Eventually her son William would join her and help run the vast business.

The family's generosity and progressive viewpoints are extremely evident in Charlie and Andy's research. According to them, one of Charles and Louisa's daughters helped start the Tennessee School for the Blind, while one of their sons helped establish the all-African American Meharry Medical College. Another daughter, Emma Louise, delivered a stirring pro–Civil Rights speech at her commencement at Vassar College, well before 1900.

When Prohibition hit Tennessee early, in 1909 rather than 1919, the family moved their production to Louisville, Kentucky, at 100 East Main Street. The Green Brier Old #5 Distillery became barrel storage, and their Nashville location provided offices only. They sold the remaining Tennessee stock legally, in barrels, at least through 1915. When national Prohibition hit, the family got out of the liquor business entirely, until 2006 when Bill, Charlie, and Andy visited the old Green Brier site and changed their stars to align with the family's past.

"We're still learning about the history," says Charlie earnestly. "I just got hold of a full bottle of rye from 1899." He shows off old marketing calendars and letterhead, old engravings and lithography, some of which the brothers plan on bringing back for current use. It gives a feeling of intense nostalgia. Charlie and Andy recently found a descendant of the cooper who made barrels for Charles Nelson. "It's just a really exciting thing," says Charlie.

The history is part of what makes this story, of course. There's no question the current Belle Meade Bourbon is a delight to drink, but everyone in the Nashville area is looking forward to the moment Nelson's Greenbrier Distillery, in its second incarnation, starts bottling its very own whiskey.

Nelson's Greenbrier Distillery Cocktails

Tennessee Toddy

2 ounces Belle Meade Bourbon
¾ ounce fresh lemon juice
½ ounce honey syrup*
¼ ounce maple syrup
4 dashes Angostura Bitters
Hot water

Blend all ingredients in a hot drink mug. Garnish with lemon oils expressed over the top of the drink.

*Honey syrup
Use a ratio of 3:1 honey to warm water. Mix until incorporated.

Vow of Silence

2 ounces Belle Meade Bourbon
¾ ounce Carpano Antica
  vermouth
¼ ounce Benedictine
Dash Angostura Bitters
2 dashes Peychaud's Bitters

Serve without ice in a chilled cocktail glass. Garnish with lemon peel expressed over the drink.

Buggy Whip

1 ounce Belle Meade Bourbon
½ ounce Cointreau
½ ounce Berentzen Apple
Dash Angostura Bitters
Champagne

Build in champagne flute. Garnish with a long lemon pigtail.

POPCORN SUTTON DISTILLING

830 US 25W, Newport, TN 37821; (423)
832-8501; popcornsutton.com

P opcorn Sutton is another excellent effort to revive Tennessee's illegal whiskey culture. As with several others, distribution is currently limited, with seventeen states in the mix, but with the new plant in Newport, Tennessee, in Cocke County, it shouldn't be long before you can purchase it in all fifty. As of this writing, tourism at the Cocke County location was not yet available, but they are working toward it, with dates likely available in late 2015.

The Product: Popcorn Sutton XXX Tennessee White Whiskey

Popcorn Sutton is a name spoken with true reverence in the hollows of East Tennessee, one of the twentieth century's best-known wildcatters. Depending on your point of view, he was either something of a patron saint of moonshine or someone with a boundless disregard for the law. To some, he was both. What is clearest about his life is he left behind a recipe for moonshine that he passed on to Popcorn Sutton distillery owner Jamey Grosser before he died in 2009.

Marvin "Popcorn" Sutton, born in 1946, spent a lifetime making illegal shine, got caught a few times, spent time on probation, and, in the late 1990s, when illegal distilling was still commonplace in Tennessee, decided he wanted to make sure people knew about his culture. He claims to have come from a long line of moonshiners in Appalachia (he was born in western North Carolina, across the state border) and firmly believed in the tradition with all his heart.

Sutton wrote an autobiography on the subject and his experience in the illegal liquor trade in 1999, and at the same time released a video on VHS on the same subject. Afterwards he appeared in several now-cult broadcasts and documentaries, including *This Is the Last Dam Run of Likker I'll Ever Make* (2002) and *The Last One* (2008; it received a Southeast Emmy Award), and some of the footage from these was used later on the Discovery Channel reality series *Moonshiners* in 2011.

In 2008, after a cancer diagnosis, Sutton was arrested by federal agents and charged with illegally distilling spirits. He asked the judge presiding over the case to let him serve out his sentence under house arrest, given his health, and friends petitioned on his behalf, but the judge refused. On March 16, 2009, Sutton took his own life—rigging the exhaust pipe of his prized vintage Ford Fairlane, turning the key, and dying of carbon monoxide poisoning. He preferred to go out on his own terms, rather than spend eighteen months in a penitentiary. Though incredibly tragic, it also underlines Popcorn Sutton's powerhouse legacy in the moonshine world.

Travis Hixon, distiller for the Popcorn Sutton distillery, says the distillery itself had already taken the first steps toward existence before that point, when one of the founders and owners, Jamey Grosser of J&M Concepts, sought out Sutton hoping to talk with him about moonshine. He managed to get in touch with Popcorn through his parole officer, and the two developed a friendship. Hixon says Sutton hoped to pass on his legacy, and Grosser was someone who could help him do that.

Sutton shared his recipe, his methods, and all the details with Grosser in a partnership, and when Sutton died, Grosser committed to carrying on. He knew he wanted to open a larger distillery now that the state's laws had changed to allow for craft distilleries, but when he got started it was still not permissible to build a distillery in Cocke County near where Popcorn had actually lived. It was, however, reasonable to open a Nashville location, so that's what he opted to do. Grosser had a still and equipment made to Sutton's specifications and was ready to go, but he needed the help of a good master distiller.

That's where Travis Hixon comes into the story. Hixon already had an established reputation in Nashville's craft brewing sector, having spent fourteen years at Blackstone Brewery, one of the city's oldest microbrewers.

Hixon started like most of Music City's best microbrewers did, as a home brewer, something he did for about three years before he decided to make a real go of it. Back in the 1990s, when his interest in homebrew turned into something he was truly passionate about, he decided to make a career of it and went to study at Chicago's Siebel Institute of Technology, the oldest and most established brewing school in the United States (founded in 1872).

When he finished, he returned to Nashville and went to work at Blackstone, brewing up excellent beer (my dad and I made a regular habit of hitting Blackstone for post–Titans game beer when we left the stadium, before I got married—we know Hixon's product well).

Beyond the brewing, he played a significant role in getting the company's new packaging brewery and bottling facility up and running. In total he worked with Blackstone for fourteen years. A few years ago he left the brewery and immediately found himself consulting, as he looked to see what the next opportunity might be. Out of the blue, he says, he got a call from Jamey Grosser.

"At the time I had an academic basis in distilling, and it was a skill I was interested in developing and adding to my knowledge base," says Hixon. He took the job and went to work at the Nashville facility, but unsurprisingly, they quickly outstripped the capacity of the small space and knew they had to find something else if they were going to increase the capacity of their distilling.

Fortuitously, Cocke County finally voted in favor of changing their own distillery laws in 2012, and the company decided it was the right time to move back there for production. Grosser and Hixon settled on a piece of property in Newport, Tennessee, about eight miles from Popcorn Sutton's home, where his wife, Pamela, still lives.

"We started building in January 2013," says Hixon. "By March 2014 we had our first mash going." It's been two years of burning the candle at both ends for Hixon and the Popcorn Sutton crew, but it's paying off. The new facility, with the equipment built to the late Mr. Sutton's specifications, is now producing at ten times the capacity of the Nashville distillery (they still operate in Nashville as well, but production has moved here to Newport).

Hixon is notably reticent when I ask him about the recipe they're using, and whether it's "a corn or a sugar shine." He clearly believes in transparency when it comes to whether distillers are making their own product or rectifying and bottling, but the mash bill, the old Sutton recipe, that's something else. And perhaps that's as it should be. There's cachet in a bit of mystery, and Popcorn Sutton has plenty of cachet to bank on, between that and its namesake's near-mythic status.

"It's definitely a proprietary recipe," Hixon tells me. "It's all traditional ingredients, handwritten from him, and we're using equipment he designed and the method he taught Jamey Grosser."

While the single product, Popcorn Sutton's Tennessee White Whiskey, has done well for the fledgling distillery, there are new products arriving on the market, all of them with their roots in Sutton's original repertoire. His widow, Mrs. Pam Sutton, is the inspiration and source behind a new line of flavored products worth the tasting, with her name on them as well—there are currently six starting to appear on the market: Mrs. Sutton's apple pie, peach, watermelon, mixed berry, blackberry, and cherry.

There are more internal projects going on, Hixon says, based on things like products Sutton made for friends at the holidays and the like.

What, I ask Hixon, do you want people to know about the product you make?

"Know that it's the re-creation of the recipe from Popcorn himself," he says. "We're true to it; we're not trying to 'innovate'—or do anything else unless he did it himself. We make sure the spirit tastes right, that's our primary goal.

"This is a heritage spirit; we're trying to preserve that tradition. This was a lifelong mission of his; it's a big part of the moonshine legacy. There's a whole story around it, as moonshine really becomes a thing of the past, and there are fewer and fewer connected to that tradition left to preserve its history."

He makes it clear they do every aspect of production here. "We're not outsourcing any part of the liquid—and I believe that shows in our product. There's no smoke and mirrors. We make it from scratch, and I think what we do makes it a premium product."

Hixon adds that they're very pleased to be settled in in Cocke County, and that the folks in Newport, Tennessee, knew Sutton well and remember him. "All the people around here knew him; we get job applicants at the plant all the time that have stories about him. And we like that we can bring the benefits of his legacy back here and share them with the local community in Newport."

In early 2015 John Lunn, master distiller at George Dickel, announced he would be moving to Popcorn Sutton as the new master distiller there. While this move was surprising, it is exciting to everyone in the region, underlining the potential of the small distillery under Lunn's exceptional talents. Expect good things—very, very good things. As mentioned earlier, the distillery had not yet opened for tourism as of this writing, but there is a small retail shop ready for shopping right now. Distillery tours are planned in the future, so when you expect to be in the area, make sure you check availability via the Popcorn Sutton website or call the distillery directly.

Prichard's

11 Kelso-Smithland Rd., Kelso, TN 37348; (931) 433-5454

The Fontanel

4105 Whites Creek Pike, Whites Creek, TN 37189;
(615) 454-5991; prichardsdistillery.com

Prichard's falls between the old, established distilleries like Jack and George, and the newcomers that made their way after the laws changed in 2009. Phil Prichard found one of the few Tennessee counties that would welcome a distillery in the 1990s and got his business up and running. Today you have two potential locations to visit—the larger distillery in Kelso or the smaller one at The Fontanel in Nashville. Regardless, take the time to check out the Sweet Lucy Liqueur and discover a very different and exciting side of Tennessee distilling.

The Products: Double Barrel Bourbon, Tennessee Whiskey, Double Chocolate Bourbon, Rye Whiskey, Tennessee Malt Whiskey, Lincoln County Lighting, Crystal Rum, Fine Rum, Private Stock Rum, Peach Mango Rum, Key Lime Rum, Spiced Cranberry Rum, Sweet Lucy, Sweet Lucy Cream, Sweet Lucifer, Fudge Brownie Cream, Praline Cream Liqueur

Prichard's is unusual in Tennessee in that when Phil Prichard set out to create what would become the third-largest distillery in the state in the late 1990s, he wanted to make rum, not whiskey. It must be admitted, Prichard's has done a fine job of it, though in the ensuing fifteen years, they've also brought a host of other good products to market from their distillery at Kelso. In summer 2014 they opened an additional small, boutique distillery at The Fontanel, the former home of singer-songwriter Barbara Mandrell just north of downtown Nashville, which is now a major attraction, with a gorgeous little inn, concert venue, and more.

As I interview Prichard, he's just overseen the installation of two cypress fermenting tanks at the Fontanel location, which he'd brought from New York the previous day. He's a larger-than-life character, and that only plays into the promotion of his prod-

uct—the day I first met him, at the Fontanel opening, he was decked out nattily in a white linen suit, still crisp on one of the hottest days of the year.

I ask him how he managed to find himself in the distilling business—a third career for him after a first in the dental industry and later the telecom business. "At the tender age of fifty-seven, I decided it was time for a change," he says. In a casual conversation, his cousin Mack had suggested, "My dad always thought we could make rum here in Tennessee from locally grown sorghum molasses." That idea stuck firmly in Phil Prichard's mind and changed his trajectory.

"It was like a burr under the saddle; there was enough of an invitation there that the idea never went away," he admits, though the idea came between his stints in the dental world and that of telecommunications. Eventually he found himself walking out of the business world, renting an office in Memphis, where he then lived, and raising money for a distillery.

"About 1997 I started really aggressively pursuing it. I walked into my friend Bill's office, he was in the banking business, and said, 'Bill, I want to build the first distillery in the state in fifty years and make rum.' And he chuckled at me. But by August 1999 I had committed and decided I needed partners. I walked into my first meeting with potential stockholders in the company and walked back out again with $75,000 in my pocket, and that's the money I started the distillery on.

"You look at the entrepreneur as being the guy who has the idea, but I'll tell you what—entrepreneurship is also the folks who put up the money to make it happen—they were special people."

Prichard was looking to create a Tennessee first in many ways, and a lot of actors had to come together to make it work. "Tennessee had funny laws at the time," Prichard says. "I call it a kind of Prohibition hangover."

Members of the Tennessee Alcoholic Beverage Commission viewed the idea favorably, even though at the time, distilleries were permitted in just three of Tennessee's counties (that law was amended in 2009). One woman on the commission reputedly commented, "I've never had the chance to vote on a distillery in Tennessee . . . and I vote we approve it," and her fellows agreed. Even so, having a distillery even in Moore, Lincoln, or Coffee Counties where it was legal required a referendum of the same sort needed to approve liquor sales by the drink and package stores (some twenty-six of Tennessee's counties remain dry). Moore County, home of Jack Daniel's, is still dry, thanks to a quirk that also requires a minimum population of 32,000 to even have a referendum.

Prichard says they tried first to find a location in Coffee County, but a couple of naysayers went to the media with negative commentary. The upside was that once the news got out, other communities called with offers of welcome. Lincoln County's Mayor Jerry Mansfield called Prichard and suggested he come take a look at an old school building in Kelso; it turned out to be a godsend.

Kelso is fairly tiny, like many of the towns where local distilleries are thriving, but the location proved perfect. "If I'd gone into an engineering firm to ask for all I needed in a small craft distillery—room for the stills, an office, a bottling facility, a warehouse, someplace to act as a visitor center, I don't think we could have come up with a better design."

The old cafeteria transformed to house the distilling equipment, the gym became the warehouse, two old classrooms were combined to create the bottling space, while two more took on the office roles. The old library-cum-music room served as the visitor center. Before 1999 was out, the company had released their first product—an aged rum.

"Making rum will take two years to find out if it's good, and then we have to sell the product," says Prichard, speaking of the usual time lapse involved between distilling and actually getting a product on the market. He made the choice to age that rum in fifteen-gallon barrels, which exponentially accelerated the aging process.

Digressing onto the topic of making rum, Prichard asserts that while there are more than 2,000 rum distilleries operating across the world today, the vast majority of them use blackstrap molasses to create their product. Almost all rum comes from molasses, and Prichard discovered that sadly he couldn't use sorghum molasses to make his product, because legally, rum must be made with sugarcane to be called rum, and efforts to fight that definition would have caused further delay.

He opted instead to use what he considered a cleaner, finer product than blackstrap—sweet table molasses, which included 90 to 95 percent fermentable sugars, compared to about 30 to 35 percent for the blackstrap.

Rum was the drink of choice on the colonial-era East Coast, much of it made in New England, and according to Prichard, that sweet table molasses was the chosen source for production. "It makes a rum Thomas Jefferson once called 'poor man's brandy,'" says Prichard. "It was very involved for the colonists to make white table sugar; they used a process that was like the old-fashioned candle dipping, dropping strings into diluted molasses, letting the sugar crystallize, and removing it manually. It was incredibly expensive to make white sugar, so most Americans at the time used sweet molasses for nearly everything, including to mix with yeast for their bread, not white sugar the way we do."

Making rum from sweet table molasses like the colonial model isn't common. Prichard speculates they were one of the first contemporary distilleries to revert to the method, helping to reinvent the American rum competition category.

He points out they make use of pot stills; using blackstrap would require a column still that could refine the heavier, more particulate-filled product more effectively. He feels the characteristic flavor of rum is better obtained through his methods.

Like many of the smaller distillers currently operating across Tennessee and Kentucky, he's largely self-taught. He credits a book called *The Lore of Still Building* for giving him concrete ideas about how to make rum, and he quickly found himself trying to figure out the ratio of water to molasses for a proper level of dilution (a 15 percent solution turned out to be right for the yeast).

"There's a point where you're undergoing the school of hard knocks, where you're standing over your wife's canning pot on the stove with white dog dripping out and you just kind of grin," he says. "But when you're making it on a kitchen stove, you really don't understand what you're doing . . . and you have to have some sense. You start, then you call your best friend and say, 'hey John, come taste this,' and before long you have no idea who's going to be coming through your front door. Thoughts don't quite go through your head right, so I'll just remind people if they plan on making it at home, go get the experimental permit and do it legally, there are stiff penalties for making illegal alcohol."

As things progressed, Prichard took advantage of AllTech in Lexington, where founder (and owner of Town Branch Distillery) Pierce Lyons was teaching distilling classes. He connected with large Midwest grain alcohol manufacturers who helped and advised him, and also with engineers who understood what kind of still he'd need.

When Prichard committed to making rum in the late 1990s, vodka was the darling product of the alcohol market, whiskey and bourbon were still in the doldrums, and rum had a slow but very steady 3 percent annual growth rate. It seemed a wise choice.

By 2003, when Kentucky-based still-maker Vendome Copper and Brass's Tom Sherman visited, he told Prichard that he'd sold a new still to a nearby potential whiskey distiller. Realizing the whiskey market had rebounded, the company bought equipment and set out to make a new product.

"Whiskey's a different animal," muses Prichard. He understood the process involved grains—especially corn, which is a starch, not a sugar, with the cell walls broken down by heating nearly to boiling. Consulting with Pierce Lyons, he came to the understanding that you need the two enzymes alpha and beta amylase, naturally found in malted barley, to do the job—cook the corn, add the rye, then the malted barley at the end. "Then it's like a miracle; it tastes like sugar water, it converts the starches to sugar, and it's ready to make alcohol." For Phil Prichard the ships were on the horizon, and Prichard's made whiskey.

Since then they've added a variety of products to their line worth investigating. Without a doubt the Crystal Rum is worth a sample (it's found a regular place in my home bar very easily). The big deal, however, has been Sweet Lucy Liqueur.

"This is purely just an exclamation of joy," Prichard says. "This dates back to the duck blind with my dad; he used to make his version with whiskey, oranges, peaches, sugar all macerated and left to sit, then poured back in the bottle to take with you. Drink it in a cold duck blind at the end of the day, and it warms you up 'Sweeeeet Lucy!' Maybe in a slightly less Christian duck blind, you might say 'Sweet Jesus.'"

Sweet Lucy has become the number one seller for Prichard's, and anyone who's had it with a little lemonade topped with club soda on a hot summer day can tell you why it keeps its popularity year-round. Cream liqueurs are also hitting it big, and the Sweet Lucy Bourbon Cream Liqueur has made a market impact as well.

Coming up in winter of 2014 is the spicy version of Sweet Lucy, made to compete with the growing popularity of

cinnamon whiskeys across the country. This one uses ginger, not cinnamon, and it goes by Sweet (wait for it) Lucifer. Sweet Lucifer makes use of a very appealing new devil duck logo, the "born in duck blind" theme. It's pretty adorable.

The distillery's number one dollar generator is likely the Double Barrel Bourbon, but it's the new flavored creams that are building excitement at the Nashville Fontanel location, where the Chocolate Fudge Brownie Liqueur has taken off. By the time you read this, there will also be a New Orleans Praline. Fontanel has put a lot of product on the map for them.

Over the years, Prichard's has also seen the rise of the new crop of Tennessee distillers, and Prichard says it started after the laws changed in 2009. "I admit when [State Senator] Bill Ketron came to me to talk about it, I was originally just a little jealous," he says. "But you ask me today and I couldn't be happier. A rising tide raises all ships—that's been proved. I support it; it's good for all of us."

Widespread distribution across the country means you have a good chance of picking up Prichard's products, even though they're not on the scale of a Daniel's or a Dickel. That's a good thing. Visitors to either distillery can get a good sense of what the Prichard's craft culture is all about. Even the small-scale, vintage feel of the Fontanel, with its French-style alembic still and cypress mash tubs, makes sure you have a true distillery experience.

"My dad once said, 'If you're proud of it, put your name on it,'" says Phil Prichard. "I never put my name on my sign in the dental business, but I do now. It has my name on it, and I durned well better make a good product."

Prichard's Distillery Cocktails

Sweet Lucy Julep (Horse Racing Version)

2 ounces Benjamin Prichard's
  Sweet Lucy
Several sprigs fresh mint
Powdered sugar

In a metal mint julep tumbler, gently press mint, then fill tumbler with finely crushed ice. Add Sweet Lucy and top off tumbler with more crushed ice. Garnish with a sprig of fresh mint first dipped into cold water and then into powdered sugar.

Summer Sweet Lucy Julep

2 ounces Benjamin Prichard's
  Sweet Lucy
Several sprigs fresh mint
Powdered sugar
Soda water

Same basic recipe as above but use a tall Collins glass instead of the traditional mint julep tumbler. After topping glass off with crushed ice, add a splash of club soda.

There's also a ready-made version, as it happens: Stuff a good-sized jar with fresh mint sprigs. Pour in a whole bottle of Sweet Lucy and store it in the refrigerator. Serve up as often as necessary, over ice, with or without club soda.

SHORT MOUNTAIN DISTILLERY

8280 Short Mountain Road, Woodbury, TN 37190;
(615) 216-0830; shortmountaindistillery.com

Short Mountain epitomizes what illegal moonshine used to be and what today's legal shine can be. Billy Kaufman and his crew absolutely make use of the old-fashioned illegal recipes—the kind that use sugar as the primary ingredient and go down so very smoothly. Kaufman is a member of the family that created the Samsonite luggage brand and, following the lead of his grandfather, he puts a coin with the "Golden Rule" on every bottle—"do unto others as you would have them do unto you." It's a maxim he lives by—which is fortunate, because a nice person would definitely introduce a friend to Short Mountain's distinct shine.

The Products: Authentic Tennessee Moonshine, Prohibition Tea, Apple Pie Moonshine

Most of us think we know what moonshine is, but honestly, we are laboring under the misconception that anything we buy in a liquor store labeled "Shine" is moonshine. Real moonshine—the illegal kind that got made all over when Tennessee opted for Prohibition ten years before the rest of the country—isn't quite the same as unaged whiskey, and it certainly isn't the same as the tweaked neutral grain spirit most of us are buying in those mason jars. Not that those things are terrible—they have their place in the liquor firmament, mind you—but this is about the real deal when it comes to what illegal shine is and was.

Billy Kaufman and his people at Short Mountain get that, and they're aiming to educate our palates. And thank heaven for that. This stuff is good.

Getting to Short Mountain involves a rural drive, no matter where you're coming from, but Woodbury and the surrounding area, all hills on

Photo courtesy of Short Mountain Distillery

the edge of the Tennessee plateau, happen to be incredibly gorgeous in just about every season. As I pull into the distillery, just out of view from the road thanks to abundant foliage, the drive is temporarily nearly blocked by a couple of pickups, one filled with fresh corn. I hop out, hoping to buy some, and meet Billy Nokes, who refuses to let me pay him for said corn because he's running for Cannon County commissioner, and his friend Can Nichols, who's running for trustee. Nice guys, who will still give a girl corn, even if she's from Williamson County.

As you walk around the distillery, you'll notice everything here is fairly small and rustic looking. There's a stage off to one side, clearly for concerts, that might double for use on the old *Hee Haw* TV show. It's beautifully wooded, and a trail to the back of the distillery proper leads down to the limestone spring where Short Mountain sources its water.

Kaufman bought this property after moving to Tennessee some thirteen years previously with the intent of turning it into an organic farm. As he worked, building relationships with local farmers, he made the discovery that most of the older farmers in the area made or had made moonshine in the course of their careers.

He developed friendships with many of them, including Ronald Lawson and Ricky Estes, who he would eventually bring in to share their experience with his master distiller. His goal centered around finding ways to help local farmers improve their economic situation. It turned out making moonshine did that, just under the auspices of the new state law this time.

Kaufman had put serious effort into creating his own organic farm, meanwhile, installing erosion protection and water conservation systems, and working to meet the necessary requirements to protect streams, wildlife, and drinking water. His commitment to that kind of purity and quality hasn't flagged as he's moved into the distilling business.

In 2010 Kaufman, great-grandson of Samsonite luggage company founder Jesse Shwayder, brought his brothers, David, Ben, and Darian, in as partners and started Short Mountain Distillery with the aim of making legal moonshine in the unincorporated Short Mountain community between Woodbury and Smithville, Tennessee. The laws for microdistilleries in the state of Tennessee had only recently changed, and Kaufman and company had to collect the necessary signatures to get the issue of a county microdistillery on the ballot. The referendum passed, and in 2012 Kaufman opened up.

Sitting in the tiny, vintage-style tasting room at Short Mountain, Kaufman waxes poetic on what moonshine really is and where it's going. At the time, I'd been under the impression that "moonshine" was essentially the same thing as the distillate being bottled at some of the big distillers and sold as "white whiskey" or "white dog" or "white lightning." I was in for an education.

There's a sign on the wall in the tasting room that says the site has been "declared haunted" by the Stones River Paranormal group. I have no trouble believing there are a few old-timey bootleggers whose ghosts kick up their heels in the chairs out front, still enjoying the smells from the still.

"We're one of the few distilleries out there that makes all the alcohol we sell; we are not buying neutral grain spirits," Kaufman begins emphatically.

He's pointing out what most people don't realize—that the vast majority of those jugs and mason jars you buy in the liquor store labeled "moonshine" are not made from traditional recipes at all. Most of them, Kaufman will tell you, are neutral grain spirits produced in the ethanol plants of big agriculture states, then bought up by liquor companies, tweaked to the needs of human consumption, and then, in many cases, flavored "as if it were Kool-Aid."

This isn't unique to moonshine; it's exactly what many of the flavored vodkas you're buying also come from, and many so-called "craft distillers" buy it and make a very popular product from it. You probably consume it on a regular basis, with a bunch of different labels affixed to it, and chances are you really enjoy some of it. But the point being, it's not the same thing as old-school moonshine of the sort that's been made in the backwoods of Tennessee, Kentucky, and Virginia for more than a century.

"There's this idea out there, in part because of the ethanol use, that clear spirits don't have any taste to them. That's a myth," Kaufman tells me. "Moonshine—the sugar shine we're making especially—has a taste. Real, traditionally made vodka, the kind coming from Russia and Poland, tequila from Mexico, they have a taste."

With the popular flavored vodkas out there, the ones aiming to woo you with flavors of whipped cream and cookies and such, they want those flavors to dominate, and neutral grain spirits make that easy for producers. But those aiming to make true, unflavored spirits have a different job to do—and Kaufman is one such maker.

He digresses into a discussion of current politics and the competition between mega companies Diageo, owner of Tennessee's second-largest whiskey producer, and Jack Daniel's, owned by Brown-Forman. Diageo aims to change the laws and regulations governing what constitutes Tennessee whiskey, making the process simpler and cheaper. The big companies, of course, are concerned with their markets for a wide variety of spirits, not only in the United States but around the world (particularly the rapidly expanding Asian markets), and that's playing out in the distilleries of Tennessee, large and small.

The state's craft distillers objected, their perspective being that watering down the rules for whiskey doesn't do them any favors as producers. They like the stringent set of rules that define just what Tennessee whiskey must be, and the quality assurance that comes with those regulations. "It gives Tennessee whiskey a distinct classification, like scotch or Kentucky bourbon," says Kaufman.

Kaufman, at this writing, is also president of the state's Distiller's Guild.

What he wants now is to see the same kind of serious guidelines drawn up for a product to be called moonshine as are now designated for a product to be called Tennessee whiskey. "All whiskeys are classified except shine," he says with quiet emphasis. "What you get on the market calling itself moonshine is all too often the cheapest liquid someone can find and sell. You have no idea what it is when you buy it.

"The history of 'moonshine' is that it's an illegally made spirit; in Tennessee that means something. Prohibition for us started earlier than most of the nation [in 1909], so by 1919 when Prohibition passed nationally, we already knew what we were doing when it came to making spirits. Here in Cannon County, we've been making a sugar shine for more than one hundred years now. It's not a neutral grain spirit, it's not a rum or vodka. People made it from sugar and corn, mostly, but back then a clever shiner could make shine out of anything he needed to. Got a truckload of doughnuts? Turn them into shine. Lots of peaches, same thing. It's about taking an excess of agricultural product, whatever it is, and turning it into something that could last."

As Kaufman tells it, there are three kinds of self-proclaimed moonshines made today. The first is real moonshine. It's made illegally, and it comes from old recipes and traditions, especially here, deep in rural Tennessee—mostly made with sugar and corn, sometimes with other things.

Secondly, there's the legal version of the same thing—the stuff he's making now with his master distiller Josh Smotherman and his advisors from the old school of illegal shine, Estes and Lawson, from a traditional recipe handed down from the guys who made the illegal stuff. The difference is that he's inspected and taxed and follows all the procedures the state wants him to—the agriculture inspection, the plant inspection, the Tennessee Bureau of Investigation, the ABC board.

And finally there's version three, the novelty "moonshines" that are "just moonshine by name," according to Kaufman. Largely, these are the products you get sold in kitschy containers like jugs and mason jars, which are mostly neutral grain spirts. They're fun, but it's a misnomer to call them moonshine.

"The thing is, the expectations [from consumers] aren't high here," says Kaufman. "Most people today expect shine to be harsh and expect that they won't like what they get—so when they don't like what they try from those mason jars, there's

Photo courtesy of Short Mountain Distillery

no surprise. But if it's well made, shine is *not* harsh. Anything *made poorly* is harsh, just like most well-made spirits are smooth. A good moonshine is as good as any fine clear spirit to mix in a cocktail. I suspect that's what makes Tennessee whiskey so successful worldwide in part; it's much easier to blend in cocktails than scotch."

Ultimately, what Kaufman is getting at is that moonshine's reputation isn't good. It comes from people's experience with bad novelty products randomly labeled as moonshine, and from the mythology built up around the stories of poisonings from back in the days of Prohibition.

"Moonshine has no identity," he says. "I want to change that. I want a spirit that calls itself moonshine to require documented proof that it [that is, the recipe] has been made illegally."

Having brought in serious old-school family legacy bootleggers with nearly a century of experience in making it between them, Kaufman has solid evidence. If you're looking for the kind of cachet, the kind of bona fides that a whiskey has in a moonshine, folks, this is it.

"It is," he says, stating his opinion in no uncertain terms with exceptional passion, "completely '*ridonkculous*' to sell neutral grain spirits as moonshine. If there was no distinction for what made a whiskey, you'd see the same thing—mediocre product would start showing up on the market instantly. It's illegal to call something whiskey that's *not*, there are regulations, and that's why the Tennessee whiskeys are up in arms about keeping them. But that's what they do with moonshine."

In Kaufman's view, if people want to make those things, that's fine, but don't use the moniker moonshine for them.

For Short Mountain it's been a labor of love, quite honestly, to compete in this market. Theirs is a high-quality product made to heightened specifications at a time when companies with huge marketing budgets are calling themselves craft moonshine distillers, but not making real, traditional moonshine.

It ain't cheap to start a craft distillery for real, whether you're bargaining in cash or in time committed. Add to that the reality that only about 30 percent of new distilleries survive after the first ten years, and you begin to understand why it's so important to Billy Kaufman to get the word out about what real moonshine is, and to ask the public to taste test.

Of course, the cool part is that Short Mountain is one of the handful of moonshine distilleries you can actually visit and see the product being made. With many of the others, that's not an option, although you may see bottling and do taste testing. "Our biggest asset right now is that we're here, we're real, you can show up and walk around," says Kaufman.

While there are plenty of brands of moonshine—and I say "brand" meaning they have magazine ads and billboards and all the shiny bells and whistles—when it comes down to it, there are very few distillers of moonshine, especially if you require your moonshine to be the kind of thing Kaufman describes—based on the illegal product and incidentally smooth, drinkable straight, the sort of thing you'd sip instead of shoot, and with a long history behind it.

Kaufman spends his money paying his people and building a distillery and getting it right, and there isn't much of a marketing budget, as he admits ruefully. Hopefully, with this book you'll go looking for his product.

Sugar is expensive, and it's the primary ingredient in moonshine. Unlike corn it needs to be bought already processed, and that comes with a price tag (by the way, they do mill their own corn). But sugar is crucial, in part because once, when everyone made it illegally, sugar was easy to buy.

"Back in the day, the general store in Cannon County sold more sugar than anyplace else in the state," says Kaufman. The revenuers and the law mostly kept their backs turned, it seems—anyone with observation skills could make a good guess at who was making shine. But oh, sugar makes for smoothness, and while it's expensive to legally buy those pallets of sugar and make a sugar shine, it's worth it to anyone who wants a decent drink.

Fortuitously, word is getting out anyway. The day my father and I visit, there's also a film team from Australia shooting a documentary at Short Mountain. The product is getting word of mouth beyond the borders of East and Middle Tennessee. One hopes that with it will come a new understanding of what moonshine is all about.

That's important, in part because it's needed to keep this kind of business alive. Short Mountain isn't cheap. A 750 ml bottle sells for about $32, and that's underpricing, but it's what the market will bear, especially when lots of people don't realize the quality difference between this and the flavored neutral grain spirits they're buying at the liquor store. And that's a shame.

Of course, it's the taste test that proves it. I have to admit, even after all this talk, I feel a little trepidation as my father and I and Mark, the Australian filmmaker, all reach for a small tasting. I follow the same rules I have at the high-end distilleries, respectfully sniffing, sipping, chewing the spirit.

And it's outstanding. There's a splendid bit of caramelized sugar on the nose—which is almost floral (that's the sugar)—and more on the palate, with a little hint of mint behind it. It couldn't be called harsh or rough for any reason. I am more than mollified. The reactions from my dad and

THE OLD-TIMERS—
RICKY ESTES AND RONALD LAWSON
TALK SHINE

The real true secret behind Short Mountain's success is a couple of old-school illegal moonshiners who've gone legit, teaching Billy and his distillers the secrets they learned over decades of wildcatting (from which they have since retired). Sitting down to talk with them feels like entering another world, and indeed it is in some ways. I must admit I never asked their ages, though you can make an educated guess based on their stories of the 1950s and 1960s, but suffice to say they've been at their trade for a good long time, and they know how to make excellent sugar shine.

I interview them as they're sitting in a couple of wooden rockers, jugs in hand, just after the Australian filmmakers have gone on their merry way. They have the kind of thick Appalachian accents you imagine from movies, except the actors never quite pull it off. Estes's is so thick I sometimes have to ask him to repeat himself, while Lawson's is easier on my citified Nashville ears. Both of them are an absolute joy to speak with; they're nice guys, thoughtful guys. Neither may have had a lot of formal education, but they're kind, well spoken, and they have no problem making a quick joke.

I ask them how they got into making moonshine in the first place. (They frequently use the word "whiskey" to describe it.)

Photo courtesy of Short Mountain Distillery

"It was quick money, for one thing," says Ricky Estes. "Make it today, sell it today. We had to sell it right away. It takes money to age the stuff, and we were poor folk, selling it was how we really survived."

Lawson jumps in. "We always kept the same clientele; there were about four or five bootleggers we sold to that bought strictly from us; there was bond and trust between us. The illegal stuff, when we were doing it, we did all on our own, bought the ingredients, made it, sold what we made. Now that we're here and what we're doing is legal, we're just working; we don't handle everything."

Estes digresses a little as we talk about his accent briefly.

"Ask him to say flyswatter," says Lawson, grinning. Ricky Estes laughs and comes out with a word I can't begin to type. He is completely unfazed by the issue. "They're a lot of big words I just can't say," he says matter-of-factly. "I don't have much education. I've never been out of Tennessee. All I know is right here we have some good moonshine, and I know how to make it and taste it."

Ronald Lawson also knows good shine, and he's been making it since he was a teenager. "I was about sixteen, and me and a friend were working at the same place. We got laid off, and we were driving around drinking beer when we had the idea for it. Now, his family made shine, and that gave us the start.

"It took us a week and a half to get all the stuff together and set up a still in the woods. This was back in the 1960s. Me and him made whiskey [his word for it] for a long time. We were in and out of it for quite a while. I ended up working in public works and then making shine at night. That's how I got started.

"The recipe we used, it was what my buddy's family had been using forever. It's the same one we use here today. Ricky made it the same way I did, and that recipe is over one hundred years old, I know for sure."

"I guess I've got a long story," says Estes. "My whole family did it. My daddy and my mama came from big families; they got married and had six kids—two girls, four boys—and all of us made shine. Some of us got caught. I got caught the first time when I was eighteen, I think. Anyhow, that's how it began. I started going to the still at eight or nine years old. I'd go and cut wood for daddy, pull the limbs from trees with my older brothers.

"I've been at it a while. I got blowed up in '91, left me off work for a year, in the burn center for nineteen days. That happened sometimes. Then they went and legalized it, and Ronald got me a job here, doing the same kind of thing. I've just always enjoyed moonshine—the rest of my brothers, they all quit. I never quit for too long at a time; I always came back.

"This is an old recipe." Estes indicates the jug he's holding. "If you wonder why they call it moonshine, I believe it comes from doing it all at night, using the light of the moon and the dark to hide the smoke from the still. That ain't for sure, but that's my idea of where it came from. I'd even seen my daddy use a storm or a foggy day to get the still fired up so we could work in the daylight. We usually kept a couple of stills; that way if one blew up, we could just move to the next one." If a still overheated or was generally running too hot, he explains, it could blow up. He adds that shine in a jug shouldn't do that, but if you leave it in the heat of the sun it can crack the bottom right off.

Both Ronald and Ricky say they tend to drink other things as well. Ricky says he favors beer. Ronald Lawson laughs, and says thanks to his Native American blood, he tries to avoid overindulging at all. "If I drink too much, I get rowdy," he laughs.

They reflect on the way moonshine figured into their daily lives. "When people came to visit, my daddy got half a gallon from under the bed," says Ricky Estes, "They'd pass the jug around, then a cup of water from the well to follow it. Nobody ever got drunk, on a day off they'd just talk all day on the porch. It was about chasing it with well water . . . I was never a big drinker myself."

"There are lots of people who think moonshine is nasty, I know," says Ronald Lawson. "There are all sorts of stories about people who go blind or get sick—but not the people who had a good maker. If it's made well, it's as good a drink as you can get. There's a lot of myth out there, but the sickness, that's a thing of the past."

There's also the medicinal quality, of course—a spoon of shine, a spoon of honey, according to Estes—something that the "old people" still do on occasion.

If anything can surprise these two, it's perhaps the growth of artisan cocktail trends using their product. Lawson tells the story of going to an event at the Grand Ol' Opry, where the bartender made him something using Short Mountain "clear whiskey" as he calls it—cranberry juice, Red Bull, a little cherry juice. "That was *the* best drink," he says. "Honestly, I usually drink shine straight, but I'd asked the bartender to mix me up something. Let me tell you, it's every bit as good as tequila or vodka. You can make the best Bloody Mary or margarita with it."

When you ask them about women and whiskey: "My thought was always that it was a man's drink," says Lawson. "I think I sold to one woman bootlegger the whole time I was working illegally. But here and now, women buy it all the time. I hear, 'Hell, that ain't for my husband, that's for me.' But I think it's just never been out in the open for women before."

The pair are sipping lightly from clear glass jugs during the interview, jugs that contain the latest product Short Mountain's been working on, Distiller's Select. "It's only been run through the still one time, but there's no need to double distill—it's pure," says Lawson.

"They think double distilling purifies it more," he adds. "But shine don't like a whole lot of heat; it'll have a bad burn. Let that heat stay down, you'll get good, sweet corn moonshine. To me, this is the best whiskey, before it's double run."

Holding up the jugs, the pair proceed to show me how beads of bubbles tell you about alcohol content without any formal measuring device. "When it's right, you want it building a bridge—beading cleanly from one side to the other."

As we finish up, Lawson offers this: "We make all our whiskey like we did in the woods. From scratch, distilled like the old-timey way it was done. You're getting authentic moonshine; this is just legal."

Mark are the same (you can't help noticing Billy's grin behind his not-hipster-but-kinda-retro mustache; he's known all along what this moment would bring for a response). Once you taste, you start getting the whole deal about it being a "premium" product, on a par with a higher-end whiskey, bourbon, or scotch.

We follow it up first with the Apple Pie—also smooth and sweet and delish, and made for girly drinks. When the apple and cinnamon can do the job of merely complementing the flavor, instead of covering it up, it's amazing the difference between this and some of the other products out there. At 40 proof, it's also reasonably innocuous—it won't knock you flat like some of the "apple pie" concoctions I've been handed by well-meaning friends at parties or in bars.

Then there's the Tea. Iced tea beverages have proliferated on the market lately, but this one is special, in part because it's not overly sweet, and also because it actually *tastes* like tea. I know, shocking, right? The secret is really just strong-brewed Lipton tea—and perhaps the fact that Kaufman is a tea drinker and knows what tea is supposed to taste like. My notes on this from the tasting say "lovely!!!" Says it all really.

If you look at the bottles, you'll notice a silver coin embedded in the top. The Kaufmans borrowed the idea from their great-grandfather, of Samsonite luggage fame, who enjoined his people to live by the golden rule—"do unto others as you'd have them do unto you." It's a good sentiment that gets lost in today's world all too often.

Frankly, I'm more than willing to let them give moonshine to me anytime, and I hope I'm nice enough to return the favor by sharing it. Because it turns out that moonshine, the real stuff, isn't something designed to be shot quickly, or made to hurt your delicate stomach. It's as fine a sipping liquor as you could ask for, if made right. Lesson learned.

Short Mountain Distillery Cocktails

White Mule

1 ¼ ounces Short Mountain
  Moonshine
¾ ounce coffee liqueur
3 ounces half-and-half

Mix the first two ingredients, then blend in the third over ice.

Tennessee Stud

1 ¼ ounces Short Mountain
  Moonshine
2 ounces lemonade
2 ounces Coca Cola

Mix all three ingredients over ice, stir, and garnish with a fresh slice of lemon.

Southern Peach

1 ounce Short Mountain
  Moonshine
1 ounce peach schnapps
1 ounce simple syrup
3 ounces Sprite

Blend the first three ingredients over ice, then top with Sprite or lemon-lime soda of choice. Garnish with a canned peach slice in the glass.

SPEAKEASY SPIRITS /
PENNINGTON'S DISTILLERY

900 44th Avenue North, Nashville, TN
37209; tennesseesippingcream.com

In a few short years, Speakeasy Spirits has gone from making a single product—Whisper Creek Tennessee Sipping Cream—to being a much larger
scale producer, making both their own and contract labels. As this book went
to press, they were breaking ground on an impressive new distillery facility in
West Nashville, with the aim of giving some of the state's larger producers a
run for their money and bringing in tourism as well. While Whisper Creek
is divine, the idea of the coming whiskeys and ryes holds a lot of tantalizing
promise, especially as they're already laying down barrels.

Products: Whisper Creek Tennessee Sipping Cream, Pennington's
Strawberry Rye, Pennington's Wheated Whiskey (forthcoming circa 2016),
Pennington's Rye, Pennington's Traditional Tennessee Whiskey, Picker's
Vodkas

Produced by Speakeasy: Battlefield Bourbon

The first time I spoke with Jeff and Jenny Pennington about their North
Nashville distillery, some two years ago, they were committed very specifically to making their own cream liqueur. They'd paired with Mike Williams, then owner of Collier and McKeel, to distill whiskey at the location.
Together they had committed to an ambitious vision for a distillery, and
they aimed to work together, bringing in other businesses at their campus
and creating a hub. By fall 2014 the business had changed rather dramatically, but the strong vision had only grown and solidified.

In part, change came because Mike Williams sold Collier and McKeel,
though he continues to produce whiskey (more on that below). Speakeasy

is still bottling for Collier and McKeel at this juncture. Meanwhile, in July 2014 Speakeasy brought in a new partner in the form of Tommy Bernard, well known across the state as the owner of Horizon Wine and Spirits, one of Tennessee's best-known distributors. Together the Penningtons and Bernard launched a momentous plan—the construction of a large-scale distilling facility in West Nashville off Briley Parkway—potentially making them the third-largest producer in the state.

Coming as it does at a moment when Tennessee whiskey couldn't be in higher demand, it seems a prescient move. The potential for expansion in the international market is astronomical, and the domestic market isn't shrinking either. Tennessee whiskey itself is soul searching right now, so the addition of another sizable distillery dedicated to the old-school rules of production will impact that.

The competition, and resultant political impact, over the definition of Tennessee whiskey itself has put the two larger brands at odds with each other (see the introduction to this section), and the smaller craft distilleries now find themselves with a distinct opportunity to have their say and impact the making of the state's signature beverage for a long time to come.

Small-batch and craft distilling is also a very new thing here—something that has emerged over the past five or six years. Previous to this, all the way back to the Depression and Prohibition, the whole mystique of the state's whiskey sprang fully formed from macrodistilleries like Jack Daniel's and George Dickel. Pennington's Distillery, the second incarnation of Speakeasy Spirits, may never be truly macro on the scale of Jack and George, but they'll be putting out a pretty significant quantity of legitimately small-batch whiskey—think in terms of the scale of something like Woodford Reserve and you won't be far off.

To return to the beginning, Speakeasy Spirits, lately creators of Whisper Creek Tennessee Sipping Cream, belongs to Jeff and Jenny Pennington. By the summer of 2012, they'd built a campus for spirits distillation and study on 44th Avenue North, and they aimed to grow it into something extraordinary.

Jeff, son of Nashville restaurateur extraordinaire Jay Pennington, and Jenny had met after college when working for rival liquor distributors Best

MIKE WILLIAMS, CHANGING TENNESSEE
LAW, AND COLLIER AND MCKEEL

Mike Williams may easily be the real mastermind behind the sudden reality of small-batch spirits as a growth industry in the state. He proudly acknowledges ancestry from a couple of gents named Collier and McKeel, who back in colonial days fled to Tennessee to avoid the spirits taxes imposed prior to the Whiskey Rebellion. According to Mike, a genial, well-spoken storyteller, when he was fifteen, he had a school science project that involved collecting and comparing Tennessee water samples.

"I fell behind," he says. "So one Saturday, my dad packed us in the car for a road trip down to the Jack Daniel's distillery. He'd stop every fifteen minutes or so, and I'd grab a sample of the nearby water in baby food jars. When we got to the distillery, I think I shocked everybody by pulling out my baby food jar and taking a sample at the Cave Spring. Well, when we got home, I discovered that the sample water from the spring was the same as the water on our property. So I told my dad we ought to build a distillery."

Of course, some of the secret to good whiskey is in the limestone-filtered water. That's what makes Jack and George, and it's what makes Kentucky bourbon, and if new distilleries down here are going to keep up, then good water is a key principle. But from that moment on, distilling whiskey became a dream for Mike, even as he built a career that included a decade spent in the Tennessee legislature, the last Democrat for a long time from the red-tinged and wealthy Williamson County, then work as a lobbyist afterwards. On his fiftieth birthday his wife, Nancy (director of the Downtown Franklin Association), told him it was "now or never" if what he really wanted was to have his very own distillery. Mike decided to give it a go.

That meant not only throwing himself into the logistics of creating a distillery and learning to distill whiskey but also getting the law changed so he could do it legally in Williamson or adjacent Davidson County (Metro Nashville).

We have a running joke in the South that since Prohibition ended, the strict religious types and the bootleggers have had an "arrangement"—as it were—that made it hard for legitimate busi-nessmen to set up proper distilleries. While that part of it may be tongue in cheek, at least in the current climate, there's no question the law as written made it unnecessarily complex to open a distillery. (See the chapter on Corsair Artisan for more stories about the efforts to change the law.)

Originally, Tennessee law insisted that for a city to have a distillery, a petition signed by 10 percent of the registered voters in said city was required. That done, a ballot referendum on said distillery was held, which needed to be won by a super majority in a year in which the governor was also elected.

When Mike Williams jumped into the fray—eventually joined by Darek Bell of Corsair Artisan (at the time doing his distilling in Bowl-ing Green, where he and Andrew Webber still make bourbon), plus the folks at Prichard's and the Penningtons—he used the skills he'd learned as a member of the legislature to turn himself into a lobbying tour-de-force. After an exceedingly long debate, the law changed to allow distilleries anywhere that liquor by the drink and package stores were already allowed and in operation. Some forty-two Tennessee counties opted in, and Governor Bredesen signed it. The governor then signed a barrel of Collier and McKeel to commemorate the occasion.

Williams began his operation with Darek Bell up at the Corsair facilities at Marathon Motor Works, but that location was quickly out-grown. He moved over to Speakeasy and began producing with them, with his whiskey providing the base for Whisper Creek. In 2014 Wil-liams sold Collier and McKeel to the California-based North Coast spirits group but remained to run the company here and returned his production to Corsair Artisan's Nashville location. As of this writing, Speakeasy still does the bottling for him, and relations between all three businesses are strong.

Also as of this writing, Collier and McKeel is available in more than twenty states and has gained Australian distribution. Of note, celeb-rity endorsements of the product include thriller author W. E. B. Grif-fin (who also happens to be my whiskey loving dad's favorite author). Visit them at collierandmckeel.com.

Brands (Jenny) and Horizon (Jeff). The Romeo and Juliet of the local beverage industry eventually came out publicly as a couple, then Jeff left Horizon to start his own company, Dynamic Digital Designs. After tremendous success, Jeff sold DDD to Uniguest six years ago; he stayed on for a year until it in turn was sold to SouthComm. Meanwhile, Jenny started Speakeasy Marketing, aimed at the spirits, wine, and beer industry. By then the couple already knew they wanted back into the spirits industry seriously, this time with their own brand.

After Jeff left Uniguest, the couple took a trip to celebrate, visiting Europe and the Caribbean, relaxing but also planning their next move. Upon their return, aware of Mike Williams's and Darek Bell's spearheading efforts to change the state distillery law, they saw their opportunity and jumped in.

"Mike was making artisan whiskey, Darek had his small-batch liquors, Billy [Kaufman] down at Short Mountain in Woodbury was making moonshine. We had other ideas—we were interested in liqueurs, cordials. We came up with the idea of a truly outstanding, whiskey-based cream liqueur—'Tennessee Sipping Cream,'" says Jeff. And thus was Whisper Creek born.

Knowing most cream liqueurs are really mostly vodka- or rum-based (with about a half percent whiskey for flavor), the Penningtons set out to create something truly whiskey-based.

They called in their friend Chef Deb Paquette, currently at Etch in downtown Nashville, and together they whipped up an all-American version of what's often called "Irish" cream. The end result is a classic Paquette layering of flavors dominated by notes intrinsic to whiskey itself—caramel, vanilla, burnt molasses—all of which you'll pick out of the whiskey they distill at Speakeasy. Underneath they blended in truly Southern flavors: fig, sorghum, smoked pecan, apple, and persimmon.

The results? Look for a rich taste and a smoother, less oily mouth-feel than more traditional cream liqueurs. It has a distinct taste profile, emphasizing the natural whiskey elements, instead of the chocolate and coffee tastes predominant in the current market's numerous Irish creams. Jeff and Jenny know they have something special on their hands.

In 2012, as Whisper Creek was just going on the market, Mike Williams, Jenny, and Jeff showed me around the campus at Speakeasy. Even at that early stage, it was vibrant with activity and excitement, all set inside a huge converted Quonset hut in a quiet northwest Nashville neighborhood off Charlotte Pike. (Collier and McKeel whiskey was already well on the market by this point in 2012.) Bottling of Whisper Creek was days from starting, but Jenny showed off her bottle designs. She's got a great eye, and much of the packaging that comes out of Speakeasy has her imprint on it.

After a quick tasting of Whisper Creek, and a chance to see those first bottles (echoing the shape of a nineteenth-century Tennessee ceramic jug), we wandered from the large conference room through the building, stopping in the well-equipped lab where chemist Neil Hilton works before exiting out into the Quonset hut, nearly big enough to be an airplane hangar. There, whiskey can be made from start to finish.

By the next visit I make, in 2014, the space will be almost unrecognizable, the equipment upgraded and the space filling up with barrel storage, and a large decking constructed to give the master distiller and his crew ready access to the still and mash tubs.

Here the Tennessee white corn is ground, then cooked in the 1,500-gallon mash cookers (where the barley and rye are added), fermented in the traditional wooden fermenter, and distilled with the help of the six hundred-gallon pot still (made of course by Vendome Copper in Kentucky—the go-to source for distillers everywhere). Hidden in a very large cupboard space is "Papa Smurf," the huge steam generator that powers everything.

The process has not changed much over the two years since I've been there, other than the obvious improvements in materials and equipment as the business has expanded. There is still the very personal devotion to making sure things are done right, and Jeff Pennington and his master distiller have come a long way themselves, mastering the distiller's art.

In 2012 Mike told me, "We operate entirely by taste here. You can do that with small-batch whiskey, not like at the big distillers, where they control everything by computer—we don't have the high volume that requires those computers." The newly made, 140 proof whiskey, he explained to me, is dripped five times through sugar maple charcoal, at that time made from trees his dad got in Humphries County. That's true Lincoln County Process, as is required of Tennessee whiskey. Then it's barreled in small barrels (where it achieves flavor and color faster than in large barrels) to age properly.

In those days Mike Williams and Jeff and Jenny Pennington foresaw the Speakeasy "campus" could potentially house other new craft distillers or would-be craft brewers, and help others with similar dreams realize their goals.

By 2014 Speakeasy had begun producing and packaging a variety of small-run spirits for other companies as well as making as much Whisper Creek as they could. Pennington's Strawberry Rye also had been introduced and had taken off spectacularly.

With Mike gone and with the recent expansions, Jeff and Jenny's team has nearly outgrown the space, even though they've just ordered a new column still for vodka production. At this juncture they're renting some 5,000 square feet of storage space, and with the upgraded equipment, they're laying down about two and a half barrels daily of distillate to age. Looking around, you can see the racks where they've built as much additional barrel storage as they can and the large containers full of white dog waiting to be barreled. Jeff says they're expecting a load of nearly three hundred barrels in about six weeks. Everything is more complex and growing rapidly.

"At this point we have more than two years of experience under our belts," says Jeff. "We've got distribution in thirty-three states, Canada, and Mexico with Whisper Creek, and we're in a good place with all that, so it's a good time to challenge ourselves."

The commitment to whiskey making is now fully under way, though they hope to get no less than four years of aging on the whiskeys before you'll see them released. They've got their yeast strains, and the whiskey products promise to be distinctive—a Tennessee bourbon whiskey without the charcoal, with a mash bill of 18 percent wheat, 22 percent malted barley, and 60 percent corn; and a high rye Tennessee whiskey with lots of spice—25 percent rye, 70 percent corn, 5 percent malted barley. The final product will be a straight rye.

The products that go into the whiskey are largely local—for example, they're sourcing the Tennessee white corn from Renfro Farms.

The mash bill choices show the influence of both Four Roses and Maker's Mark on the Speakeasy palate, but Jeff says he's a longtime Maker's fan. They also express gratitude to Bill Samuels at Maker's Mark and Jim Rutledge at Four Roses, both of whom advised and consulted with them.

As Tommy Bernard says, "We've got to make really great whiskey, because we're going to be drinking it for the rest of our lives." Jeff provides that quote, saying it came as they were sitting in a bar, looking at the other brands behind it. He adds, "You can't really be the guy known for making one whiskey and ordering someone else's."

The team is more settled; in addition to Jeff as CEO and Jenny as CMO, Jesse Meeks now works as master distiller, coming over from Popcorn Sutton, and Carter Collins is director of plant operations. (There's also distillery dog Shafer.) The big deal is perhaps the arrival of partner Tommy Bernard.

When he sold Horizon Wine and Spirits to Warren Buffet's Berkshire Hathaway, Bernard stayed on as a consultant for a couple of years, then found himself keeping an eye on his friends at Speakeasy, especially when they launched the Pennington's Strawberry Rye through Horizon. As the distillery got a lot of positive buzz and, most notably, a lot of sales, Bernard met with Jeff about a potential investment, and they came to good terms (the Penningtons remain majority owners).

"He has a direct line to so many people, having owned a big distributorship for thirty years," says Jenny. "He was Jeff's first boss, and now he stands to be a mentor to him in a new way. Tommy also brings a lot of credibility to us as a small supplier, and his capital investment will allow us to make and age whiskey for real."

The presence of the affable Bernard, who wanders comfortably in and out of the meeting in jeans, his dog at his side, gives the company the chance to imagine a larger potential. Already past the space capacity for the Speakeasy campus, in fall of 2014 the company acquired land in northwest Nashville (officially in Ashland city), near Briley Parkway off Interstate 40; they're got architectural renderings and are ready to break ground in early 2015, assuming everything comes back approved from the zoning board.

The point of this distillery isn't simply laying down larger quantities of whiskey, although the process has already begun for the aforementioned three new products, but to appeal to tourists and help make the Nashville area even more of a distillery tour destination.

"We're looking at having 200,000 people a year through the new location, and providing thirty to forty jobs in the process," says Jeff. The new space will spill across five acres, including the two-story distillery building with a special outbuilding for the stills, complete with a sizable event venue, retail space, a bar, a taproom connected to a tiny microbrewery, and even a couple of bocce ball courts, as Jenny reports with glee.

There will also be a restaurant on the premises—likely helmed by Jeff's dad, Jay Pennington, who's got more than twenty years of stellar restaurant development under his belt in the Nashville area, and whose name is an instant draw to local diners. The views from the restaurant, on the second story, will include the Nashville skyline.

As they plan for the facility, they've also begun work on new products that should be available by the time this book hits the shelves, including Picker's Vodka—in unflavored, blood orange, and blueberry. These will be made with real fruit juice, a cut above the usual flavorings in that kind of product, and the flavors promise to be a little more distinctive than the usual variety lined along the liquor store wall. Having had the blood orange variety, I can tell you this is tailor-made for custom cocktails, and like nothing else on the market.

A collection of cordials is also under way, including their takes on things like amaretto, and extending beyond to watermelon, peach, and the like. "We aren't making these for the larger market; they're more of a local thing," says Jenny, showing off the new bottle designs. "All the bars and restaurants in the area purchase this kind of thing at high volume, and for us it's low margin, low price—something we can do to make sure there's a local product option." Given the Nashville market's endlessly expanding restaurant and food scene, this looks like a very smart move, playing into the local food movement from a cocktail standpoint.

They've thrown out other ideas that aren't that far from production, artisan cocktail makings like an aged Sazerac, for example, since they aim to produce more rye-based and high rye products.

"Ultimately, this distillery is also about making Tennessee something as competitive for the tourist market as Kentucky's fantastic bourbon trail," says Jeff. "But in terms of production, I think there's certainly room for five or six million-case-per-year distilleries in Tennessee, given the size of the market, and I'd like us to be one of those. We feel like we have a very good team, and great understanding of the market itself. I think there's room for a lot of the young distilleries to really make it, including us, Corsair, Prichard's. . . . Some of the smaller places—Popcorn's, Short Mountain, Tenn South, they have really interesting things happening too."

Mercury Rising

This is my own take on the mule made with Pennington's Strawberry Rye. You can use any ginger beer, but I use Buffalo Rock, made in Birmingham from a Civil War–era recipe. The name comes from the city's iconic statue of Mercury.

2 ounces Strawberry Rye
1 can Buffalo Rock ginger ale

In an 8-ounce glass, pour the rye over ice, then add ginger ale to top. Garnish with a lime twist.

Whisper Creek Hot Chocolate

1 cup milk
$\frac{1}{3}$ cup semi-sweet chocolate chips
2 ounces Whisper Creek Tennessee
   Sipping Cream

In a saucepan over medium heat, heat milk until simmering. With a whisk, blend in chocolate chips until melted, add Whisper Creek and serve.

Whisper Creek Irish Coffee

1 (6–8 ounces) cup black coffee
Whisper Creek to top

This is the most basic of concepts, top your coffee with anywhere from a tablespoon to 2 ounces of Whisper Creek—you don't need sugar or anything else. Fantastic.

BATTLEFIELD BOURBON

Battlefield Bourbon isn't a typical Tennessee spirit. Instead it combines the notion of traditional whiskey with the recognition of the American Civil War sesquicentennial, thanks to the efforts of *New York Times* best-selling author Robert Hicks. Hicks, best known nationally for his books like *Widow of the South* and for his contributions to magazines including *Garden & Gun*, epitomizes the need to preserve our culture—including the overwhelmingly painful moments like the Civil War, whose repercussions are still being felt 150 years after its end.

If you don't live in a part of the country where the War Between the States was fought, you might not be as aware of the events that have taken place between 2011 and 2015 to commemorate the war and the many people who lived through it. There is an old adage that says those who don't learn history are doomed to repeat it, and the acknowledgement of this history helps us to recall—and hope to understand—a moment when we as a nation allowed ourselves to fracture.

Tennessee and Kentucky were contentious places, producing factions that fought on both sides of the bloody conflict. We had our share of gracious-appearing plantations and horse farms hiding and profiting from the ugliness of the slave trade, and also independent-minded folks who wanted the union preserved and had no use for slavers. At the time the war broke out, we were already producing bourbon and whiskey with methods in tune with what we're still doing today, albeit rougher and less precise.

For historians and preservationists, remembering those times and continuing to secure the memories of those who died—black and white, Northern and Southern, free and enslaved—is vital to the fabric of our country today. For Hicks, whose biography includes exceptional efforts to help preserve the site of the brutally bloody Battle of Franklin, the effort to create Battlefield Bourbon as not only a remembrance, but also as a fund-raiser for battlefield preservation, has been a highly personal one.

Most people have never heard of the Battle of Franklin, if they don't live here, but a shocking number of people died on both sides here on November 30, 1864. If you have heard of it, it's from Mrs. Mead's line to Mrs. Merriweather in the movie *Gone with the Wind*, remarking on Rhett Butler having survived it.

Hicks has been one of the driving forces behind battlefield reclamation "for more years than I want to count," he says. He's always been a bourbon aficionado, and he thought perhaps he might be able to effectively merge his love for bourbon and his passion for preserving American history.

"I decided to go with the allotment model, like Pappy Van Winkle does, and put the product out once a year in small quantities. Once I did that, it became a matter of finding bourbon. When it came to that, I had two concerns. First, as good as the bourbons being sourced out of Indiana are, and make no mistake, they are good, I wanted a Tennessee-made, Tennessee-aged product, one that could be bottled and sold here.

"Beyond that, to me—though I'm a fan of the older bourbons— the best taste really comes from the seven- to nine-year ones. I like an eight-year-old bourbon. The last thing I want to do is discover it tastes like I'm licking the inside of an oak barrel. Now, as I say that, I have a bottle of Pappy here on the counter, but I have to tell you that I'm fond of the twelve year or the fifteen year, it's less woody." (Those not fans of rare, super premium small-batch Pappy Van Winkle should know the prized versions are twenty and twenty-three years old, respectively.)

The source of the bourbon was tougher than deciding to create it. Fortunately, Hicks had plenty of connections around the industry. The best lead, however, came when Hicks's longtime friends J. T. and Susan Andrews Thompson (among other concerns, owners of the historic Lotz House in Franklin) ran into Jenny and Jeff Pennington at a cocktail party. The couple also had an interest in the battlefield bourbon project.

"J. T. told me they were looking at building a whiskey project that would help raise the profile and awareness for battlefield preservation and reclamation," says Jenny Pennington. "It looked like it might be a good fit, and Jeff and I are both actually from Franklin." In the end, Jenny also helped design the distinctive packaging for the product.

The concept presented was that Battlefield Bourbon would be a true Tennessee bourbon released perhaps once or twice a year to commemorate various battles of the Civil War. The first iteration would remember, of course, the Battle of Franklin.

The most interesting aspect is that the bourbon would be proofed with water from a spring on the battlefield site. "Once we had the bourbon sourced, I wanted to proof it with water from the battlefield. It was a happy accident that I decided I wanted it at 91.2 proof before I was using that water, and then we decided to use the water from the spring to cut it. It's water from the place where boys of both sides were found the next morning, having bled to death—you get thirsty when you're bleeding out, you need water. And you know, it made a much sweeter bourbon, again a happy accident that made it good."

The water from this release likewise came from Franklin, but for next year's release, the water will come from Shiloh, or perhaps Chickamunga—other Tennessee battlefields. Each release will follow in the same format, with water and focus given to a different battle.

Hicks's opportunity for bottle design was, as he puts it, icing on the cake. The type face comes from the cover of his novel *The Widow of the South*; the image is a popular nineteenth-century rendition of a scene from the battle; and while Hicks always planned on a wooden cork, his friend Justin encouraged him to add the words "lest we forget" to it. That motto appears on monuments to the dead across both North and South.

The first release has proven incredibly successful. Even with a very premium price, according to Hicks and the Penningtons, the distributors sold out of their limited number of bottles (a grand total of 1,864) within a few hours, and the entire stock had disappeared from retail shelves within a couple of days. "It's just amazing," says Jeff Pennington. "Buyers were reacting to this like it was Pappy Van Winkle—I hope this kind of response continues."

I'm so happy I chose to put out 1,864 bottles, but I wish I had put out more," says Hicks. "The Wednesday before Halloween we released it, and I prayed it would all sell by Christmas. On Monday the distributor called me and said they'd sold out. Why not put out more? But then, the number seems right, too."

Hicks wants you to know that this is not just Tennessee whiskey, but Tennessee bourbon whiskey. "We can create good bourbon down here too," he says.

He lists his own favorites as the Van Winkle, Blanton's, and then adds, "But I love Jack Daniel's too—I've always been a huge fan and always will be. I may not be able to write like William Faulkner—none of us may—but I can drink like him. Heh, back in his day, though Four Roses in the United States was swill—now the Four Roses Single Barrel is excellent, add that to my list."

New York Times best-selling author, battlefield patron, and now the mastermind behind a new bourbon release—Robert Hicks has plenty to celebrate in life.

Franklin's Charge

Among Robert Hicks's many contributions to historic preservation is his extraordinary effort to save and reclaim the land on which the Battle of Franklin took place. If you can't get your hands on a bottle of Battlefield Bourbon this year, consider donating to his charity, Franklin's Charge, and helping to preserve Civil War sites. For more information or to make a donation, visit franklinscharge.com.

Franklin's Charge is a 501(c)(3) Tennessee nonprofit corporation organized in 2005 and dedicated to preserving America's threatened Civil War battlefields in Williamson County, Tennessee.

TENN SOUTH

1800 Abernathy Road, Lynnville, TN 38472;
(931) 527-0027; tennsouthdistillery.com

Tenn South really is the new kid on the block. They bottled their first whiskey in October 2014, and they're going like gangbusters these days. The brainchild of an engineer and a radiologist who thought they could do it themselves and proved it, the distillery is a testament to their powers of invention. Clayton James and Old King Corn whiskeys join their already excellent moonshines, vodka, and gin in helping to define a promising new venture and maintain the strong spirit of traditional Tennessee whiskey.

The Products: Clayton James Whiskey, All Purpose Shine, Blackberry Shine, Apple Pie Shine, Peach Shine, Abernathy Gin, Black Mule Vodka

Lynnville, Tennessee, lies seven miles off Interstate 65 at exit 27, not far from the Alabama line. It's a small place in a charming little town, close to the Railroad Museum and an old-fashioned ice cream parlor, near a cluster of antiques shops. At this writing, their first aged whiskey isn't in the bottle yet, but it soon will be. They do, however, make some mighty fine unaged spirits, which pay the bills while the whiskey ages in proper Tennessee fashion.

"For a long time there were just the two dynasties in Tennessee whiskey," says co-owner Clayton Cutler, a former engineer turned distiller. "Then the laws changed, and it became apparent that a common man, if he had fortitude, could make himself a part of the whiskey business in this state."

Along with his brother-in-law, radiologist James Brady Butler, the two struck out, as Cutler says, forging their own way along—tasting, researching brands and distilling techniques, visiting with other distillers, meeting consultants, and going to conferences. In 2011 they started their work in earnest, buying twenty-eight acres in Lynnville and bringing in or building all the necessary equipment, then began distilling. In early October 2014, they launched their whiskey.

Both residents of Columbia, Tennessee, about twenty minutes north of Lynnville, they originally aimed to open the distillery there, but when the laws changed in 2009, they didn't automatically allow for distilleries everywhere, and Maury County, where Columbia is located, voted against them. Giles County and Lynnville, meanwhile, welcomed them with open arms—including Dan Speer, executive director of Giles County Economic Development.

(It's worth noting that in mid-2014, Maury County changed its laws, and a new craft brewery is on the way there—evidence of the fact that the state's fledgling distillery and microbrewing culture has actually taken off and is building supremely valuable tourist appeal.)

As with most young distilleries, for Tenn South there existed the question of revenue. Whiskey takes years to produce, and somehow or another you have to pay for your equipment and premises in the meanwhile, let alone the rest of living. Cutler and Brady felt very strongly that they didn't want to source their whiskey. It's a tough choice, because it means the public develops a taste for something potentially quite different than what you end up producing under the same name a few years later.

Tenn South opted to instead produce unaged spirits immediately, for the purposes of cash-flow generation. The first—in summer 2013—was their All Purpose Shine, produced from a traditional Tennessee moonshine recipe dating back decades, not simply white dog from their whiskey distilling. As has been noted elsewhere in this book, true shine of the sort made by bootleggers is not the same thing as unaged whiskey.

"We're making this without technology," says Cutler. "It's a true heritage process, the shine of a hundred years ago. It's just ground white corn, Giles County water, and sugar. We do start with a sour mash, but we don't cook the corn either. It tastes this way deliberately, nothing like raw whiskey—that's not what we're making. We proof it to 100 proof, but this is

our theory of shine, and we figure that the bootleggers were caught in the woods most often [by the revenuers] from the column of smoke from the still. There's no real reason to have two columns of smoke from cooking corn, it just increases the risk of revealing your location and getting caught. Everyone local knew who was making shine anyway, based on the amount of sugar they bought. But they tended to turn a blind eye."

Tenn South's mix, he says, is half corn, half sugar, fifty-fifty. "There are some folks these days producing some stuff that's 95 percent sugar; but frankly, that's not moonshine, that's essentially a kind of rum," he says.

His wife, Cindy, who serves the distillery in a variety of roles from bookkeeper to marketing manager, adds that the sour mash provides a little hint of anise on the finish that's nice. This is quite true, but don't expect the anise taste to dominate.

The resulting shine, when I taste it, has a caramelly nose and goes down with brilliant smoothness, with just the faintest hint of that anise note on the finish. I suspect if you aren't looking for it, that isn't how you'll identify it, barring being a professional whiskey taster.

TASTE OF TENNESSEE

Over the past two years, Cary Ann Fuller has worked tirelessly to create an entirely new event, the Taste of Tennessee, at the Tennessee State Fair in September. Taste of Tennessee brings together the vast majority of the craft brewers and distillers in Tennessee for a two-night event—one night focused on beer, the other on spirits. The goal of the event is not only to get the different businesses talking with one another—in most cases they do that already—but also to show the public at large the potential impact of spirits and beer production on the state.

Unlike Kentucky, Tennessee has resisted its distilling heritage following Prohibition. To put it bluntly, most of the people living outside major metropolitan areas or cities where distilling is taking place may not even be aware that it's going on. The choice of the Tennessee State Fair as a site brings in a goodly portion of that demographic, because while the fairgrounds themselves are in Nashville, the attendance comes from all corners of the Volunteer State.

Added to the clear shine came Apple Pie, Peach Pie, and Blackberry—all at 50 proof. Each of these is made with real fruit juice and real fruit, not artificial flavorings, and there's none of the powdered kid's drink taste about them. Notably, there is sediment, real sediment, in the bottom of the jar, which seems truly refreshing in place of the abundant artificial color in clear liquid that's typical in some mass production "shines."

Frankly, each one makes a fine drink-alone beverage as well as cocktail-making material. I have to admit a distinct preference for the Blackberry, because the vanilla note on the front gives it a sense of fresh cobbler, and because some of the sour-tart note of actual blackberry blends nicely with the sweet.

The Apple Pie is very apple, with a hint of cinnamon on the front and a hint of vanilla on the finish. Cocktail lovers pair it with ginger ale or ginger beer, says Cindy Cutler, while cooks love it as a reduction with pork loin. Peach Pie, meanwhile, has a hint of citrus on the nose, but the flavor is very, very peachy—and that's just fine. Cindy suggests pairing it with iced tea, sweet or unsweet.

The Blackberry (no "pie"), as mentioned, has a pleasant tart note and works well paired with a little Guinness beer. Lynnville has an annual blackberry festival, so like most of the rest of Tenn South's products, it's a nod to the place that inspired it. Of note, Tenn South's merchandise includes some darling ceramic shot glasses (ok, slightly larger than shot glasses) that reference the old shine in a ceramic jug trope.

Moving beyond shine, the Black Mule Vodka—its label and name a tribute to Columbia, Tennessee's annual Mule Days festival—is corn-based with an incredibly clean nose and just a hint of corn sweetness on the finish of an otherwise very, very clean vodka. Though comparatively new, the amount of pickup by bars and restaurants in Middle and East Tennessee that Black Mule has seen indicates its fast-growing word-of-mouth popularity. You can understand why—it makes for a smooth martini. It took a gold medal in 2013 at The Fifty Best (thefiftybest.com).

Finally there's the Abernathy New American Gin. The mockingbird label pays homage to Tennessee's state bird (all the labels save the whiskey are the work of Nashville artist Bob Delavante), and Abernathy to Abernathy Road, on which the distillery rests (in turn named for the Abernathy family, who helped found Lynnville). This one is Dr. Butler's baby, and it's a gin with a mix of nine botanicals that make it very specifically a Tennessee thing, a Southern thing.

If you're an old-school, juniper-forward, citrusy gin lover, this might not be your profile, but if you like gin with serious flavor, for heaven sakes, toss your preconceived notions and try it. The juniper's there, but it lacks the astringency of some gins. Among the ingredients are pecan, orris root, angelica, cassia, coriander, cardamom, and citrus. It's aimed for a Southern palate, not a New England one (to name a region where gin is a more traditional spirit than whiskey). There's a light nose, a citrus note, and a hint of nuttiness on the finish. While "New American" isn't a true gin category quite yet, in terms of competition judging at any rate, that's coming. It's worth noting that like the All Purpose Shine, the Abernathy Gin won a bronze medal from the American Craft Distillers Association. Cindy Cutler says the trend in bars is to mix it with Blue Moon beer and a twist of orange.

This brings us to the whiskey—two types, Clayton James and Old King Corn. At this juncture I'm waiting to taste the finished product, but indications are it will be something good. Clayton James obviously takes its name from the founders, and the mash bill makes use of locally grown white corn.

To be true Tennessee whiskey, the Lincoln County Process needs to be part of the equation, and it surely is at Tenn South. Clayton Cutler says his technique with small batch is a bit different than the big distillers, and while Tenn South sources so much from this region, they opt to purchase their charcoal from a lumber company in New England. The company harvests sugar maple trees that have been used for sap for years when they are past production point and need to be cut and the area replanted. Most of those trees go for lumber, but those unsuited for lumber are turned into charcoal, and that's what Tenn South makes use of in their Lincoln County Process.

Guests at Tenn South can see the entire process at the small facility, including the hand bottling (still too small to justify any mechanized assembly line bottling). The only thing they're secretive about is the yeast strains, but that's not a surprise—it's what everyone is secretive about.

"We are the 'hands-on' tour," says Clayton Cutler. "We'll give you all the details of what we do and how we do it; we jokingly say it's the TMI tour. Come here knowing as much or as little as you like; we'll make you comfortable asking any questions you have."

Lynnville itself makes an excellent day trip from Nashville or Huntsville; it's small and personable—as is the distillery. If you go on a Saturday, expect the kind of touring groups you expect at larger places—motorcycle enthusiasts, car clubs, and the like. Cindy Cutler says of late she's even seen the non-drinkers stop by—church groups who just want to know what's going on, even if they have no intention of tasting. I hope when you visit, your goal is well and truly tasting.

TENN SOUTH DISTILLERY COCKTAILS

Tenn South MoonTini

2 ounces All Purpose Shine
1 ounce olive juice
Dash dry vermouth

Shake and strain into a chilled martini glass. Garnish with blue cheese–stuffed olives.

Black Moon Martini

2 ounces Tenn South Blackberry
 Shine
1 ½ ounces half-and-half
2 ounces cranberry juice

Shake all ingredients together with ice and strain into chilled cordial glasses. Garnish with a dash of cinnamon and a few frozen blueberries.

TROY AND SONS

At Asheville Distilling Company,
12 Old Charlotte Highway, Asheville, NC; (828) 575-2000

Troy and Sons aren't in Tennessee, but their strong ties to the state and to Nashville in particular suggest they belong in a book that's talking about Tennessee spirits, and whiskey in particular. Music producer Dub Cornett is a vital part of the Nashville culture, and he's made Troy and Sons a Nashville beverage—which really wasn't hard, as it suits our character. Troy Ball, a Vanderbilt grad, also has significant Nashville ties, and she is one of only a handful of notable women distillers in the region. While you may have to cross over to Asheville to visit, it's worth the trip, and the whiskey has some historical secrets to make it special.

The Products: Platinum Small Batch Moonshine, Oak Reserve, Blonde Whiskey

To start, you must completely disabuse yourself of the notion of white lightning, white dog, call it what you will—an unaged whiskey distillate of the kind that's referred to as moonshine in its extra-legal variety—as a fiery beverage that goes down hard and sits harder in your gut, served up out of a mason jar. The proverbial good stuff, even back in the day and certainly as made now, is smooth, made with the best corn, a fine sipping liquor, if you will.

Troy Ball, of Troy and Sons distillery in Asheville, North Carolina, gets that. She's not alone among the new breed of artisan distillers making something clean and flavorful, but she stands out. And with her Nashville ties, including a quiet partnership with legendary music producer Dub Cornett, she aims her product at everyone who's rediscovering the whole notion of white lightning in the modern distilling world.

From Texas, Troy came to study at Vanderbilt in Nashville and loved the city that brought her back again and again, even after her marriage to Charlie Ball and three children. In college she earned a business degree and ran the Vanderbilt *Hustler* newspaper. Accepted to grad school at Vandy, she ended up returning home to work in the family business.

Troy and husband Charlie moved their family to Asheville in 2004. Two of their sons have disabilities, and the climate proved much better for them (the extraordinary oldest son, Marshall, now in his twenties, has made a remarkable career for himself as a writer). The Balls' real estate business suffered the same trials that the whole industry did in 2007 and 2008. To deal with the stress, Troy developed a new interest—distilling.

In 2008 an eighty-year-old man told her about the "real" homemade white lightning and moonshine whiskeys, and about the differences in taste. Intrigued, Troy headed to the state archives and read about the fellas back in the day who were well respected for their quality liquor. Prior to Prohibition, North Carolina had the nation's highest percentage of distillers; today it's limited to artisans here and there. Troy set out to find the guys who still knew what it took to make the good stuff and decided that she wanted to try it.

Enter John McEntire, a seventh-generation corn farmer still somehow producing a rare white heirloom corn dating back to the nineteenth century (once, white corn was for eating, yellow for livestock). "John is the loveliest man ever, kind, jolly, just terrific," declares Troy. And his corn really is the be all and end all.

The Balls took some of McEntire's heirloom corn to the University of Tennessee for analysis. "They shucked the corn and ran it through their machines," she says. "Their eyes got real big. They asked to do another ear . . . they'd never seen a corn like this." Higher in fat, lower in starch than modern corns, this heirloom seed had survived on McEntire's farm for more than a century, while time and big corporate hybrid corn after 1945 passed it by.

"We use it in all our batches, mixed with other white corn—we can't grow enough. It won't take the heat and grow elsewhere, it needs the Southern mountains." With the help of her research, John McEntire's corn, and the support of her husband, Charlie (now the master distiller), in the midst of a recession, Troy Ball became the only woman in the country with a distillery making whiskey on her own. She is a star, as Dub Cornett says, and her charm and powerful belief in her own product are the selling point for many people when they discover the spirit.

Dub Cornett, producer for John Prine, Townes Van Zandt, Lucinda Williams, and other category-defying Nashville artists, met Troy through friends in Nashville early in the process. The two hit it off, and Cornett became supporter, cheerleader, and then partner. He recognized at once the need to take a "highbrow approach to a 'lowbrow' product." He reasoned that here would be plenty of folks working to make "grandpappy's whiskey." The goal of Troy and Sons would be to do it really, really right.

The Virginia native from the Appalachian mountains was soon traveling regularly to Asheville to visit family and dropping in on the Balls, listening as Charlie Ball moved from saying "you all are crazy" to turning himself into a talented distiller along with his wife.

"I just feel lucky to be part of it," says Cornett modestly. But he promotes the amazing whiskey like crazy, helping to get prominent placement for it on TV and in film. "He's wonderful," says Troy.

"[Troy] making whiskey is the same as someone writing and singing a great song. She's not someone who just decided to do it; she's what quality is all about," says Cornett. "Allan Benton is the same thing with his bacon [www.bentonscountryhams2.com]. And it's a sustainable business; we wanted to be the Tom's Shoes of booze." For Cornett, the best of Southern and "hillbilly" have made something classic.

Cornett and Ball met, he says, through mutual friends from Texas. Troy came from Austin originally, and when a friend talked to Troy about whiskey a bit, the instant response was, "Oh, you should meet Dub!" Cornett says coming from Austin, Troy and Charlie had watched the rise of other micro-spirit brands like Tito's, and they stuck in Troy's mind, "a little nugget in her subconscious," says Cornett. At the time, in Nashville, Charlie was deeply into real estate and had little interest.

Cornett, meanwhile, took a very different view, and predicted accurately that the distilling culture in Tennessee would take off after the laws changed. He saw the culture and the vision that was developing, he says, and he thought it would appeal to Troy. When she determined she had a potential product, Cornett told her, "I don't need my name in anything, but let's see if we can make this work." He remains reticent about speaking publically, preferring all the credit go to Ball.

"She did the lion's share of the work. I was company adviser and philosopher. She wanted to do something different, and she needed to be the face of it—I mean, why not have an incredibly smart woman as the powerhouse here? And she is one."

Ironically the company almost settled on a Tennessee site, in Sevierville near Gatlinburg, but it didn't feel right to them. One of the spots they looked at now belongs to Ole Smokey, and it's suited them well in the tourist mecca, but for Troy and Sons in their quest for location, it just wasn't right. The Asheville decision has been a good one, in terms of the kismet discovery of the heirloom corn and the way in which it aided the Ball family and their children's health.

When it came time to find a still, Charlie Ball finally got on board. He'd previously been with Dell and built computer factories, says Cornett. "The pair of them are about as self-sufficient as anyone I've met."

Charlie's research indicated that the Germans have always done local schnapps distilling, and their methods seemed best suited to what Troy and Sons aimed for, getting only the heart of the whiskey with precision. The odyssey to find the still clearly led him down a new path, since he now fills the role of master distiller.

Ultimately what they're producing is a true white whiskey. It doesn't fit into the "moonshine" category, either of the type being made by Short Mountain and Tenn South or the more commercial style of Ole Smokey. "It's the base of every good whiskey; we just make it good at this stage. It's our own approach; we made our own version," says Cornett.

"We are a true craft distiller from the word go," says Cornett. "We talked about the option to make it cheaper; we didn't do it. We went all the way, we wanted a provenance for our product and we got one, we elevate it, make it better—down to the elegance of the bottle."

The larger Nashville tie was established thanks to a relationship with the city's Lipman Brothers, Music City's oldest local spirits distributor. Margaret Lipman got on board early on, after a promising note on Troy and Sons in *Garden & Gun* back in 2011, and contacted the distillery. The Nashville tie deepened, and Lipman is now "almost like family."

Among its products, Troy and Sons offers its Platinum Moonshine and Oak Reserve moonshine whiskey—extraordinary spirits both. Made with John McEntire's Crooked Creek white corn, mountain spring water, and a whole lot of effort, only 50 percent of the distillation makes the bottle—the toxin-filled head is discarded, as well as the end run, and with it the burn that makes harsher moonshine. Just the heart of the run is used, producing a drink so smooth bartenders can't believe it. There's a reason this was the first shine ever to appear on Disney's properties, among other prestigious sites.

The Troy and Sons Platinum is billed as a premium moonshine spirit (use it like you'd use vodka, if that confuses you at all) made with Appalachian spring water. As mentioned above, you're going to find it smoother than a typical shine, and I've got no problem with that. It doesn't have the heat I've come to expect with unaged whiskeys, a definite plus, especially if you're drinking it straight.

Meanwhile, Troy and Sons Oak Reserve is aged in bourbon barrels, giving it a trace of the warm amber color you'd expect in an older whiskey, and really lovely flavor notes of oak, caramel, and maple sugar. There's also the Blonde Whiskey, which melds Tennessee-style with European-style processes to produce a truly intriguing hybrid of Turkey Red wheat and white corn, distilled no less than a dozen times and aged in oak barrels, minus the char, for a blonde color and a lovely aroma of caramel and vanilla. This is a whiskey a girl can get behind.

Troy Ball, along with husband Charlie and quiet adviser Dub Cornett, has an excellent product that very much fits into the world of spirits being created by Tennessee's promising new distilleries, even if she happens to be across the border in North Carolina. We're willing to count her as one of us.

CLASSIC COCKTAILS

Cocktail culture is all the rage and, frankly, there's good reason for that—cocktails make things interesting, and whiskey and bourbon lend themselves to mixology. What follows are the recipes for a few of the classics—the cocktails that started traditions and, in many cases, gave rise to more complex and detailed variations, especially in the current mixology craze. These, however, are pretty basic, slimmed-down versions, and I need to thank James Hensley at Nelson's Greenbrier, who a few years ago was my spirits correspondent when I edited a city magazine, for introducing me to almost all of them.

Algonquin Cocktail

Another Golden Age of Cocktails tradition, James Hensley introduced me to this ages ago, though I can't remember if he gave me this recipe or not. The original was reputedly made in the 1930s at New York's Algonquin Hotel.

1 ½ ounces rye whiskey
¾ ounce vermouth (dry, not sweet, is preferable)
1 ounce pineapple juice*

Add everything to an ice-filled cocktail shaker, shake until mixed and chilled, and strain into a cocktail glass—a martini glass works fine.

*Please note that if you're using a commercial pineapple juice, many of them are blends—read the labels to make sure what you're getting really is pineapple juice.

Bourbon and Water or Soda

The quintessential introduction: This is the way I got introduced to whiskey—and it's not a bad way to begin. These days, if I'm sipping it, it's neat or with a single ice cube. This is well suited to sweeter bourbons or Tennessee whiskeys, in my opinion.

2 ounces bourbon or whiskey
Water or club soda

Add a couple of rocks to your cocktail glass, then add your bourbon or whiskey. Top your glass or fill to taste with water or club soda. Garnish with a lemon twist.

Hot Toddy

Let me be clear, this is my variation on the hot toddy. When my husband or I have a head cold, I'm likely to make it in a big coffee mug with far more hot water to soothe sore throats. If you want to be festive with it, add a bit of cinnamon stick, clove, or nutmeg. Yeah, I'm the girl who has whole nutmegs and graters in my cabinets. If you can find it, a dash of ground grains of paradise, a spice not used much after the nineteenth century, is nice too.

1 teaspoon honey*
1 ounce lemon juice
2 ounces whiskey or bourbon, to taste**
2–3 ounces boiling water, to taste

In your tea or punch cup, mix the honey and lemon juice, pour in your whiskey, then add boiling water, stirring to dissolve the honey. Garnish with a lemon wheel if you like. If you want to add spices, a cinnamon stick garnish, a couple of cloves, and a grating of nutmeg are nice. If you're sickly, add them all, and double the amount of water and lemon juice.

*A note on honey—sadly, these days most of your grocery store honey is full of adulterates, and probably mostly *not* honey. Buy it from a local farmers' market and be sure you have real honey. I buy from my neighbors at TruBee Honey, who have a fantastic new bourbon barrel–aged honey that makes the best cocktails you've ever had, and it's pretty awesome on homemade biscuits too. (Order it at www.trubeehoney.com.)

**This is also nice with some of the flavored bourbons and whiskeys out there. If you like sweet, try it with Jack Daniel's Tennessee Honey (likewise, use about half the actual honey the recipe calls for); it's also pretty lovely with Knob Creek Maple Bourbon.

LOCAL INGREDIENTS

I mention using Arrington, Tennessee's **TruBee Barrel Aged Honey** (trubeehoney.com) in my hot toddy recipe. It's good for any cocktail that calls for a touch of honey—aged in bourbon barrels, it's really something special. It's wonderful for baking, serving with cheeses, and smearing on biscuits too.

Sarah Souther at **Nashville's Bang Candy Company** (bangcandycompany.com) makes some fantastic simple syrups that pair nicely with whiskey. She's next door to Corsair Artisan Distillery, and they've paired spirits and syrups on many occasions. Choose from flavors like Smoked Spiced Orange, Habanero Lime, or Ginger Rosemary, and reimagine your favorite cocktails.

Matt Jamie at **Bourbon Barrel Foods** (bourbonbarrelfoods .com) in Louisville now offers up bitters handcrafted with Woodford Reserve bourbon, and they're worth the purchase. He's also got a Smoked Simple Syrup on offer, bourbon-smoked sea salt, and other seasonings. The products are truly extraordinary, whether your plan is to use them for cocktails or cooking.

Lynchburg Lemonade

We all know this gets its name from the home of Jack Daniel's. I think it really needs JD, but in a pinch, it will work with any good Tennessee whiskey or sweeter bourbon you have in your home bar. It's a great summer cocktail.

½ ounce fresh lemon juice
½ ounce simple syrup
1 ounce whiskey
1 ounce triple sec
Lemon-lime soda such as 7Up or Sprite
Ice

Mix together lemon juice and simple syrup to make a sweet and sour mix (you can use the pre-made, but this is just nicer). Mix it with the whiskey and triple sec in a pint glass (go ahead and use those mason jars or order a set of beverage glasses from Uncorked Glass Company in Atlanta, which is what I use). Add ice, then top with lemon-lime soda (if you want sweeter, use Sprite; fresher, use 7Up).

The Manhattan

The story is that this cocktail dates to high-society New York in the late nineteenth century, and it may have been invented for Lady Randolph Churchill (Jennie Jerome, mother of Winston, and an American-born heiress). Making this at home, I like Belle Meade Bourbon, Knob Creek, Maker's Mark, or Woodford Reserve particularly, but any good straight Kentucky bourbon will serve you well.

2 ½ ounces bourbon
¾ ounce sweet vermouth*
Dash Angostura Bitters
Maraschino cherry to garnish

Add your ingredients to a shaker or glass of ice and stir, don't shake, until well chilled. Strain into a cocktail glass and garnish with a single cherry.

*Bill Samuels at Maker's Mark insists that his one contribution to mixology is to switch the sweet Italian vermouth for Dolan's, which is drier, and to use a tiny bar spoon of cherry juice. I have to admit, this makes a fine cocktail. Try it some time.

Mint Julep

I've been to so many steeplechase and horse events down here, I can't remember when I was first introduced to the mint julep. This is a pretty streamlined version, but if you ask a good mixologist, there are plenty of variations around. My friend Paul Koonz of Lexington suggests the proper way to make this drink is to pour your bourbon into a glass with a rock or two, throw away the mint, and drink. I'm not sure that counts as a cocktail, but it's not a bad idea.

WHISKEY, BOURBON, AND CHEESE

Everyone pairs wine and cheese, but it occurred to me that whiskey, bourbon, and cheese might be just as lovely a thing to do for the holidays, especially—even if the holiday is "hey, it's June 3rd" (or April 8th, or any of the 365 options). I asked my friend Kathleen Cotter, cheesemonger extraordinaire at the Bloomy Rind in Nashville and founder of the city's Artisan Cheese Festival, what she thought ought to be done for the occasion.

"Pairing cheese with liquor can be a little tricky as the intensity can overpower the cheese," she says. "Bourbon and whiskey do have some characteristics that play well with cheese, though, such as caramel/butterscotch, smoke, and various fruity notes. Likewise, look for cheeses with more flavorful profiles, such as hard, aged goudas, cheddars, and blues, and it's best to avoid rich, buttery cheeses like camemberts.

"My cheesemonger cohort and whiskey aficionado, Tim Gaddis, shared some of his favorite pairings with me. **Angels Envy** with **L'Amuse Gouda, Bulliet** with **Capriole's Mont St Francis, Woodford Double Oak** with **Rogue Creamery Smoky Blue,** and **Knob Creek** with **Ted from Kenny's Farmhouse.** As with all pairing, the fun is trying out different combinations to see what you like best!"

10 mint leaves (I like mine fresh from my garden, but you can find them in the produce section of your grocery.)
1 teaspoon simple syrup
4 ounces bourbon

Ideally use a julep cup, but if not, go with your rocks glass. Muddle the mint and syrup. Fill the cup with crushed ice or small ice cubes, add the bourbon, and stir till it's nice and cool.

If you're in Nashville, come by and visit. "We also have a few cheeses and accompaniments that have the whiskey already in them. **O'Banon from Capriole Goat Cheese** in Indiana is a small round of fresh chèvre wrapped in **Woodford Reserve**–soaked chestnut leaves, imparting that delicious bourbon flavor without overwhelming the cheese.

"**Sequatchie Cove Creamery** makes a robust, natural-rind blue that is finished by wrapping the wheels in **Chattanooga Whiskey Co.**–soaked fig leaves, lending a sweet punch to balance out the spicy blue. And to round out your whiskey-themed tasting, try Nashville's **Bathtub Gin Tennessee Whiskey Cherry Tomato jam,** which is perfect with an aged clothbound cheddar."

If you aren't in the area, the cheeses mentioned can be found at these websites:

capriolegoatcheese.com
facebook.com/sequatchiecovecheese
threeringfarm.com/cheeseroom.htm
http://kennyscheese.com
Or visit thebloomyrind.com and see what Kathleen has available!

Old-Fashioned

The Old-Fashioned is newfangled these days—everyone has their own version of it. The last few I've had have been served with an overabundance of skewered fruit—orange slices, cherries, and more exotic options including pomegranate seeds. I like to skip those and have a nice clean variation.

1 sugar cube or a teaspoon of sugar (or to taste—if you like sweet, add a little more)
2–3 dashes Angostura Bitters
1 piece lemon zest (use organic lemons!)
Orange slice
1 maraschino cherry or bar spoon of cherry juice
2½ ounces bourbon

Saturate the sugar with your bitters. Using an Old-Fashioned glass, mix the saturated sugar with the lemon zest, orange slice, and cherry juice and muddle neatly. Add ice (crushed) and then add the bourbon; stir to chill.

Sazerac

The original version of the Sazerac, as made in New Orleans, uses cognac—but given the origins of bourbon whiskey, it seems fitting that at some point in the late nineteenth century bourbon became the spirit of choice. The original also involved that most daring of beverages, absinthe (and you can indeed substitute Corsair Artisan's Red Absinthe effectively for the Pernod), but when it became illegal in this country, other anise-flavored spirits stepped in to fill the role.

1 sugar cube
2–3 dashes Peychaud's Bitters
2 ounces bourbon
½ ounce Pernod, Herbsaint, or other anise-flavored spirit
½ ounce lemon juice (fresh squeezed, preferably)

Saturate your sugar cube with the bitters, then add it and the bourbon, anise liqueur, and lemon juice to an ice-filled glass (crushed ice is preferable). Stir until chilled. Garnish with a lemon twist.

Whiskey and Coke

Yeah, you probably know this as Jack and Coke, and I'm completely behind that, but you can truly get away with using any whiskey you like.

2 parts Jack Daniel's or other Tennessee whiskey or sweeter Kentucky bourbon
3–4 parts Coca-Cola*

Add your whiskey to a tall glass of ice and top with coke; stir to chill. Garnish with a lime wheel or lime wedge.

*Why the Coke brand? Aside from tradition, Coke is a little less sweet than most of the other big colas, but if you like sweet and have another cola of choice, go for it.

Whiskey Sour

This is one that goes in and out of style, and it seems to be in again right now. Be honest, we all remember our college days with blended whiskey and sour mix, right? This is not that. It's cleaner and fresher.

2 ounces bourbon or whiskey
1 ounce fresh-squeezed lemon juice (if you're using prepackaged, use less, about ¾ ounce)
½ ounce simple syrup, or to taste

Add all ingredients to a shaker and shake thoroughly to mix. Strain into a chilled glass. Garnish with lemon. I add a dash of Fee Brothers lemon bitters every now and then, just for fun.

WOMEN AND WHISKEY

Don't tell me whiskey and bourbon are strictly a man's domain, just don't. We're way past all that—as whiskey writer and blogger Chuck Cowdery says, we need to move past the notion that a spirit can be gendered, period. With the appearance of the artisan cocktail movement especially, women have moved into the world of brown spirits like never before, and we've discovered we like them, and we're not leaving them behind.

There's a Carrie Underwood song of recent popularity that includes a line about a pickup artist cheating on his girlfriend, who buys his bar-room conquest "some fruity little drink 'cause she can't shoot whiskey." The larger implication is obviously that a cocktail is an inferior beverage, and shooting whiskey is what badass women do. In exploring the whiskey world, with all due respect to Underwood's awesome voice, let me say with confidence that every single distiller and bartender I've talked to has essentially negated this line.

Oh, not that women don't drink whiskey—and bourbon—quite the contrary; the interest in what was once considered almost wholly the purview of men has never been greater. But the line misleads because it suggests that the right way to drink good whiskey is to shoot it, and that cocktails are somehow a sign of weakness.

Women drink whiskey and bourbon because they like it. In cocktails, straight up, or with a rock or two.

You only shoot bad whiskey, and every woman I know who drinks whiskey knows it, and so do the men. And artisan cocktail culture, especially with bourbon and whiskey at its heart, is a thriving good that introduces many, many new people to some mighty fine spirits. As Jimmy Russell at Wild Turkey says, the way to drink whiskey is the way you like it.

The notion of shooting whiskey just perpetuates a bad stereotype of the tough guy in the bar in the Old West, slamming the strongest thing they have just for the pain and the burn. It's Buck Owens singing "Cigarettes, and Whiskey, and Wild, Wild Women" and Clint Eastwood tossing back something horrible but bracing, and acknowledging the burn. Let that image go.

The quality of today's bourbons and whiskeys is such that this sort of thing is ridiculous. The smooth, mellow products being produced today appeal to drinkers of fine-quality beverages, and there's no excuse for drinking something raw, rough, or bad.

It is still something of an anomaly to see women associated with whiskey, even though women have been part of the equation for years, indeed since the beginning, whether you're looking at Margie Samuels's powerhouse role at Maker's Mark, the old-school pre-Prohibition distillers like Louisa Nelson, who took over after her husband's death, or the many women who are working as distillers today in Tennessee and Kentucky, including Allisa Henley at George Dickel, Troy Ball at Troy and Sons, and Andrea Clodfelter and Karen Lassiter at Corsair Artisan.

The rise of cocktail culture has certainly contributed to the appeal of brown spirits to women, but this isn't the very beginning of a relationship between women and whiskey, it's just the first time the demographic has truly been acknowledged as a target market.

"There are a lot of cultural factors at work here," says Larry Kass at Heaven Hill. "It's much more acceptable—and much more stylish—for women to seek out well-made spirits, and that's not just whiskey. In the past we've given them permission with things like obscure Italian liqueurs; now women have become a driving force, and they've taken the opportunity to delve in and explore. Interestingly enough, women actually have better noses than men and are better tasters, and that may be part of the appeal. A lot comes into play, including an expanded social license to try bourbon."

Kass adds that the arrival of the flavored bourbons and whiskeys on the market have had some sales driven by women as well, things like honey and cinnamon versions of the spirits. "But I'd argue that it isn't the honey flavor," he says. "The spirits are being appreciated in and of themselves—and frankly plenty of the flavored stuff is sold to men."

"There have been women distillers for a long time," says Allisa Henley at George Dickel in Tennessee. "Most people just don't know about it, but I think now there's more awareness being brought to us and what we do. Science has proven over and over that women have great palates, so it shouldn't be a surprise that whiskey appeals to us. And as the trend continues, more and more women will get interested in the distilling side of things, and I expect to see an influx over time."

Like Kass she credits the resurgence of "old-timey" cocktails. "Women tend to order cocktails, and when they do, it opens their minds more to whiskey. From there they learn to like it and want to know how it's made, where it comes from."

The revitalization of cocktail culture as a whole, however, is a rebirth, not just a resurgence, according to Maker's Mark's Bill Samuels. "The old bourbon customer was a very different breed, mostly older, mostly male. Now they're young, professional, urban, from an enormous number of professions, and women are a big part of that. I'm not sure there's much of an overlap between the old-school drinkers and the new ones today."

Fred Noe at Jim Beam says in the old days, women were neglected, but now they're a big part of the culture. "You never tell a lady she needs a lighter bourbon," he says with finality. "Bourbon is about acquiring a taste."

Cocktail culture or not, women of Gen X and Millennial generations have also grown up taking cues from Dad as much as Mom when it comes to their drink of choice. And in some cases, even our Boomer-generation moms had adopted brown spirits before it was officially fashionable.

If you start asking women of all backgrounds and professions, you'll find that more like whiskey than do not, I suspect.

My friend Jean Pace Hovey says it well (she's the author of several Southern-themed novels for Crimson Romance under the moniker Alicia

Hunter Pace, with cowriter Stephanie Jones). "There's just something so Southern about drinking Wild Turkey. I cut my adult teeth on it when white wine spritzers were the tony thing. I never could drink them or those drinks that put one in the mind of pureed fruit salad," she says. Jean has always been one of my foodie heroes, she cooks like nobody's business, and she makes a mean Bloody Mary because she knows what spicy means. I wish very much I could put Jean and Jimmy Russell in a room together at some point; I think they'd have the most interesting of possible conversations about bourbon.

"I'm from Kentucky and we drink bourbon because, well, tribalism," says Sarah Rae Parker-Rhea of Louisville. "So I think I naturally developed a taste for it over other types of whiskey from sheer exposure, although my mother has since defected to scotch. I keep 1792 in the house for everyday drinking, and for a special occasion I might pick up some Booker's or some of the double-oaked Woodford Reserve. Of very few things in my life, choosing to drink bourbon didn't seem to be a gendered thing when I was growing up or now. I hadn't really thought about how gender-neutral the whole thing was until now."

"I love whiskey and bourbon, but I can't remember when I started drinking them," says Deborah Brown of Raleigh, North Carolina. "I've ordered Manhattans since college, and then my Kentucky uncle taught me to switch over and make them with bourbon. My favorite bourbon is Woodford Reserve, especially the Masters blends—I had a maple-cured one once that was amazing, and my current bottle is the double-oaked. It was fun in college to watch people (especially guys) be impressed if I ordered something besides white wine or an umbrella drink, but mostly I just liked the taste and having something I could sip slowly."

Nashville artist Sandy Spain, from the Boomer generation, says, "When I was in the corporate world, I had to appear not to be weak. But to be honest, I hated the assumption I would want a silly girly drink or wine just because I was female. I like to taste the difference in the brands, and the type. I like it to be just plain or with a few cubes, so I don't lose the flavor of it. It also helps a lot to have a liquor salesman as a close friend, and I get to sample some of the new offerings."

On the other end of the age spectrum, twenty-something Mary Kate Smith (last seen on SyFy's *King of the Nerds* in 2014—the feisty, pretty science grad student) says, "I'm a big whiskey gal these days, and it started because it was something I could share with my father." I'm right there with her—my dad introduced me to scotch, and that led to whiskey and bourbon in time.

"My father enjoyed his Jack Daniel's when I was a kid, and I would have a sip or two," says architect Marilee Lloyd, currently of Sewickley, Pennsylvania. "When he'd order or make a Manhattan or a Rusty Nail, I'd get a sip too. I began to enjoy the cocktails before finding that I had a taste for bourbon or whiskey straight (often, now, with a drop of water). I still like Jack Daniel's (partly nostalgia, I expect), but I prefer Basil Hayden's for sipping, Maker's Mark for a great Manhattan. Another bourbon I enjoy is Woodford Reserve. Leopold Brothers makes a nice small-batch American whiskey."

"I like Knob Creek with a couple ice cubes or straight for passing around a fire. It also makes a good Manhattan," says Andi Houston of Gainesville, Florida (www.greenbasket.com). "I recently tried a cocktail in a restaurant in Georgia with ginger beer and lime that knocked me out it was so good, but I can't remember the name—a "mule" maybe? I totally agree about the gender thing though. People always seem surprised when my husband orders the sweet drinks and I order a dirty martini."

Anne Koonz, the woman who introduced me to AllTech and Town Branch, says, "My grandfather and father were whiskey and bourbon drinkers, mostly Jack and Wild Turkey. I guess I mostly just grew up with it. I got a wider taste after moving to Kentucky. My husband, Paul, introduced me to everything; now my favorites are Pogue and 1792, but I like to try everything. The honey bourbons are awesome, especially chilled over ice cream. I also like that I can sip on one glass for a while and make it last, rather than drinking quickly, which is what I tend to do with sweet things and wine."

The bottom line is that every woman who drinks bourbon and whiskey comes to it from a different perspective. It's far more complex than saying it's a trend of the moment—it's no more a trend than the whole rise of brown spirits is—it's something that's in demand and going to be around, much like wine will continue to be a vital part of the alcohol culture, or any other major spirit.

The reason for talking about women and bourbon is because it ultimately underlines part of the reason that bourbon and whiskey have returned to such prominence. There's been an undoubted improvement, steadily, to the quality of the spirits in the years since World War II and the true recovery from Prohibition, as brown spirits became cleaner, less bitter, more drinkable, and smooth across the board.

As the interest in whiskey has taken off again worldwide, it's grown a new audience—not just older gentlemen but a group of young, diverse people interested in the spirits for their taste and the culture behind them for its craftsmanship and its attention to detail. And the daughters of some of those whiskey- and bourbon-sipping Southern men have been brought up by dads who didn't save the savoring of it for their sons, or by moms who broke a whole lot of old gender rules.

If you look at your local paper or web news page, chances are you'll see ads for a plethora of events with titles like "Women and Bourbon" or "Whiskey Girl's Night Out"—distributers have also come to understand the value of the female market, and advertising is being tied as much to women buying the products as men. The times are changing, and women are a target market.

As this movement continues, look for more women drinking the products of all these distillers, more women in the industry, and our culture reaching a point in time where shooting whiskey in a bar is a forgotten image, replaced by elegant sipping from a rocks glass by men and women alike.

And with the enormous artisan cocktail culture still impacting the whole world—from Japan to Russia to the United States—in a huge way, it doesn't matter what you like your whiskey and bourbon with—Coke, in a Manhattan, or taken neat. The part that matters is you've developed an appreciation.

INDEX

Van Winkle, Julian "Pappy," 24, 59
Veach, Mike, 60, 114, 160
Velvet Elvis cocktail, 153
Vendome Copper and Brass Works, 74, 172, 195
Versailles, KY, 3, 105
Very Old Barton (Barton 1792), 10, 11
vodka, 16–17, 179, 198–99
Volstead Act, 23, 67, 115, 145
Vow of Silence cocktail, 162

Wadelyn Ranch Distilling, 3
Waynesburg, KY, 3
Webber, Andrew, 115, 120, 121, 123, 193
Wheatley, Harlen, 23–28
whiskey. *See also* Tennessee whiskey
  blended, 8, 29, 34, 99, 151
  smoked, 126–27

and women, 187, 227–32
Whiskey and Coke, 225
Whiskey Rebellion, 192
Whiskey Row, 6, 41
Whiskey Sour, 226
Whiskey Thief Distilling Co., 3
Whisper Creek Hot Chocolate, 200
Whisper Creek Irish Coffee, 200
Whisper Creek Tennessee Sipping Cream (Speakeasy Spirits), 118, 190, 191, 194–95, 196, 197
white dog, 73, 116, 178. *See also* moonshine
white lightning, 15, 212. *See also* moonshine
White Mule cocktail, 189
Whites Creek, TN, 168
white whiskey, 215. *See also* white dog
Wilderness Trail Distillery, 3, 4

Wild Turkey, 2, 3, 25, 85–94, 230, 231
Willett Distillery, 3, 4, 95–104
Williams, Mike, 115, 120, 122, 190, 192–93, 194–96
Wiseman, Jeff, 15, 18
women
  and bourbon, 55, 90
  and cocktails, 63–64
  distillers, 126, 133, 212
  and whiskey, 187, 227–32
Woodbury, TN, 116, 117, 176
Woodford Mule cocktail, 112
Woodford Reserve distillery, 2, 3, 5, 66, 105–12, 191, 230, 231
Wright, Pete, 15, 16, 18

yeasts, 31–32, 36, 72, 147–48
Yellow (Four Roses), 33, 37